ISLAMIC LEGAL METHODOLOGY
A NEW PERSPECTIVE ON UṢŪL AL-FIQH

IIIT, P.O. Box 669, Herndon, VA 20172, USA • www.iiit.org
P.O. Box 126, Richmond, Surrey, TW9 2UD, UK • www.iiituk.com

Library of Congress Cataloging-in-Publication Data
    Names: Kazemi Moussavi, Ahmad, author. | Mavani, Hamid, author.
    Title: Islamic legal methodology : a new perspective on Uṣūl al-fiqh /
       Ahmad Kazemi Moussavi and Hamid Mavani.
    Description: Herndon : The International Institute of Islamic Thought IIIT,
       2023. | Includes bibliographical references and index.
    Identifiers: LCCN 2023030990 (print) | LCCN 2023030991 (ebook) | ISBN
       9781642055672 (paperback) | ISBN 9781642055665 (hardback) | ISBN
       9781642053517 (ebook)
    Subjects: LCSH: Islamic law--Interpretation and construction--History. |
       Islamic law--History.
    Classification: LCC KBP440.3 .K39 2023 (print) | LCC KBP440.3 (ebook) |
       DDC 340.5/909--dc23/eng/20230804
    LC record available at https://lccn.loc.gov/2023030990
    LC ebook record available at https://lccn.loc.gov/2023030991

Layout and design by Saddiq Ali

Printed in the USA

Islamic Legal Methodology
A New Perspective on Uṣūl al-Fiqh

Ahmad Kazemi-Moussavi *and*
Hamid Mavani

LONDON • WASHINGTON

CONTENTS

Acknowledgements

This book has largely been researched and written by Ahmad Kazemi-Moussavi whilst teaching Islamic law at the International Institute of Islamic Thought and Civilization (ISTAC) in Malaysia during 2000-2004. He wishes to acknowledge with gratitude all the professors and students with whom he discussed many of the topics included herein during his tenure at ISTAC. He is especially grateful to Professor Muhammad Naquib al Attas, the founder of ISTAC, for his unceasing support and encouragement. He also extends his gratitude to Professor Mohammad Hashim Kamali for his inspiring works and teachings on Islamic law. Sincere thanks are due to Assistant Professor Hamid Mavani for reviewing the entire work and updating the materials. We are indebted to Professor Mohammad Faghfoory and Mr. Anthony Arcangeli for their gracious assistance with editorial work on parts of the book, as well as to the IIIT Publication Department for carefully reading the entire work and offering the necessary suggestions.

Endorsements

Uṣūl al-fiqh is one of the major Islamic traditional sciences that has not received as much attention in scholarly works written in English as it deserves. The present work goes far in filling this lacuna. In a very scholarly and at the same time Islamically authentic manner the author deals in clear language with the main theses of *uṣūl al-fiqh*, both Sunni and Shia and includes recent developments rarely mentioned in other works. The author is to be congratulated for adding an important text to the copies of works in English dealing with Islamic Law and its principles as well as with legal methodology.

SEYYED HOSSEIN NASR
University Professor of Islamic Studies at the George Washington University, Washington DC, USA

Islamic legal methodology (*uṣūl al-fiqh*) has been one of the most influential branches of Islamic Studies since the 10th century. Jurisprudence (fiqh), interpretation of the Qur'an (*tafsīr*) and tradition (ʿilm al-ḥadīth) are based on this methodology. Ahmad Kazemi-Moussavi has thoroughly reviewed the development of this methodology in different schools of theology and jurisprudence (*kalām* and fiqh). This book covers both the classic and modern *uṣūl al-fiqh*. Kazemi-Moussavi does not restrict himself to the traditional understanding of legal methodology, in contrast he expands the border of this methodology to include hermeneutics. Kazemi-Moussavi successfully introduces the development of concepts integrated into Islamic legal language for general readers. This is a good work and serves as an introductory text for students of Islamic studies in the course of *uṣūl al-fiqh*.

MOHSEN KADIVAR
Visiting Professor of Islamic Studies at Duke University, USA

Moussavi has constructed an insightful narrative of the history and methodology of Islamic jurisprudence. He departs from the conventional format and chapterisation of titles to a new, more interesting yet accurate presentation of themes and chapters. The work provides comparative reviews of the doctrines of the various schools and scholars of Shariah, both Sunni and Shia, as well as parallel developments in Greek logic and philosophy, Jewish thought, and western jurisprudence, all in an objective and readable style. A significant feature of this book is its balanced coverage of both the classical and modern contributions to the discipline presented in a coherent and progressively evolving fashion. Students and scholars of Islamic studies and *uṣūl al-fiqh* will find reading this richly rewarding. The book is eminently suitable for a university text book on the subject.

MOHAMMAD HASHIM KAMALI
Founding Chairman & CEO International Institute of Advanced Islamic Studies (IAIS), Malaysia

Foreword

The International Institute of Islamic Thought is pleased to present this important work on *Islamic Legal Methodology: A New Perspective on Uṣūl al-Fiqh*. The science of *Uṣūl al-Fiqh* is fundamental to the Islamic experience and deeply rooted in Islamic Law, elucidating the derivation of rulings from the Qur'an and Sunnah, through various juristic tools and methods. It employs both reason and revelation to work for the betterment of human society. This work discusses the historical development of the legal methodology for the interpretation of the Shariʿah, and analyzes proposed reforms by modern Muslim scholars.

Written in a clear and lucid style, it is hoped the book will benefit both general and specialist readers alike, increasing their awareness of the field as well as exploring modern scholarly Muslim discourse on the principles of Islamic Jurisprudence and challenges faced in the modern context.

Since its establishment in 1981, the IIIT has served as a major center to facilitate serious scholarly efforts. Towards this end it has, over the decades, conducted numerous programs of research, seminars, and conferences as well as publishing scholarly works specializing in the social sciences and areas of theology, which to date number more than six hundred titles in English and Arabic, many of which have been translated into other major languages.

We would like to thank Dr. Ahmad Kazemi-Moussavi and Dr. Hamid Mavani for their cooperation throughout the various stages of production, and all those who were directly or indirectly involved in the completion of this book. May God reward them for their efforts.

IIIT

September 2023

Introduction

WITH THE increased attention paid to Islamic law in recent decades, there is a need to further understand the methodology Muslims employ when deducing a legal ruling based upon static and immutable universal ideals and norms (e.g., justice, equity, and the sanctity of life) known collectively as the Shariʿah. However, as this remains the provenance of the Divine or in the "mind of God," it is essentially inaccessible and thus that which is accessible is no more than the result of a person's utmost intellectual endeavor and exertion (ijtihad). In other words, the only possible result is a tentative fallible approximation of the ideal Shariʿah[1] (i.e., fiqh) that must be interrogated, corrected, and revised both critically and continually if it is to remain relevant in changing times, contexts, circumstances, and customs.[2] This critical distinction between the timeless Shariʿah and mutable jurisprudence allows for a mechanism that can review and revise juridical opinions in the light of new information. And so fiqh, the result of juridical reflection reached by scholars of the Shariʿah at a certain time and in a certain context, is always changing, is always in a dynamic process of "becoming" rather than of "being." Therefore it is in constant need of elaboration and evolution (*taṭawwur al-fiqh*).[3]

Ijtihad, which relies upon a legal theory and hermeneutic principles, generates positive or substantive law (*furūʿ*). Being a combination of Islamic law, ethics, and rituals, the Islamic legal-moral-ritual code stands as the major source of inspiration, identity formation, and social cohesion for Muslims. Islamic legal thought developed alongside juridical authority, the holders (*fuqahāʾ*) of which were assigned by Muslims to deduce legal rules from the normative Shariʿah. To evaluate such authority, Muslims gradually developed a legal methodology (i.e., *uṣūl al-fiqh* [the foundation of jurisprudence]) by which they could frame the sources of law and their legal language, and provided the grounds for elaborating on the law's logic and objectives. The language of the primary sources, namely, the Qur'an and Sunnah (the Companions' reports of the Prophet's (ṢAAS)* words and deeds [hadiths]), became the subject of verbal analyses designed to reconcile and harmonize the revealed texts with the legal rulings (*aḥkām*) while either devising law ("rule creation") or post facto "rule justification."[4] Charles Pierce refers to this logic as "abduction," which he defines as "studying facts and devising a theory to explain them," and Rumee Ahmed affirms: "In works of legal theory, then, jurists were less concerned about *discovery* and more concerned about *justification*."[5] By developing the law's secondary sources, in addition to the Qur'an and the Sunnah, namely, *ijmāʿ* (juristic consensus) and especially *qiyās* (analogical reasoning), several new components were integrated into the legal methodology and provided greater flexibility and discretion in correlating the revealed texts to the legal rulings. However, the authority of "verbal demonstration"[6] or "signification" remained central to the legal methodology. Modern approaches to a text's form and content have made it possible for scholars to reexamine this methodology outside its traditional boundaries.

This study has two goals: to (1) summarize *uṣūl al-fiqh*'s rise and development from its rudimentary form to its advanced and mature phase by articulating the contributions of eminent jurists on key intellectual debates in order to find out how this genre eventually placed exclusive authority in the texts' "verbal demonstration" and (2) present a schema of reforms, new hermeneutics, and epistemology proposed by modernists to bring about foundational changes in Islamic legal methodology so that they can bypass the authority of the legal language. In studying the historical evolution of this discipline, we will explore the cause and scope of its expansion in the works of jurists, who gradually incorporated numerous principles from logic, exegesis, theology, philosophy, Arabic grammar, and other

---

*(ṢAAS) – *Ṣallā Allāhu ʿalayhi wa sallam*. May the peace and blessings of God be upon him. Said whenever the name of Prophet Muhammad is mentioned.

fields. Social exigency and expediency also prompted jurists to amend its format and content by merging their theoretical and social considerations into their legal methodology. Finally, we will survey the legal approaches of some contemporary authors in order to present their critical evaluation of this discipline's traditional methodology and their proposed reforms so that it can better address modern issues. The focus, however, remains on how scholars reshaped and reimagined their legal methodology by echoing the requirements and needs of their own era.

The link between the law's linguistic aspect and time-honored knowledge can be seen in the works of most Muslim scholars who dealt with the same principles of *uṣūl al-fiqh*, although in quite different formats and expressions. For example, we will observe how the diffusion of formal logic forced Abū Ḥāmid al-Ghazālī (d. 505/1111) to significantly change both the language and format of his legal methodology (Chapter 5). More importantly, we will examine how Abū Isḥāq al-Shāṭibī (d. 790/1388), benefiting from his knowledge of inductive reasoning, incorporated the law's higher objectives (*Maqāṣid al-Sharīʿah*) into his legal methodology (Chapter 6). But at the outset, one must ask what prompted Muslim jurists of the second/ninth century, such as al-Shāfiʿī (d. 204/819), to develop a methodology for deriving legal rules.

Islamic legal methodology arose out of the need to formulate a systematic and rigorous approach to deriving legal rules, one that was both stable and in harmony with the textual sources. This ultimately resulted in the supremacy of the sources of the law – the Qur'an and Sunnah – over the customs, conventions, and practices that had been incorporated over time. According to al-Shāfiʿī, the best known exponent of canonizing the Hadith, his primary juridical concern was to establish a precedent for the Qur'an's legal authority, and particularly that of the Sunnah, over the uncontrolled use of independent reason and the preexisting customs of Madinah as normative (i.e., setting the interpretative semantic rules). His goal here was to harmonize the conflicting ways of understanding these sources' texts and reports and to ensure a formal consistency in the new law's application. Jurists gradually expanded the scope of *uṣūl al-fiqh* by borrowing and adapting concepts and applying principles from theology, exegesis, logic, philosophy, Arabic grammar, and other disciplines. This persuaded the authors to adopt various formats for organizing the contents of their proposed legal methodologies.

Jurists expanded and modified this discipline's contents either by adopting new elements from other ones or by shifting the emphasis from one aspect of legal methodology to another. The hierarchical considerations for the law's sources can be viewed as the point of departure for this genre of writings at the turn of the third/ninth century, provided that Shāfiʿī's detailed defense of the Sunnah is held to be a rudimentary legal theory on the sources' authority for deriving legal rules. This emphasis, however, drastically shifted to semantics and practical interpretations in the works of some Ḥanafī jurists in Baghdad during the fourth/tenth century, beginning with Abū al-Ḥasan al-Karkhī (d. 340/951; Chapter 3). Before this shift, Muʿtazilī theologians such as ʿAmr ibn Baḥr al-Jāḥiẓ (d. 255/ 869; Chapter 2) included the relationship between reason and revelation in *uṣūl al-fiqh*. The next phase of major change, that of incorporating epistemological elements of Aristotelian deductive logic into the legal methodology or theoretical jurisprudence, started with Ẓāhirī Ibn Ḥazm (d. 456/1064) and expanded and blossomed with al-Ghazālī, who simultaneously provided a new format to his own methodological approach.

At the same time, the standard arrangement of *uṣūl al-fiqh*'s contents was gradually evolving. This began with Shāfiʿī's synthesis between rationalists or people of opinion (*ahl al-ra'y*) and traditionalists (*ahl al-ḥadīth*) and reached its peak with a standard hierarchical format of what were judged to be the essential sources for acquiring legal knowledge: the Qur'an, the Sunnah, and semi-independent legal reasoning (ijtihad) buttressed by the first two sources. This kind of vertical formatting originated with Shāfiʿī's approach to presenting a new theory of epistemology and hermeneutics of the Sunnah versus the living traditions of his time, although it was very rudimentary and he probably did not anticipate that it would later on become *uṣūl al-fiqh*. The contemporary author Robert Gleave regarded Shāfiʿī's *Risālah* as "an attempt to delineate a typology of interpretive efforts" as follows:

> Unlike its contemporary texts, the *Risāla* is more than a collection of solutions to problems (legal and theological) with *obiter* com-ments revealing self-reflection. Rather, it is an attempt to delineate a typology of interpretive methods through the investigation of particular legal examples, regularly utilizing the literary device of an interlocutor in order to demonstrate the need for consistency in the application of these methods. This is not to say that it qualifies as a work of *uṣūl al-fiqh* as understood in subsequent Muslim scholarship, but it is the case that many of the interpretive methods outlined in the *Risāla* are found in the later *uṣūl* tradition in more elaborate and sophisticated formulations.[7]

The second arrangement provides a horizontal scope and divides the legal methodology into four parts: (1) the legal norm, (2) the sources of the law, (3) the method of perceiving the law, and (4) the practitioners of the law (i.e., *mujtahid*s). This format is based on al-Ghazālī's innovative proposal, which broke away from his previous formats and arrangements. Most post-al-Ghazālī authors, such as al-Āmidī (d. 631/1233) and Ibn al-Ḥājib (d. 646/1248; Chapter 5) and up to the modern era, adopted the third arrangement, which combines the two previous ones. The fourth arrangement divides the methodology into two parts: (1) literal (i.e., linguistic interpretations) and (2) rational indicators, which takes into account the levels of human understanding of the sources and is subdivided into knowledge (*ʿilm*), suppositional (*ẓan*), and doubt (*shak*). This way of arranging the materials has continued, particularly among Imāmī jurists, from the nineteenth century onward (Chapter 8).

The Muslims' encounter with modern scholarship has fostered a new genre of intellectual approaches to Islamic legal theory, one that recognizes a critical role for human reason in legal deliberation.

Unparalleled in terms of scope in traditional Muslim thought, it has influenced the Muslim discourse on legal methodology in two important aspects. First, some reformists seek to bring about serious reform without discarding the entire legal theory by aligning the epistemology, hermeneutics, and sciences with contemporary requirements and needs. In this respect, AbdulHamid AbuSulayman (d. 2021), Taha J. Alalwani (d. 2016), Hashim Kamali, and others have worked to give a broader and more substantial role to the principles of public welfare (*maṣlaḥah*), the prioritization of issues, and the law's higher objectives. Kamali particularly seeks to harmonize the existing instruments of legal methodology with today's social realities – to merge "government ordinances" with ijtihad and to incorporate "statutory laws" with *ijmāᶜ*.[8] Second, other reformists are applying modern hermeneutical methods of law that allow a revealed text's nature and presuppositions to transcend its literal meaning. Mohammed Arkoun (d. 2010), Abdolkarim Soroush, Mojtahed Shabestari, Nasr Hamid Abu Zayd (d. 2010), and others have proposed ways of applying modern epistemology to legal theory. Even though they have not yet devised a specific method for applying modern hermeneutics, their critical discourses nevertheless offer new avenues of understanding the revealed law.

We now turn to the formative period in which Shāfiᶜī played such a pivotal role in canonizing the Qur'an and Sunnah for deriving legal rules, a process that reached maturity in the eleventh century with the expression "the consolidation of the schools" (*istiqrār al-madhāhib*).

CHAPTER 1

The Advent of an Islamic Legal Methodology

UṢŪL AL-FIQH appeared as a distinct and functional legal discipline at the turn of the fourth/tenth century; however, its birth and growth can be traced back to the advent of the Islamic legal-moral-ritual code in the first/seventh century. Concurrent with the development of jurisprudence (fiqh), Muslims began to debate ways of understanding and applying new rules. It seems that the problem of "conflicting laws," particularly that of abrogating (*naskh*) some of the Qur'anic rules, concerned the nascent Muslim community the most and brought the necessity of instituting an orderly understanding of the Qur'an and Sunnah when deriving legal rules to the fore. A hadith reported by Ibn Sallām (d. 224/838) includes Caliph ʿAlī b. Abī Ṭālib's (d. 40/661) warning to a local mediator: "One should not engage in settling a case if the abrogated verses of the Qur'an are not known to him."[1] Clearly, "conflicting laws" were among the first elements that encouraged the formulation of a structured and stable methodology, for the knowledge of abrogation is a prerequisite to understanding the applicable legal norm.

The next important factor was the interplay between the prophetic and the lived traditions (*ʿamal*) of Madinah's Muslim community. The Prophet endorsed a substantial amount of the pre-Islamic Arabs' living traditions, but as he was the one who defined his community's normative practice, he also abrogated a sizable number of those that could have interfered with and distorted the prophetic traditions. This problem, in addition to the discrepancies in hadith reports, caused the next generation to begin sifting them and interrogate Madinah's communal tradition to determine their utility and authenticity. The *Kitāb al-Sunan* (The Book of Traditions) and similar books composed during the second half of the first/seventh century testify to the steps Muslims took to devise a more stable and systematic legal hermeneutic. The formal inclusion of *qiyās* (analogical reasoning) paved the way for a wider yet harmonious interpretation or legal hermeneutic.[2] However, its application caused an outbreak of opinionated debates, the rampant use of unfettered speculative reasoning, and the sidelining of Hadith, all of which eroded "a secure and autonomous communal tradition connecting the present-day community to the moment of revelation."[3] This was, in turn, countered by the rise of traditionalism, as reflected by invoking the prophetic hadith reports to discipline the supposed arbitrary legal hermeneutic.

All of the aforementioned factors contributed to the gradual evolution and refinement of Islamic legal theory and legal hermeneutics. Ibn al-Nadīm has listed the titles of treatises written on abrogation (e.g., *Kitāb al-Nāsikh wa al-Mansūkh*), the Sunnah of the Prophet (e.g., *Kitāb al-Sunan*), and the discrepancy of tradition-reports (*ikhtilāf al-ḥadīth*), some of whose authors belong to the first/seventh and the second/eighth centuries.[4] To this genre, we may add two non-extant works by the great Ḥanafī scholars Muḥammad ibn Ḥasan al-Shaybānī (d. 189/804)[5] and Qāḍī Abū Yūsuf al-Anṣārī (d. 179/795)[6] under the rubric of *uṣūl al-fiqh* and *ijtihād al-ra'y*. The extant works of al-Shāfiʿī reflect the ongoing debates in their embryonic form.

All of the above-mentioned Ḥanafī scholars, as well as Abū Ḥanīfah (d.150/767) and Shāfiʿī, sought to ensure consistency, harmony, coherence, and stability in the law's interpretation and to rein in what they regarded as "speculative reasoning." However, none of them intended to establish or anticipated what later came to be known as *uṣūl al-fiqh*. The use of *uṣūl* co-joined with *fiqh*, *dīn*, *ʿilm*, or ḥadīth has an intricate history in the Arabic language, one that does not necessarily correspond to their present meanings. Al-Shāfiʿī used *ʿilm al-uṣūl* in his *Kitāb al-Umm*[7] to mean "knowledge of the sources," but not in the sense of a methodology, to which his *Risālah* made a significant contribution. Current scholarship is still trying to determine his precise role in developing both a systematic legal methodology and jurisprudence. Notwithstanding this, one can assert that his hermeneutical proposals and the theoretical foundation he provided, both of which invest the Qurʾan and the prophetic hadiths with normativity when deducing legal rules, enabled his students and others to develop a systematic methodology that was rigorous and more "scientific" than relying on the amorphous Madinan practice, tradition, and collective memory of that city's Muslim community or invoking *ra'y*.[8] El Shamsy notes that the term *aṣḥāb al-Shāfiʿī* (al-Shāfiʿī's disciples) was in vogue during the early third/ninth century, which suggests the birth of a distinct and identifiable school of thought.[9] We shall survey the ongoing debates after reviewing his theoretical framework.

A Synopsis of al-Shāfiʿī's Methodology

Al-Shāfiʿī's approach to a methodical understanding of the revealed sources' authority begins with God's five announcements of those norms (*bayān*) that explain the bilateral connection between the Qurʾan and prophetic Sunnah and how it leads to legal knowledge on specific cases. Central to his approach is that the exclusive "authority of the revelatory sources" should prevail over the community's living traditions and customs in order to produce a sense of commitment to the religious law. Al-Shāfiʿī includes the two supplementary sources of *ijmāʿ* and *qiyās* for acquiring legal rulings for any cases not addressed in the revelatory texts.

I.   As the first topic of his argument, he provides five modalities of God's statements of norms (*bayān*)[10] in the form of five possible permutations of the Qur'an and Sunnah:

a. What God communicated via the Qur'an in the explicit and univocal form of a *naṣṣ* (e.g., the obligations to pray and fast) as well as indisputable prohibitions (e.g., intoxicants).

b. What God revealed in the Qur'an is enough for fulfilling the obligation. Therefore, the Sunnah only provides additional but non-essential details. He cites the example of how one can perform *wuḍū'*.

c. What the Qur'an ordained and the relevant details provided by the Sunnah (e.g., how to perform the ritual prayers).

d. What can be established only by the Sunnah because the Qur'an is silent about it.

e. What Muslims should find out through their interpretive activity (ijtihad) based on the Qur'an and Sunnah, either individually (*qiyās*) or collectively (*ijmāʿ*).[11]

II.   Al-Shāfiʿī then turns to meaning analysis and denotation of the revealed texts, after which he introduces the general (*ʿāmm*) and particular (*khāṣṣ*) types of *bayān*. In this chapter, which seems to be the first of its kind in Islamic jurisprudence, he tries to harmonize some conflicting verses of the Qur'an and the Sunnah via particularization.[12]

III. The appearance of abrogation: Al-Shāfiʿī sets a categorical condition that the Qur'an may be abrogated only by the Qur'an, and the Sunnah only by the Sunnah. To him, an abrogated ruling cannot be left without a better replacement. He also discusses cases that are abrogated in part by the Qur'an and in part by the Sunnah or *ijmāʿ*.[13]

IV.   The revealed text (*naṣṣ*) and the Sunnah lay down the duties (*farā'id*): Shāfiʿī gives examples of these duties to show how some verses look general (*ʿāmm*) when, in reality, they are meant to be particular (*khāṣṣ*).[14]

v. Discrepancy of the Traditions: In response to a question on discrepancies among tradition reports, al-Shāfiʿī presents another account of how a Muslim can recognize lucid and ambiguous rulings in addition to the general, particular, and abrogated ones in cases of conflicting laws. He also discusses the reports of the Companions' practices and concludes that only the Sunnah of the Prophet can set laws for the community and that those laws must be followed.[15]

vi. Chapters on knowledge of traditions and ways of authenticating solitary or single-transmitted traditions (*al-akhbār al-āḥād*). Al-Shāfiʿī equates the verification of the just nature (*ʿadālah*) of a hadith transmitter to that of legal testimony (*shahādah*). However, with some caution, he does legitimize the validity of *āḥād* tradition-reports.[16]

vii. Consensus (*ijmāʿ*): al-Shāfiʿī's main concern here is how to obtain consensus on reporting or understanding the Prophet's traditions.[17] Twice in this chapter, he argues that the entire community cannot agree on an error when it comes to understanding the Sunnah, without basing it on a similar tradition-report attributed to the Prophet: "My community [will] never agree on [an] error." One may suggest that either al-Shāfiʿī was unaware of the report or that the report was built upon his words at a later date.

viii. Analogy (*qiyās*): al-Shāfiʿī tends to restrict *qiyās* to those cases that can be connected to an established Qur'anic verse.[18]

ix. Ijtihad: al-Shāfiʿī encourages the practice of ijtihad for both applying and interpreting the Qur'an and Sunnah, citing 2:144, "Turn your face toward the Sacred Mosque," which encourages Muslims to find the proper prayer direction. In his account, *qiyās* appears as part of ijtihad.[19]

X. Juristic preference (*istiḥsān*): al-Shāfiʿī advances this juristic principle in order to exclude it from the class of juridical rational or textual indicants (*adillah*). He considers *istiḥsān* a matter of taste and preference (*taladhdhudh*).[20]

XI. Juristic disagreement (*ikhtilāf*): al-Shāfiʿī divides this into forbidden and permissible disagreements. The former seeks to create schism (*tafriqah*) in the community, whereas the latter is a matter of differing opinions and interpretation. This topic was later developed into a distinct jurisprudential discipline under the rubric of ʿ*ilm al-khilāf*.[21]

The constitutive elements of this sketch underline al-Shāfiʿī's efforts to advance the Qur'an and Sunnah as the exclusive canonized sources of revelation. Jurists should interpret the former without the mediation of local traditions and lived practices as part of the hermeneutical repertoire and should use the Hadith to complement and elucidate the Qur'an, especially its multi-vocal and polyvalent verses. Relying on the textual sources as foundational also precluded the arbitrariness of individual reasoning in deducing law. Disillusioned and alarmed by the rampant use of speculative reasoning and reliance on the lived practice of Madinah's Muslim residents due to the lack of a methodical reading of legal sources, al-Shāfiʿī accorded primacy to the Qur'an and Sunnah and established ways of interpreting and harmonizing them partly by introducing the crucial element of "ambiguity,"[22] which provided greater interpretive flexibility, in order to reconcile the verses, hadiths, and legal rules to the revealed textual sources. By quoting 3:78, 2:79, and 4:50 and 52 and arguing for the necessity of learning and exerting effort to deduce knowledge (*al-ʿilm wa al-ijtihād*), he was hinting at his trajectory, one that would seek to establish a hierarchy of sources that prioritized the two primary sources in relation to analogy, consensus, and *ra'y*.[23]

The thrust of his argument in *al-Risālah*, despite its being imbued with contemporaneous juridical debates, is to establish the legal authority of the Qur'an and Sunnah and to demonstrate their consistency with the already existing legal rules. According to him, both of these primary sources occupy a central place in Islamic legal thought, whereas ijtihad and *qiyās* are supplementary and auxiliary.[24] His chapters on general (*ʿāmm*) and particular (*khāṣṣ*) ijtihad, as well as the discrepancies among hadith accounts related to the same incident, are part of his legal hermeneutics. The hierarchy of the sources (i.e., the Qur'an, Sunnah, and ijtihad) was generally known to Muslims, but al-Shāfiʿī's conviction in the harmony of revealed laws led him to establish a more explicit arrangement. In the words of El Shamsy: "The locus of collective memory, hitherto diffused in the realm of oral culture and ritual performance, thus shifts to written texts ..."[25] It is important to state here that the idea of "four sources of law" was not clearly set in early Muslim thought, that legal consensus (*ijmāʿ*) had yet to acquire a definitive form,[26] and that the application of *qiyās* remained delimited. Although al-Shāfiʿī apparently had no intention to formulate a distinct category of sources, as his interpretive theory was still rudimentary, the sequence of his rational discussion brought *ijmāʿ* and *qiyās* to the fore in such a manner that later authors could surmise four distinct sources of law.

The ideas that al-Shāfiʿī promoted in his *al-Risālah* faced resistance from some quarters and were hard pressed to find a receptive audience among the nascent Muslims as a whole. Apparently, it was no easy matter to convince his adversaries of the Qur'an's supreme authority, and especially that of the Sunnah, when those two sources differed from personal opinions and the community's living traditions. Al-Shāfiʿī's emphasis on textual-based reasoning, the innovative nature of which his students and other scholars developed further, shows the absence of such a practice among his contemporaries.

Some have argued that his legal-theoretical method of establishing the primacy of these two core sources seemed to have had only a slight impact on his fellow jurisprudents and up until the beginning of the fourth/tenth-century milieu. However, ample evidence suggests that his students[27] preserved his intellectual legacy, and "there are numerous reports of *al-Risālah* being known and circulated and used and disputed in one version or another throughout the third/ninth century."[28] Sherman Jackson provides evidence of several Mālikī texts with the title *Radd ʿala al-Shāfiʿī*,[29] and Murteza Bedir demonstrates that Ibn Abān (d. 221/836) had addressed al-Shāfiʿī's work early on by taking him to task for relying on and considering solitary narrations as authoritative when formulating the law, suggesting thereby that al-Shāfiʿī's work did garner some influence.[30] Thus, one can argue that the ostensible gap in the study of *uṣūl al-fiqh* between the time of al-Shāfiʿī and Ibn Surayj's (d. 306/918) students may be illusory. Wael Hallaq posits that, among other things, the direction taken by such contemporaneous traditionist trends as Hanbalism and Zahirism did not allow al-Shāfiʿī's paradigm to gain acceptance.[31] Moreover, he challenges the merit of those modern authors who credit al-Shāfiʿī with being the main architect of Islamic legal theory by claiming that *al-Risālah* predominantly elaborates upon the prophetic hadiths' privileged status in legal reasoning, in which non-Sunnah topics appear only sporadically.[32] He corroborates the idea that this text was essentially written in defense of, or as an apologia for, the Sunnah.[33] But this criticism seems to address al-Shāfiʿī's intention rather than his actual achievements, for although al-Shāfiʿī was obviously inspired by the contemporaneous genre of writings such as *Kitāb al-Sunan*, to which his *al-Risālah* essentially belongs, some of his own methodological principles were foundational and innovative in jurisprudence. Although an outgrowth of *Sunan* writings, in fact, one should not underestimate the many inspiring and creative concepts that he advanced in this text that turned out to be vital in terms of advancing *uṣūl al-fiqh* from the fourth/tenth century onward.

Importantly, al-Shāfiʿī is commonly held to be the first one to set forth the rules of the general/particular (*ʿāmm/khāṣṣ*) as a hermeneutic device and for integrating them into a legal theory to accommodate certain Qurʾanic verses.[34] This view should be retained, despite the fact that the Persian author ʿAbdullāh ibn al-Muqaffaʿ (d. 139/756), who translated Aristotle's *Peri Hermeneias*, had presented the concepts of "universal" and "particular" with the same terms in his Arabic exposition of logic some ten years before al-Shāfiʿī's birth.[35] Indeed, the ideas and modes of expression found in *al-Risālah* show no sign of any influence from these philosophical sources. Nevertheless, this does prove that the *ʿāmm/khāṣṣ* dichotomy was present in another form in the Arabic literature of that period. This dichotomy in logic was later expressed by terms such as *kullī* and *juzʾī*.

In his studies of various early Muslim works, Norman Calder (d. 1998) put forth a radically revisionist thesis: The *Kitāb al-Umm* and *al-Risālah* were unauthored school texts composed over generations by multiple authors and initially appeared as a response to the ongoing problems and perceptions that emerged and disturbed those scholars who were intent on preserving the prophetic legacy.[36] Regarding the many "refinements" developed in the early Islamic period, he proposes redating *al-Risālah*, in its present form, to the turn of the fourth/tenth century, when it began its "liberating influence" on the literary tradition of fiqh.[37] Christopher Melchert confirms Calder's redating by emphasizing that the al-Shāfiʿī school originated during the third/ninth century.[38] Attributing the text's appearance to the school rather than to al-Shāfiʿī himself, he tries to explain the supposed absence of its influence during the third/ninth century. It does not seem, however, to deny the fact that the original author is responsible for the bulk of the work. Moreover, Calder's argument is open to challenge. For example, the term *ʿillah* (efficacious cause) in the sense of *ratio legis*, which was in common usage during the third/ninth century, is starkly absent in *al-Risālah*,[39] an indication that the language al-Shāfiʿī employed in writing this section was that of the late second/eighth century. Instead of *ʿillah*, al-Shāfiʿī (or his student Rabīʿ ibn Sulaymān, who recorded his teacher's discourses[40]) used such terms as *maʿnā* (meaning) and *asbāb al-qiyās* for "the elements of analogy."[41]

Some have posited that *ʿillah* began to be applied in Islamic jurisprudence after Aristotle's *Analytica Priora* was translated during the early third/ninth century.[42] This can be confirmed by comparing the translation of "logic" in the work of Ibn Bihrīz (d. 205/820) with that of Ibn al-Muqaffaʿ (d. 139/756). The former applies this term in the sense of an "effective cause," whereas the latter lacks such an expression.[43] Yet questions raised about *al-Risālah*'s delayed influence and possible redating can hardly deny that al-Shāfiʿī's major contribution to the legal-theoretical method that grants normativity to the Qur'an and Sunnah inspired generations of scholars to further develop his work and construct a systematic legal methodology. Elsewhere, Calder brings forth evidence of the existence of the ʿamm/ khāṣṣ dichotomy within the Jewish hermeneutic tradition: "the text known as the Thirteen Middle of Rabbi Ishmael shows a similar concern with this basic device."[44] He nevertheless acknowledges that this phrase in *al-Risālah* "is locked into a Muslim structure of thought and shows no signs of outside influence."[45]

Jonathan Brockopp's recent research on third/ninth-century Egyptian jurisprudence provides evidence that al-Shāfiʿī's thought influenced his students' writings.[46] Brockopp's examination of a compendia (*Al-Mukhtaṣar*) written by al-Shāfiʿī's student Ismāʿīl b.Yaḥyā al-Muzanī (d. 264/877) indicates that this did occur in cases of applied law (*furūʿ*), but not in terms of giving primacy to the Qur'an and Sunnah. Rather, this work is a familiar mixture of Hadith, individual reasoning, abstract rules, and quotations from al-Shāfiʿī.[47] This corroborates Hallaq's thesis that the first generation of al-Shāfiʿī's students were not affected by *al-Risālah*. Nevertheless, we learn from *Ta'rīkh Baghdād* that his Makkan Companion ʿAbd al-ʿAzīz ibn Yaḥyā al-Kinānī (d. 240/854) included the concepts of ʿumūm/khuṣūṣ (general and particular) and *bayān* (statement) in his book.[48] This supports the idea that later scholars adopted al-Shāfiʿī's method of particularizing some of the Qur'an's conflicting verses long before they adopted his way of concretizing the Sunnah into the prophetic hadiths. The reason for this delayed impact, as Hallaq has suggested, lies in the intensity of traditionism during the first half of the third/ninth century, partly due to the institution of the inquisition (*miḥnah*), which did not conform to al-Shāfiʿī's semi-rational proposal at this point.

Joseph Lawry's new reading of *al-Risālah* suggests that the "four sources" theory (i.e., the Qur'an, Sunnah, consensus, and analogy) is not found in the text and that there is no support "for a reduction of his legal theory to a four-part scheme or hierarchy, or to anything which even resembles a four-part, three-part, or even – except heavily qualified – two-part scheme or hierarchy."[49] By rearranging al-Shāfiʿī's hierarchy of authority [of law], Lowry finds most of them to be "out of context" as they "represent secondary, corroborative authority." He therefore concludes that *al-Risālah* is nothing more than al-Shāfiʿī's theory of *bayān* – "an attempt to describe, down to the last detail, the divine architecture of the law."[50]

Concerning his "no support for four sources theory in *al-Risālah*," one should know that Muslims never reached any consensus on the law's exact sources, except for the Qur'an and Sunnah (with some qualifications). Although *ijmāʿ* was soon added, its scope and the legitimacy of those who practiced it remained undefined, as its character and content were unknown to them. These sources were more obscure during al-Shāfiʿī's time, because the Sunnah was not necessarily related to the Prophet and no specific term had been created for consensus. In fact, al-Shāfiʿī used *ijmāʿ* and *ijtimāʿ* interchangeably,[51] and *qiyās* had yet to be distinguished from ijtihad and *ra'y*. Except for the Qur'an and Sunnah (according to al-Shāfiʿī's understanding of the latter term), the difficulty of finding an explicit statement of the "four sources" theory in early Muslim works should not be regarded as surprising.

Lowry's findings that "al-Shāfiʿī's lists of authority [of law] represent secondary, corroborative authority" is in line with Hallaq's suggestion that non-Sunnah topics appear inadvertently in *al-Risālah*. These assessments have led some contemporary authors to undervalue this work's contribution. And yet this evaluation cannot undermine the fact that its corroborative presentation of the Shariʿah's authoritative sources inspired scholars from the late third/ninth century onward to develop the formal methodology that would engender more consistency and stability in terms of understanding the revealed law. The impetus behind this was, in actuality, the theoretical work *al-Risālah*, regardless of whether it is called *bayān* or *uṣūl al-fiqh*.

If al-Shāfiʿī's *al-Risālah* is considered a major step in the development of Islamic legal methodology, one should examine the variance between his method in his re-presentation of legal norms contained in his *al-Umm* in comparison with Mālik ibn Anas' (d. 179/795) *Al-Muwaṭṭaʾ*, written some twenty years before the former. The first noticeable difference is that al-Shāfiʿī, unlike Mālik, does not speak exclusively in the language of hadith reports. Instead, he adds his own generalizations to the reports and, more than Mālik, places the relevant verses at the beginning of the respective topics. For example, in the case of congregational prayers, al-Shāfiʿī first quotes 5:58 and 62:9[52] and then concludes that the prayer is obligatory according to the Book and the prophetic traditions,[53] whereas Mālik relies exclusively on the language of hadith reports and rarely includes his own opinion of them.[54]

On the legality of taking zakāh from an orphan's property, al-Shāfiʿī applies the principle of generality (*aṣālat al-ʿumūm*) on the grounds that the Qur'an and Sunnah did not particularize this act. In addition to positing the first two sources, he also suggests some of the Companions' reports (*āthār*) or the undisputed word of common Muslims and a legal analogy, if applicable, as the evidential basis (*ḥujjiyyah*) to support his view.[55] Such a listing of the sources of legal authority, which is in line with al-Shāfiʿī's mode of argumentation in his *al-Risālah*, is absent from *al-Muwaṭṭaʾ*. By the "undisputed word of common Muslims" al-Shāfiʿī means the tradition-reports delivered by them, a recurring statement in *al-Risālah* that gives weight to the "words of the commonalty of Muslims" (*qawl ʿāmmat al-muslimīn*). He believed that this *ʿāmmah* usually does not agree on error,[56] which proves that *ijmāʿ* was not fully conceptualized during his time.

Almost a century after al-Shāfiʿī presented his *al-Risālah*, Abū al-ʿAbbās Ibn Surayj (d. 306/918), a prominent jurisprudent of Baghdad, dedicated his courses to promoting al-Shāfiʿī's jurisprudence and methodology. He felt that the elegance (*ẓarf*) of these teachings had been overlooked or corrupted by al-Shāfiʿī's immediate students, especially al-Muzānī.[57] The commentaries on *al-Risālah*[58] written by Abū Bakr al-Ṣayrafī (d. 330/942), al-Qaffāl al-Shāshī (d. 333/947), and Abū Isḥāq al-Marwazī (d. 340/951), all of whom were students of Ibn Surayj, were enough to popularize the legal methodology that they deciphered from it. Of course, they also made their own intellectual contributions. But as none of these works are extant, we cannot compare their structures with those of their contemporary Muʿtazilī and Ḥanafī counterparts, upon which we will focus in the following chapters.[59]

CHAPTER 2

The Approach of Muʿtazilī and Ashʿarī Theologians to Islamic Legal Methodology

PARALLEL TO the methodological efforts of the Shāfiʿī school, Muslim theologians of the early Muʿtazilī and Ashʿarī schools took a keen interest in *uṣūl al-fiqh* and tried to develop its rules further by reason-based legal arguments and by assimilating dialectical theology (*kalām*). Both of these schools can be grouped under the "rational" trend of Islamic thought, despite their difference on the role and scope of human reasoning. The former gives a central place to it, whereas the latter places it after the revealed sources. Melchert prefers to label the latter as a "semi-rationalist" party "who took up the tools of *kalām* in defence of traditionalist doctrines."[1] This "rationalist" approach to *uṣūl al-fiqh* gained momentum despite al-Shāfiʿī's reluctance to imbue his work with contemporaneous *kalāmī* ideas. According to George Makdisi (d. 2002), al-Shāfiʿī wrote *al-Risālah* to defend Islamic traditionalism against the then current rationalist movement.[2] Muʿtazilī rationalists, who were quite active, played a leading and pioneering role in developing theories of legal methodology right from the outset. In addition to the significant contributions of Muʿtazilī writers of the fourth/tenth and the fifth/eleventh centuries, new investigation shows that Muʿtazilī authors of the third/ninth century wrote treatises designed in an orderly fashion to cover topics of the discipline later known as *uṣūl al-fiqh*. Here, we will deal chronologically with the legal works of some prominent Muʿtazilī and Ashʿarī theologians.

ʿAmrū ibn Baḥr al-Jāḥiẓ

The renowned Arab theologian, prose writer, and prolific author on *adab* Abū ʿUthmān ʿAmrū ibn Baḥr al-Jāḥiẓ (d. 255/869) contributed, among other things, to the field of Islamic legal methodology. Born and raised in Basrah (Iraq), a center of Muʿtazilī productivity, he travelled to Baghdad to join the House of Wisdom (*Dār al-Ḥikmah*) founded by Caliph al-Ma'mūn (d. 833) to attract scholars specialized in both the religious and natural sciences. He reportedly wrote about 200 treatises on a variety of subjects, approximately thirty of which have been preserved in their entirety and another fifty only partially preserved. His extant works include Arabic grammar, lexicography, poetry, the study of animals, Islamic law and legal methodology, and other subjects. He refers to the non-extant latter work in his *Kitāb al-Ḥayawān*.

Devin Stewart, in his painstaking search for the earliest works on *uṣūl al-fiqh* or references made to them, points to al-Jāḥiẓ's lost but much mentioned *Kitāb Uṣūl al-Futyā wa al-Aḥkām* as a manual on legal methodology.[3] Before dealing with al-Jāḥiẓ's work, he quotes a passage from Ibn Sallām (a hadith master; d. 224/838) and subsequently asserts that "the concept of a complete, finite, and ordered list of the roots of the law existed already in the early ninth century, perhaps even during al-Shāfiʿī's days."[4] In this passage, Ibn Sallām enumerated the sources of legal norms (*uṣūl al-aḥkām*) as "the Book, the Sunnah and what the leading jurists and righteous ancestors who have ruled on the basis of consensus and ijtihad."[5] Missing from the list is *qiyās*, the fourth category. Stewart writes:

Al-Jāḥiẓ himself describes the work in *Kitāb al-Hayawān* as follows: "*Kitābī fī al-Qawl fī Uṣūl al-Futyā wa al-Aḥkām*" (My book discussing the principles of legal responsa and legal rulings).[6] In an extant letter, he presents the work as a gift to the Muʿtazilī chief judge of Baghdad, Aḥmad ibn Abī Dāʾūd al-Iyādī (d. 240–854).[7]

After examining the attention garnered by al-Jāḥiẓ among his various fellow scholars and their analysis, Stewart concluded that *Kitāb Uṣūl al-Futyā* "must have treated *uṣūl al-fiqh*, including, at the very least, sections on consensus, legal analogy, and ijtihād."[8] These are the same topics that al-Shāfiʿī had discussed in his *al-Risālah* some thirty-five years earlier. The distinctive and original nature of his work prompted contemporary scholars such as Stewart to distinguish the work as "a complete, finite, and ordered list of the roots of the law," which appeared to have been absent in al-Shāfiʿī's *al-Risālah*. Al-Jāḥiẓ was a student of the Muʿtazilī theologian Ibrāhīm al-Naẓẓām (d. 230/845), who had also dealt with some *uṣūlī* topics, among them *qiyās* and *ijmāʿ*, in his non-extant *Kitāb al-Nakt*, supposedly to refute their validity.[9]

Al-Qāḍī Al-Bāqillānī

Abū Bakr al-Bāqillānī (d. 403/1013) was a renowned and preeminent theorist of the Ashʿarī school of theology who subscribed to the Mālikī school of thought. A contemporary of al-Qāḍī ʿAbd al-Jabbār (d. 415/1024), he was born in Basrah but raised and educated in Baghdad, where he became a prominent judge and theologian. His knowledge of formal logic enabled him to debate on Islamic law and theology at the Buwayhid and Byzantine courts. In general, al-Bāqillānī supported the Ashʿarī doctrine of the Qurʾan's uncreatedness, inception, divine decree, and the possibility of seeing God.

He made important contributions to the theory of language, signification, and the tension between a word or an utterance's clarity and ambiguity (i.e., the hermeneutics of ambiguity). This is attested to by the fact that subsequent authors and biographers frequently referred to his work. The fourteenth-century biographer Tāj al-Dīn al-Subkī included al-Bāqillānī's *Kitāb al-Taqrīb wa al-Irshād* among the earliest works written on the Islamic legal methodology after al-Shāfiʿī's *al-Risālah* and its commentaries.[10]

In writing his *Taqrīb*, al-Bāqillānī appears fully aware of the definition and scope of *uṣūl al-fiqh*, which he defines as knowledge of both the sources and speculative indications through which legal rules are deduced.[11] Nevertheless, he does not deal with the legal sources (*adillah*) first; rather, he defines ʿ*ilm* (knowledge), ʿ*aql* (intellect), *dalīl* (indicant/signifier), and even the term *definition* (*fī ḥadd al-ḥadd*).[12] He distinguishes two applications for *ḥadd* – logical and mechanical – which mark the beginning of transferring notions from formal logic into legal methodology. Al-Bāqillānī's next chapter, "On the Essence of Human Action," is totally theological in character. In a subchapter devoted to the human perception of good and evil, he refutes the idea that the human mind has the capacity to distinguish good from evil.[13]

After these introductory remarks, al-Bāqillānī begins to set forth his eight topics under the rubric of his legal methodology:[14] (1) The divine address or oration (*khiṭāb*) as reflected in the Qur'an and Sunnah of the Prophet. Here, he emphasizes the semantic and grammatical aspects of the revealed message;[15] (2) The Prophet's practices as evidence to determine revealed laws; (3) The tradition-reports of the Prophet and their gradation; (4) The solitary or single-transmitter traditions and conditions they have to fulfill before they can be invoked as evidence; (5) The *ijmāʿ* of the community; (6) *Qiyās;* (7) The qualifications to attain the rank of a bona fide mufti whose juridical opinions can be followed by others; and (8) Prohibited and permissible actions (*al-ḥaẓr wa al-ibāḥah*).[16]

The above outline shows that his conception of *uṣūl al-fiqh* coincides with the hierarchical arrangement of the four-source theory of the law plus elements borrowed from logic, grammar, and theology. He ends by enumerating the requirements one has to fulfill in order to qualify as a jurist who can deduce rules by interrogating the sources. Al-Bāqillānī's last topic, "On the Restriction of Human Action," is evidently designed to limit the discretion of a human being's inherent independent capacity, in accordance with his Ashʿarī worldview. His legal methodology has essentially adopted the following sequence: deliberation on the sources' authority, ways of interpretation, and limits of human ijtihad as an auxiliary to the revealed rules.

Al-Qāḍī ʿAbd al-Jabbār

A stark contrast to al-Qāḍī al-Bāqillānī is provided by the renowned Muʿtazilī (formerly Ashʿarī) theologian Qāḍī ʿAbd al-Jabbār al-Hamadānī (d. 415/1024), famously known as *Qāḍī al-Quḍāt* (judge of the judges [chief magistrate]), who promoted a theological orientation to legal methodology. Representing Busrah's school of thought, he was born in Hamadān (Iran) and educated first in Busrah and then in Baghdad. The most notable student of al-Jāḥiẓ, who he frequently quotes, this Shāfiʿī jurist argued that believing in the disjuncture between God's eternal speech and the Qur'an's created words, as the Ashʿarīs did, would make God's will humanly unknowable. According to him, this would violate the Muʿtazilī principle that His speech must always provide perfect clarity so that His will could be understood correctly.

In 367/978, the powerful governor and vizier Ṣāḥib ibn ʿAbbād, a staunch supporter of Muʿtazilī theology, invited him to Rayy (part of present-day Tehran) and appointed him chief magistrate. He wrote several books on Muʿtazilī theology and Islamic legal hermeneutics, including a separate work on Islamic legal methodology, *Al-Nihāyah fī Uṣūl al-Fiqh*, that has not come down to us.[17] However, in his magnum opus the *al-Mughnī*, which is a systematic work on theology, he deals with subject matters found in legal methodology under the rubric of *sharʿiyyāt* (legal matters) to which we now turn. Governed by the Muʿtazilī understanding of justice, this human faculty attempts to fathom the inherent merit or demerit of an act as well as the divine intent.

In this book, whose opening chapters have been lost, al-Qāḍī ʿAbd al-Jabbār provides a theologically oriented legal methodology in both the selection of topics and justification for his arguments to demonstrate theological consistency. He dedicates several headings to set conditions for the divine discourse (*khiṭāb*) in accordance with his view on the fundamental role of reason and immediate access to His knowledge.[18] In his account, the divine commands and prohibitions indicate actions that are innately good or evil and therefore independent of God's command. As such, revelation's role is to show their moral status rather than provide a prescription.[19] More importantly, he situates justice as the overarching principle behind the *uṣūlī* maxims of generals/particulars (*'amm/khāṣṣ*).[20] In addition, he adds categories such as "permissible actions" (*ibāḥah*) to refer to acts that are to be regarded as permissible in principle unless there is explicit evidence to the contrary. This indicates his highly sophisticated Mu'tazilī position, in which the faculty of human reason is assigned an inherent capacity to appraise the merit or demerit of actions prior to receiving revelation on the issues. Other jurists, among them the Ḥanafī judge Abū Zayd Dabūsī (d. 430/1038)[21] and the Mālikī thinker Abū Isḥāq al-Shāṭibī (d. 790/1388), later corroborated the thread of this argument.[22] These are, however, questions in the domain of legal philosophy with which *uṣūlī* scholars were not usually concerned.

Regardless of his theological stance, al-Qāḍī 'Abd al-Jabbār's method of formatting the discipline's relevant contents is in line with the schema derived from al-Shāfi'ī's discussion of the issue. That is to say, after dealing with the Qur'an and Sunnah, which he terms *sam'iyyāt* or *nubuwwāt* (revealed guidances), he turns his attention to determining the qualifications, at least in his perspective, for a valid *ijmā'*, *qiyās*, and ijtihad. In addition to divine guidance, he boldly incorporated human reason's vital role in setting both reason-based topics for legal methodology and in structuring the revealed guidance. No wonder that the fierce Ash'arī reaction did not allow the survival of a framework that juxtaposed reason with revelation. From another perspective, this can connote the culmination of an affinity not only between Islamic theology and legal methodology, but also between revealed law and human reason.

Vishanoff makes an astute observation in this regard:

For the Ẓāhiriyyah, literalism stemmed from their refusal to look beneath the surface of language, whereas for 'Abd al-Jabbār, literalism and minimalism stemmed from his opposite stance that the meaning of God's speech is determined by the just motives that lie behind it. But despite their very different starting points, the outcome was similar: both hermeneutical theories tended to deny the ambiguity of language, and therefore did not provide the flexibility necessary for al-Shāfiʿī's project of negotiating relationships between texts and laws.[23]

Abū Manṣūr ʿAbd al-Qāhir al-Baghdādī

Abū Manṣūr ʿAbd al-Qāhir al-Baghdādī (d. 429/1037) was a Shāfiʿī jurist and Ashʿarī theologian who contributed to Islamic legal methodology as well as to jurisprudence. Born in Baghdad, he later moved to Nishapur (in Khorasan) with his father and continued his studies there. After the Seljuk invasion, he moved to Isfarain (northern Khorasan) and attended Abū Isḥāq's lectures. Upon the latter's death, he assumed the Chair of Shāfiʿī fiqh at the Mosque of ʿAqīl. He is credited with training a number of eminent students and leading scholars, among them al-Juwaynī and al-Ghazālī (see below), who attained prominence and helped foster a new trend of moderate Ashʿarism in Khorasan. The list of al-Baghdādī's works includes twenty-four treatises on theology, law, jurisprudence, heresiography, history, mathematics, and other disciplines. However, three of his extant books seem to be very important and much referred to by experts: *Uṣūl al-Dīn*, *Al-Milal wa al-Niḥal*, and *Al-Farq bayn al-Firaq*. The titles of his other works point to several methodological (*uṣūlī*) writings, such as *Al-Taḥṣīl fī Uṣūl al-Fiqh*; however, since none of them are extant, we content ourselves with examining his famous *Uṣūl al-Dīn*.

Al-Baghdādī summarizes the fundamentals of Islamic thought in fifteen principles, each of which he sub-divided into fifteen cases or theoretical-jurisprudential issues (*masāʾil*). He allocated the first principle to a general exposition of truths and, specifically, to human knowledge of them. His first question, therefore, is about the definition of knowledge (*ḥadd al-ʿilm*), which he defines according to the Ashʿarī conception of time as "a quality by which a living human becomes knowledgeable" (*ʿalīm*); nevertheless, he quotes the Muʿtazilī and other views.[24] He then classifies knowledge as follows: First, eternal knowledge of God versus human and animal knowledge. The latter is sub-divided into acquired (*iktisābī*) and necessary (*ḍarūrī*) knowledge. Necessary knowledge is that knowledge over which one has no control and which one can obtain without reasoning, because it is either obvious or sensible (*ḥissī*). Among the knowledge acquired by the five senses, knowledge received by narration (*samʿī*) is believed to be the most important in a religious system. From this point, the author moves on to an evaluation of tradition-reports (*khabar*).

Al-Baghdādī divides tradition-reports into three types: (1) *muta-wātir* (a successively reported tradition through multiple independent transmissions) that conveys necessarily reliable knowledge due to the impossibility of complicity among its narrators; (2) solitary (*āḥād*) traditions that are single-transmitter and, of course, not on par with *mutawātir*. However, they are acceptable for practice, provided that their chain of transmission is strong, for their validity is akin to the testimony of witnesses known to be just; and (3) *mutawassiṭ* (medium), which al-Baghdādī considers comparable to *mutawātir* in its validity and in terms of conveying knowledge.[25] He then presents another classification of knowledge that may be relevant although not juridically valid: (1) things that can be understood by reason either through analogy or reflection (e.g., the world's creation, the Creator's eternity, and humanity's obligation toward its Creator); (2) what can be understood by experiences and habits (e.g., medicine and crafts); (3) what is known by religious law-giving (e.g., how to perform the prayers); and (4) what is known by some people through inspiration (*ilhām*) (e.g., the talent and taste of poetry and music).[26]

Concerning the law's sources, al-Baghdādī, following al-Shāfiʿī and other precursor jurists, holds these to be the Qurʾan, the Sunnah, consensus, and *qiyās*. He adds that the Qurʾan verses may be subject to the rules pertaining to the general or the particular, the absolute or the conditional, the abrogated and the ambiguous. He elaborates on the linguistics of the Qurʾan and the Sunnah in Chapter 9,[27] where he also stipulates that *ijmāʿ* refers to the consensus of the people of each period on a juridical matter supported by the Prophetic tradition that the Muslim community will never agree on an error.[28] In Chapter 8 he deals with the miracle of the Qur'an, which he believes lies in its inherent eloquence and the revelation of mysteries related to past and future events. He refutes some Mu'tazili views, such as those advocated by Ibrāhīm al-Naẓẓām (d. 230/845), who excluded the Qur'an's eloquence from this list. Al-Baghdādī stresses the inimitability of the Qur'anic verses' ordering, not just the meaning, saying that it surpasses the poetic and lyric writings of the experts.[29]

He bases the leadership of the community (*imāmah*), the last topic of his work, on the position adopted by Abū al-Ḥasan al-Ash'arī (d.324/936): *imāmah* is a necessary law of the Shari'ah. He quotes Shi'i and Mu'tazili views in support of this idea, but disagrees with the latter's position that it is necessary due to God's grace (*luṭf*). Instead, he bases its authority on the Companions' practice. As for its legitimacy, he draws an analogy with examples from both Islam's private and public laws, such as *iqāmat al-ḥudūd* (implementation of the penal laws). In contrast to the Twelver Shi'a view that the Twelfth Imam in inaccessible and is in the phase of prolonged occultation, he emphasizes that the Imām must be apparent and accessible. In terms of this person's qualifications, al-Baghdādī emphasizes his just nature and belonging to the Qurayshī tribe; however, he excludes the attribute of infallibility on the grounds that this belongs only to the prophets.[30] The most important question of the theory of *imāmah* concerns its mode of establishment. Al-Baghdādī, like most Sunni authors, believes that the community's elite members must choose (*ikhtiyār*) a qualified person. In the case of necessity, however, he permits the choice of a less learned and qualified (*mafḍūl*) person.[31]

As such, al-Baghdādī strengthened and solidified Ash'arī thought, which caused many Muslim scholars to help establish the Niẓāmiyyah schools in Baghdad and Nishapur in 1065, almost three decades after his demise. These schools are considered the first Islamic institutes of higher learning that specifically promoted a well-balanced and systematic Ash'arī thought to confront the Mu'tazili and even philosophical trends. We will see below how al-Baghdādī's views on the authority of legal sources and jurisprudence were elaborated and expanded upon by scholars such as al-Juwaynī and al-Ghazālī, through whom Ash'arī thought survived in the Sunni world. We can observe that some Ash'arī theological positions still retain their influence in varying forms even today.

Abū al-Ḥusayn al-Baṣrī

In many ways, the work of al-Qāḍī 'Abd al-Jabbār was continued by his student Abū al-Ḥusayn al-Baṣrī (d.436/1044), who set a standard for composing legal methodology in the early period of Islamic history. A native Basran as well as a Ḥanafī who followed a Mu'tazilī creed, he studied Islamic law and theology as well as medicine in Baghdad and then traveled to Rayy and became one of al-Qāḍī 'Abd al-Jabbār's pupil. Although a staunch defender of Mu'tazilī thought, he nevertheless challenged some of his teacher's ideas on legal theory and jurisprudence and "aligned himself in his later work with the hermeneutic of al-Karkhī and al-Jaṣṣāṣ."[32] The close relation between Mu'tazilism and Ḥanafism and their influence on each other continued for most of the fourth/tenth and fifth/eleventh centuries. His work *Al-Mu'tamad* is regarded as the earliest well-balanced structure of legal methodology based on both revealed and rational sources, which makes him a scripturalist and a rationalist. His work spread far beyond Mu'tazilī circles, particularly among the Shāfi'īs and Hanbalīs of Baghdad, the Twelver Shī'ī scholar Sadīd al-Dīn al-Rāzī (sixth/twelfth century), and the Zaydīs of Yemen.[33] As will be shown in the following outline, the Mu'tazilī-influenced al-Baṣrī allocated a separate section to human reason.[34]

The Structure of al-Baṣrī's Legal Methodology

Al-Baṣrī defines *uṣūl al-fiqh* as the method of knowing the legal norms (*aḥkām*) and outlines what he considered to be the topics of its methodology and how they should be arranged. He devotes an introduction to the legal language and the difference between "real" (*ḥaqīqah*) and "metaphorical" (*majāz*).

I. Commands, Prohibitions, and Their Semantic Rules

This includes chapters on (i) the legal text's general and particular expressions, (ii) its ambiguous and explicit expressions, and (iii) the rules of abrogation. Here al-Baṣrī adds a chapter entitled "acts" (*afʿāl*), which deals mainly with the human ability to recognize good and evil (*al-ḥusn wa al-qubḥ*) with the help of reason prior to revelation.

II. Other Sources of Legal Knowledge

Comprising chapters on: (i) consensus, (ii) the traditions, and (iii) juridical analogy and ijtihad. Al-Baṣrī gives no title to this part, for it is understood that he is dealing with non-scriptural sources of legal knowledge after the Qur'an.

III. The Permissibility of Using Human Reason and Its Limits

Under the title of "*al-ḥaẓr wa al-ibāḥah*," al-Baṣrī allocates a chapter on several topics in an attempt to explain how human reasoning may arrive at legal knowledge.

IV. The Mufti-Commoners' Relations

Al-Baṣrī devoted his last chapter to rules concerning the qualifications of the mufti or *mujtahid* and the procedure for issuing a fatwa. The purpose of these postulates is to qualify and limit the scope of independent reasoning.[35]

The above outline shows the influence of theological concepts, such as people's capacity to evaluate an act's moral status prior to revelation and the permissibility of using human reason while respecting its limits (*al-ḥaẓr wa al-ibāḥah*). In al-Baṣrī's approach, Islamic legal methodology begins with the semantic interpretation of scripture and tradition, continues with the categorization of other sources, and ends with the qualification of a *mujtahid* and the scope of his authority to engage in independent reasoning in the absence of a revealed text. From this viewpoint, we may say that his methodology is founded on the capacity of the person's rational faculty to understand and interpret the scriptural and traditional sources. This scheme can, in essence, be found in al-Shāfiʿī's sketch. And yet al-Baṣrī's work lacks al-Shāfiʿī's defensive argument for the Qur'an's authority, and especially for that of the Sunnah, because by his time all schools had fully recognized their legal weight.

Comparing al-Baṣrī's methodology with al-Shāfiʿī's sketch, we may draw the following key differences that distances al-Shāfiʿī from most of the post-al-Baṣrī *uṣūl al-fiqh* works: (1) The hierarchy of legal sources is de-emphasized, as it now appears to be fully entrenched within the structure of jurisprudence; (2) The authority of the Qur'an and Sunnah is incorporated into the topics of "commands and prohibitions," for they have been established as the principal sources of legal knowledge; (3) The texts' semantic interpretation expands due to its extended scope. In other words, a new identity was being conceived based upon the words of the established texts whose authority originally stemmed from the Qur'an and Sunnah; (4) Legal reasoning's scope is wider than *qiyās* and ijtihad. The human capacity to distinguish good and evil without the aid of revelation and the sphere of allowable actions (*ibāḥah*) are now added to them; and (5) The method of expressing ideas differs from that of al-Shāfiʿī. Al-Baṣrī delivered his ideas via statements, whereas al-Shāfiʿī's style is mainly based on narrations. This is due both to the 225-year gap between them and the changed style of Arabic prose writing – transmitting words on the authority of others (*riwāyah*) to express ideas declined in value after the third/ninth century.

Although the assimilation of rational theology with legal methodology did not change the latter's character, it did provide new and expanded grounds to legal methodology. Classical Muslim authors considered the extent of the new grounds as a natural development within legal knowledge, for not only did it embrace a shared epistemological approach between theology and law, but it was also inspired by a common conviction that God's law, like Himself, is imbued with an eternal truth that must be explored through an identical approach. This is why the relation of these two disciplines is characterized as a fusion of law and theology. Makdisi considers *uṣūl al-fiqh* as eminently receptive to two rationalist instruments of methodology: logic and dialect.[36] Comparing the work of al-Baṣrī with that of ʿAbd al-Jabbār, we see that this interaction was formalized in the work of al-Baṣrī. In Chapter 5, when dealing with the trajectory of theorizing a legal methodology, we will see how it was confirmed as a shared epistemological approach in the works of Ibn Ḥazm, al-Juwaynī, al-Ghazālī, and subsequent authors.

It is noteworthy that al-Baṣrī shows no interest in using terms borrowed from formal logic to define legal terms, a trend that had started with Abū Bakr al-Bāqillānī and was developed further by Ibn Ḥazm and al-Ghazālī. Nevertheless, the solid structure of his work, delivered in clear statements, demonstrates his methodic conceptions of the materials.

CHAPTER 3

The Ḥanafī Elaboration of Legal Methodology

THE ḤANAFĪ school's decision to incorporate new and changing social realities into its methodology brought forth a new approach to Islamic legal methodology during the fourth/tenth century. This occurred in Baghdad, which hosted a certain number of Ḥanafī scholars, especially the three contemporaneous shaykhs Abū Zayd ʿUbaydullāh al-Dabbūsī (d. 430/1038), Abū Bakr Muḥammad ibn Aḥmad al-Sarakhsī (d. 490/1096), and Fakhr al-Islām ʿAlī ibn Muḥammad al-Bazdawī (d. 482/1089). The latter figure's legal pedigree can be traced to Abū al-Ḥasan al-Karkhī (d. 340/951) and Abū Bakr al-Jaṣṣāṣ (d. 370/981). These scholars shifted the emphasis from theoretical discussions on the sources' authority to practical solutions for dealing with the continued arising of new contingencies. Their goal here was to make the law's application more consistent by adding more legal maxims (*qawāʿid al-fiqh*, see below) to theories about its authority. Thus Mohammad Hashim Kamali considers this approach as deductive and "pragmatic in the sense that theory is formulated in light of its application to relevant issues."[1]

The available sources reveal that the city's Ḥanafī scholars benefited from both the Ḥanafī and Shāfiʿī works of that period. For example, they had access to the works of past Ḥanafī masters (e.g.,

Abū Yūsuf and Shaybānī) and to al-Shāfiʿī's *al-Risālah*, which was reintroduced by the Shāfiʿī jurist Ibn Surayj (d. 306/918). Among these Ḥanafī scholars were Abū Ṭāhir al-Dabbās (d. first quarter of fourth/tenth century), Abū al-Ḥasan al-Karkhī (d. 340/951), Aḥmad ibn Muḥammad al-Shāshī (d. 344/955; he infused a number of legal principles into their methodology), and others.[2] This gave birth to the related discipline of *qawāʿid al-fiqh*, which, in practice, affected the development of Islamic methodology. These principles are essentially a host of generalizations derived from important legal rulings of positive law, such as the principle of "no harm inflicted or reciprocated" (*lā ḍarar wa lā ḍirār*). This led some authors to conclude that Ḥanafī methodology focused on topics and discussions of positive law.[3] We will examine the school's early structure of legal methodology in the work of al-Jaṣṣāṣ.

Al-Rāzī al-Jaṣṣāṣ

An almost-contemporary of al-Bāqillānī, Abū Bakr Aḥmad ibn ʿAlī al-Rāzī (d. 370/981), better known as al-Jaṣṣāṣ, produced the earliest extant text on *uṣūl al-fiqh* (more than 140 years after al-Shāfiʿī's death) and the non-extant book attributed to his colleague Aḥmad al-Shāshī.[4] Both were students of Abū al-Ḥasan al-Karkhī. Al-Jaṣṣāṣ was an Ashʿari theologian who had adopted some Muʿtazilī views as well as refuted sorcery and the idea that humans would be able to see God with their eyes (i.e., the "beatific vision"). Politically he adheres to the emerging tendency among the ʿulamāʾ of disassociating themselves from the government, for he declined the Caliph's offer to assume the position of Baghdad's chief justice (*qāḍī al-quḍāt*). This tendency died out later on, for the ʿulamāʾ gradually became closely attached to the Caliph. He wrote commentaries on the works of early Ḥanafī grand masters such as al-Shaybānī and Abū Yūsuf.

Al-Jaṣṣāṣ' work on *uṣūl al-fiqh* lacks any introductory remarks on the law's sources, for their authority and categorization seems to have been taken for granted by then. However, his way of expressing ideas resembled that of Shāfiʿī, for it is imbued with debates and quotations from authoritative predecessors. He frequently applies the stated principles to examples from positive law (or establishes a rule on their basis). In these cases, his account resembles that of *qawā'id al-fiqh* or simply Ḥanafī jurisprudence. Nevertheless, the bulk of his work contains topics of legal methodology. Unlike al-Baṣrī, al-Jaṣṣāṣ provides no orderly sequence for the contents of his *uṣūl al-fiqh*. He opens the subject with the revealed texts' semantics and closes it by discussing the human exertion needed to interpret them. The influence of Arabic grammar is visible in his semantics, as he dedicates a chapter to the various roles and meanings of words such as "*wāw*" in Arabic.[5]

Al-Jaṣṣāṣ' account on legal analogy appears more detailed and well argued. He often equates *qiyās* with ijtihad, as was common in the earliest Sunni and Shi'i jurisprudential works, and defends both according to evidence found in the Companions' practice.[6] The reason for this lies not only in the Ḥanafīs' agreement with the wider scope of *qiyās*, but rather in al-Jaṣṣāṣ' elaboration of the *ratio legis* (*'illah*), which is so refined in his analysis. We know that al-Shāfi'ī, when writing about *qiyās*, used *ma'nā* and similar words, as opposed to *'illah*, for "the efficacious cause." Nabil Shehaby, a contemporary author, tried to draw parallels between al-Jaṣṣāṣ' presentation of rational and literal proofs and those of Stoic logic.[7] In his view, there is a resemblance between *'illah* and the Stoic category of "quality," if not the "common quality" of Diogenes of Babylon (d. 140/150 BCE).[8] Al-Jaṣṣāṣ' account of *'illah*, however, shows no influence from any of the logical works, although he does include *'aql* among the proofs to legitimize *qiyās* in general.[9] Shehaby's account of Stoic and Babylonian precedents points to the fact that "the efficacious cause," as well as "generals" and "particulars," were commonly understood by ancient communities. However, their ways of articulation and application were independent from each other, as al-Shāfi'ī and al-Jaṣṣāṣ' articulations of *'illah* and *'āmm/khāṣṣ* show that they are unique to them. Joep Lameer conjectures that Muslim theologians may have borrowed the concept of *'illah* from Aristotle (d. 332 BCE) as early as the second quarter of the third/ninth century or were at least inspired by his usage of the term. It was then appropriated by

Muslim jurists from Muslim theologians. He supports his latter speculation in this way: "Judging from the fact that the jurists' understanding of the *ʿilla* in terms of such a concept is *wrong*, the theologians' conceptual understanding of the *ʿilla*, on the other hand, *correct*, I conclude that the jurists must have borrowed this concept from the theologians and not the other way round."[10]

The works of al-Jaṣṣāṣ exhibited great sophistication and can be situated between rationalism and traditionalism with ample evidence of Muʿtazilī influence. He included a chapter on the permissibility of using human reason and its limits (*al-ḥazr wa al-ibāḥah*) in which he analyzed the moral status of people's actions before the onset of revelation,[11] which inevitably led him to accept reason's role in the absence of religious prescription. In addition to this chapter, al-Jaṣṣāṣ leans upon reason throughout his work, particularly in his assertions of legal analogy (*ithbāt al-qiyās*), explanations of its *ratio legis* (*ʿillah*), and assessments of the validity of solitary reports.[12] (Later Ḥanafī works deemphasize the intellect's role.) However, his *uṣūlī* rational approach does not cause him to be regarded as a Muʿtazilī thinker, as al-Baṣrī seemed to be. Although Mu'tazilī biographers labelled him "Mu'tazilī," this claim has been contested of late. Perhaps the most accurate way of depicting him may be as someone situated "between the rationalist and traditionalist tendencies in Islamic intellectual thought."[13] However, no definitive conclusions can be drawn because his *kalām* work is no longer extant. His reliance on *ʿaql* appears to be within the limits of Islamic orthodoxy. At the same time, he was also actively involved in the hadith discourse.

An Outline of al-Jaṣṣāṣ' Legal Methodology

Al-Jaṣṣāṣ defines *uṣūl al-fiqh* as a method to expound the Qur'an's meanings and their rational and textual indicants (*adillah*). He opens his discourse by discussing the semantics of words (*alfāẓ*) [of the

revealed sources], continues with juridical analogy and juristic preference (*istiḥsān*), and ends with the qualifications of a *mujtahid*:

1. Legal language: In this context, the manifestation of real or
   metaphorical meanings, its general and particularistic traits,
   exceptions, the meaning of ambiguous terms, and conjectures are
   discussed.[14]
2. The divine address (*khiṭāb*): Here, his primary focus is the texts'
   expressed or implied, real or metaphorical, intricate or unequivocal meanings.
3. The clear statement of divine norms (*bayān*): Under this title he
   discusses, among other things, the varieties of divine commands
   and prohibitions and their possible abrogation.
4. The transmission of the traditions (*akhbār*), their discrepancies,
   the evaluation of solitary reports: their contents, transmitters, and
   acceptance of *mursal* reports.
5. Consensus: Its contextuality and qualification. Here, he deliberates on the widely accepted disagreement within an *ijmāᶜ* and supports the minority view on its validity.[15]
6. Juridical analogy, ijtihad, and juristic preference (*istiḥsān*): their
   justification and varieties, and how to expound and qualify *ᶜillah*
   in *qiyās*.
7. The qualifications of a *mujtahid* and the necessity of following
   their opinions, since they come up with sound opinions even in
   the case of a discrepancy.[16]

Abū Zayd al-Dabbūsī

Both Abū Zayd ᶜUbaydullāh al-Dabbūsī (d. 430/1038) and Abū Bakr
Muḥammad ibn Aḥmad al-Sarakhsī (d. 490/1096) are greatly
indebted to al-Jaṣṣāṣ, for they relied heavily upon his work when
composing their own. As a matter of fact, some parts of their book
are copied verbatim from his work. Al-Dabbūsī, who lived about
half a century after al-Jaṣṣāṣ, spent the majority of his life in
Transoxiana and adopted a similar legal methodology. However, he
gave more weight to the context of revelation, the evidentiary value

or probative force (*ḥujjiyyah*) of the sources and reason, and argued that a jurist's interpretive activity remains only an approximation because the exact divine injunction would be almost impossible to unveil. Thus, a jurist is rewarded for his efforts regardless of the outcome being correct or not.[17]

Born in Dabus (near Bukhārā), he became the city's chief judge. Among the first Ḥanafī authors to write on the comparative laws of Islam explaining juristic disagreements (*ʿilm al-khilāf*), he also indicated his concern about the sources' validity by writing a work on *uṣūl al-fiqh: Taqwīm al-Adillah*. He first divides the legal proofs' authority into revealed and rational (*al-sharʿiyyah/al-ʿaqliyyah*) and then each of them into *mūjibah* (lit. affirmative) and *mujawwizah* (lit. permitted). The former obligates definitive knowledge (*qaṭʿ*) where no dissent is permitted, whereas the latter allows for disagreement and differing views.[18]

According to al-Dabbūsī, the law's revealed indicants include the Qur'an, the traditions of the Prophet, consensus, and *qiyās*.[19] His account on rational proofs (*al-ḥujaj al-ʿaqliyyah*) contain topics concerned with legal norms, including *mubāḥāt* (permissible acts whose commission or omission is equally legal) and *muḥarramāt al-ʿaql* (forbidden by the dictates of reason). By *ʿaql*, here al-Dabbūsī means the customary judgments or practices of his time.[20] His exact methodological topics are found in his argumentations on the revealed indicants' authority. Nevertheless, he includes in his work a number of ethico-mystical topics such as *ilhām* (inspiration) and the "state of the human heart before acquiring knowledge," which point to his gnostic inclination.[21]

Al-Dabbūsī's accounts of the relationship between reason and revelation points to his Muʿtazilī inclination, something that he appears hesitant to acknowledge. One of his most Muʿtazilī type assertion is:

> It is understood that the permittedness of having things beyond the need is an established principle by an apparent but not conclusive indication of reason (*bi dalīl al-ʿaql ẓāhiran lā qaṭʿan*); but it is still a

ground on which one is obliged to act unless revelation makes it clear that the truth is the opposite of it, which is also a possibility of reason. Thus the revelational indication becomes like an indication that specifies [the general verdict of] reason. It has the same status as the particular that comes after the general where the latter remains operative outside the specified area.[22]

Ahmed meticulously studied the texts written by al-Dabbūsī and al-Sarakhsī, Ḥanafī jurists who lived close to each other and relied upon the same intellectual heritage and yet reached very different conclusions on how to apply the law.

A case in point is the scope of reason in deriving legal rulings. Ahmed argues that the subtle differences in how they define terms may appear immaterial at first sight but that, in actuality, such differences do have significant ramifications.[23]

Fakhr al-Islām al-Bazdawī

Fakhr al-Islām ʿAlī ibn Muḥammad al-Bazdawī (d. 482/1089), another principal Ḥanafī author from Bukhārā, also pursues this course of pragmatic elaboration of legal methodology. He wrote many treatises on Islamic jurisprudence and Qur'anic exegesis; however, later Ḥanafī writers mainly cite his treatise on Islamic legal methodology. Al-Bazdawī did not define legal methodology, but rather identified it as knowledge of [general] principles (*uṣūl*) in contrast to knowledge of the applied law (*furūʿ*). His approach to legal methodology begins with an elaboration of the law's sources, in which he includes the Qur'an, the Sunnah, and consensus. He upholds *qiyās* only if it is inferred from the aforesaid sources.[24] In dealing with the Qur'an's semantics, al-Bazdawī offers a new division of the topics according to either their order of expression (*naẓm al-ʿibārah*) or their meaning (*maʿnā*). The first category is concerned with the linguistic aspects of legal words, which include topics of general (*ʿāmm*) and its particularization (*khāṣṣ*), homonym (*mushtarak*), and construed (*mu'awwal*). The second category, which is concerned with the expression (*bayān*) of legal norms, is divided into explicit (*ẓāhir*), clear injunction (*naṣṣ*), explained (*mufassar*) and solid (*muḥkam*), and their counterparts. The third category, the mode of applying (*istiʿmāl*) legal terms, comprises metaphor (*majāz*), allusion (*kināyah*), and their matching parts (i.e. "real and explicit"). The fourth category involves ways of understanding the text's purpose and meaning by [rational] endeavor and consists of reasoning (*istidlāl*) over the content of texts and their meanings by allusion (*ishārah*), indication (*dalālah*), or requirement (*iqtiḍāʾ*).[25]

At the end of this section, al-Bazdawī adds a grammatical one to the aforesaid semantics and then turns his attention to strict and concessionary laws of dispensation (*al-ʿazīmah wa al-rukhṣah*). He first divides the former into *farīḍah* (made obligatory by the text), second is *wājib* (obligatory), third is the Sunnah, and fourth is *nafl* (supererogatory). The concessionary law is divided into (1) real (*ḥaqīqī*), such as undertaking illegal actions (e.g., damaging someone's property with force and coercion) and (2) metaphorical (*majāzī*) such as shortening one's prayer while traveling. Al-Bazdawī concludes this semantic part by analyzing the divergent meanings of legal words, for he is one of the precursor jurists who recognized that some legal commands or prohibitions might implicate a contrasted legal meaning. For instance, Qur'an 2:228, "and it is not lawful for women to conceal what God has created in their wombs," implies that women should tell [their husbands] when they are menstruating.[26]

The second part of al-Bazdawī's work centers on the traditions of the Prophet. Here, he deals with the varieties of traditions, their transmitters, and cases of conflict in the tradition-reports. At the end of this part, he briefly discusses two theological questions of scriptures that came through earlier prophets and the emulation of the Companions' practices. Thereafter, he addresses abrogation and alteration (*tabdīl*), which are applicable to both the Qur'an and the Sunnah. Following the hierarchical arrangement of the law's sources, al-Bazdawī then deals with consensus, its justification and conditions, and the causes that would warrant its usage. He categorically endorses *ijmāᶜ* and its necessity, although he sets some conditions for its realization.[27]

Al-Bazdawī's last topic of legal methodology is *qiyās*, in which he includes *istiḥsān*, the position of a *mujtahid* in patching up legal norms and resolving questions of conflict in laws. In the book's closing stages, al-Bazdawī deals with questions that belong either to substantive law (fiqh) or to the "principles of law" (*qawāᶜid al-fiqh*). Among them, the role of *ᶜaql* in determining a legal norm is quite noticeable. Al-Bazdawī sets forth the question in its theological formulation, but soon turns it into a juridical question of eligibility (*ahliyyah*) to discern legal rulings.[28]

Shams al-ᶜUlamā al-Sarakhsī

Abū Bakr Muḥammad ibn Aḥmad al-Sarakhsī (d. 490/1096) was educated in Bukhārā and taught in Sarakhs (in contemporary Iran), where he was imprisoned from 466/1074 until about 480/1088, most likely because he criticized the city's ruler for allowing his officers to marry slave girls before their waiting period (*ᶜiddah*) ended. One of the last early Ḥanafī scholars, he is one of the most celebrated Ḥanafī jurists who elaborated on Islamic legal methodology's ability to respond to social change and the harmony between theory (*uṣūl*) and practice (*furūᶜ*). Besides his book on Islamic legal theory, he authored the widely cited jurisprudential work *Al-Mabsūṭ*, one of the most comprehensive Ḥanafī legal texts. It also provides an extensive commentary on al-Shaybānī's *Kitāb al-Siyār*,[29] known as the first extant work on Islam's laws of international relations and war and peace.

In his *uṣūlī* book, al-Sarakhsī preserves and sometimes enhances the close connection between substantive law (fiqh) and methodology, but lessens the theological side in favor of a more linguistic elaboration. He does not define the methodology at hand, but rather opens his work by emphasizing the importance of both fiqh and its methodology and then turns immediately to the topics of commands and prohibitions with a linguistic approach.[30] After dealing with the semantics of legal texts, he focuses on the authority of the law's sources (i.e., the Qur'an, the Sunnah, *ijmāʿ* and *qiyās*). He deals with most of the topics that fall under *uṣūl al-fiqh* by presenting an elaborate treatment of the law's sources, and frequently supports his arguments with examples from substantive law and historical precedents. He devotes two chapters to the "conflict of laws" (*al-muʿāraḍah bayn al-nuṣūṣ*) and subtitles them "abrogation."

Al-Sarakhsī's presentation of *qiyās* is quite comprehensive, as he includes in it a number of related topics such as *istiḥsān* (preference in general), *muʿāraḍah* (conflict of laws), *tarjīḥ* (preference in cases of conflict of laws), and *istiṣḥāb* (presumption of continuity).[31] His treatment of *qiyās* apparently embraces most rational argumentations that are not directly based on the revealed texts. In this connection, his discernment of *qiyās* borders on ijtihad, just as al-Shāfiʿī expressed in his *al-Risālah*. Thus it is hardly surprising that his work contains no chapter on ijtihad, whereas he allots a large introduction to vehemently defend *qiyās* according to the Companions' practices.[32]

Al-Sarakhsī's articulation of *istiṣḥāb al-ḥāl* (the presumption of continuity) is interesting and displays his pragmatic approach to legal theory. Including it under the heading of "argumentations without a proof" or a legal indicant (*iḥtijāj bilā dalīl*), he divides it into (1) The presumption of continuity in the assured absence of any contrary evidence to indicate a change in the situation. He accepts this kind of *istiṣḥāb* based on Qur'an 6:145, which states that eating meat is not prohibited, save for exceptional items like dead meat and pork. He argues that after a legal norm's applicability has been established, its continuity needs no proof;[33] (2) The presumption of continuity based on a fact against the contrary, which is based on speculation and ijtihad. This *istiṣḥāb*, Sarakhsī believes, can be used to examine an excuse or defend a recognized right, but not to establish a new claim, because it is always exposed to the opponent's counterargument; (3) The presumption of a state's continuity before searching for contrary evidence. According to him, this is a case of ignorance (*jahl*) and is unacceptable, except from a person who was unable to search. For instance, if a *dhimmī* who is unaware of Islam's obligatory worship rituals embraces Islam, he must compensate (*qaḍā*) for that which he missed. This rule does not apply to a *ḥarbī* (warlike non-Muslim) who embraces Islam and no expiation is required, because he was not in a position to be able to search; and (4) The presumption of continuity cannot be used to establish a legal norm (*ḥukm*), since it matches neither the form nor the meaning of *istiṣḥāb*. In the case of a missing person (*mafqūd*), the continuity of his life can be presumed and will be invoked as evidence in establishing his existing rights, but not in establishing a new right for him.[34]

Al-Sarakhsī's last part in *uṣūl* is concerned with the varieties of legal norms and their causes, conditions, and signs that are not directly related to his legal methodology. Most topics in this part belong to substantive law (fiqh), legal maxims, or ethical principles.[35]

Al-Sarakhsī's practical approach toward jurisprudence often prevents him from incorporating theological considerations into his methodology. Nevertheless, Wael Hallaq sees theological implications in his considering the principle of limitation of the *ratio legis* (*al-takhṣīṣ fī al-ʿillah*) invalid. This rejection, however, was motivated by his opposition to the Muʿtazili assumption that "humans have an ability to act prior to their action."[36] His work on substantive law in *Al-Mabsūṭ* shows a high degree of maturity and sophistication. He often presents law as emerging from tradition-reports. Except for semantics, he seldom applies his methodology to extrapolating rules. The tradition-reports remain his key source to elicit law, and *ra'y* plays a very circumscribed role because, according to him, jurists are too far removed from the pristine community to be able to articulate Islamic injunctions on their own.[37] In the case of limits of interpretation, he refutes the Muʿtazilī view that "Every *mujtahid* is correct (*muṣīb*) for having made the effort to discover reality," even if he comes out with an invalid response, because it is his effort that is commendable, and in this sense he is "correct."[38]

CHAPTER 4

Shiʿi Legal Methodology

THE LOCUS of authority in Shiʿi Islam resides in the Prophet and, by extension, the Twelve Infallible Imams, who are viewed as the legatees and inheritors of his prophetic charisma and knowledge. The leadership vacuum caused by the Twelfth Imam's Greater Occultation, which began in 329/941 and remains ongoing, has made him inaccessible to his followers. The *ʿulamā'*, basing themselves upon rational and traditional evidence, gradually filled this absence by claiming to be his indirect deputies until his return. Prior to this event, the Imams had played a dominant role in guiding the community as the authoritative interpreters of the divine will and the sole arbiters in settling disputes. They would remind their disciples that it is abominable and evil to utter statements on any matter without first having heard it from the divine guide: *"amā inna hu sharr ʿalaykum an taqūlū bi-shay' mā lam tasmaʿū hu minnā."*[1] As such, a number of hadith reports condemn and denounce the use of ijtihad, *ra'y*, and *qiyās* because access to the Imam brought forth an epistemology that resulted in certainty (*yaqīn*) as opposed to probability (*ẓann*). However, the Imams encouraged their followers to sharpen their rational argumentation skills in order to deduce legal rulings derived from Islam's general rules and principles. They might have adopted this approach because the Umayyad and Abbasid rulers kept them under close supervision and often under the threat of persecution, imprisonment, or extended periods of arrest. Naturally, such a hostile environment diminished direct contact between the Imams and their followers. In addition, followers who lived in distant lands had no access to them and thus could not seek a ruling or obtain clarification.

This process of transferring some of this charismatic authority and its ramifications are captured by Liyakat Takim: "In the process of divesting their authority to their close disciples, the imams were routinizing their charismatic domination and diffusing their charisma into a nascent, symbiotic structure, one that was dominated by the *rijal*."[2] This interim leadership made the transition to the Lesser Occultation (874–941), during which the Twelfth Imam's agents (*safīr*) served as the interlocutors between himself and the people, easier and less traumatic. The subsequent vacuum created by the Greater Occultation resulted in another leadership crisis, one that ultimately led to the concept of general agency (*al-niyābah al-ʿāmmah*) and the rise of *mujtahid*s.

The Imams encouraged and commanded their companions, primarily for pragmatic reasons, to engage in independent reflection based on textual sources in order to derive rulings on positive law and then formulate inferences firmly grounded in the universal principles laid out by them. Imams Jaʿfar al-Ṣādiq and ʿAlī al-Riḍā are reported to have said: "It is for us to set out foundational rules and principles (*uṣūl*), and it is for you [the learned] to derive the specific legal rulings for actual cases (*tafrīʿ* or *tafarruʿ*)."[3]

Hossein Modarressi challenges the general view that Shiʿi law remained undeveloped and unsophisticated while the infallible Imams were accessible:

> It is generally believed that Shiʿi law was undeveloped in this period which began with the Prophet and ended in 260/874. This is based on the assumption that since the Imams were present and accessible, there was no great urge to develop the practices of

independent judgment and that law was limited to the transmission of traditions. This idea is not correct."[4]

In any event, it is safe to assume that the Shiʿi legal tradition did
not emerge in a vacuum and, as such, was influenced by its extensive
interaction with Sunni jurisprudence, from which it adopted and then
modified many features to fit its doctrinal worldview. According to
Devin Stewart, "Shiite law and legal methodology started out quite
different from Sunni law, but gradually conformed more and more to
the Sunni system."[5] Among the examples he cites are the initial
rejection but ultimate adoption of ijtihad, *ijmāʿ*, and *qiyās*. The
following statement has been ascribed to Ayatollah Hosein Boroujerdi
(d.1961): "Shiʾī legal tradition is a commentary on Sunni legal
tradition"[6] but not, of course, in the sense of a blind and slavish
adoption or servile imitation that ignores its own unique features in
order to make whatever is imported harmonious and compatible.

The Shiʿi contribution to *uṣūl al-fiqh* actually began in earnest
during the first half of the fifth/eleventh century, due to the efforts of
three prominent figures of the Buyid period: Shaykh Mufīd (d.
413/1022) and his disciples Sharīf Murtaḍā (d. 436/1044) and Shaykh
al-Ṭā'ifah al-Ṭūsī (d. 460/1067). The latter wrote three distinct
treatises on *uṣūl al-fiqh*. Some contemporary authors trace Shiʿi *uṣūlī*
works to non-extant treatises of the early Imāmīs, such as Hishām ibn
al-Ḥakam (d. c. 190/805) and Yūnus ibn ʿAbd al-Raḥmān (d.
208/823).[7] Since Murtaḍā and Ṭūsī, who would have had easy access
to this genre of works, do not refer to them in their works as they did
to those of their Sunni and Muʿtazilī predecessors, we content ourselves with what we have at hand.

Al-Shaykh al-Mufīd
Muḥammad ibn Nuʿmān al-Shaykh al-Mufīd (d. 413/1022), a
contemporary of al-Qāḍī ʿAbd al-Jabbār, is considered the foremost
Shiʿi master to have applied rational *uṣūlī* arguments in rewriting the
school's jurisprudence in his principle juridical work: *al-Muqniʿah*.
He is the first scholar to move beyond the textual sources and open

the door for adopting Muʿtazilī methods and doctrines into mainstream Imāmī thought at a time when the Shiʿi intellectual community dominated the traditionist school and severely censured the introduction of reason and rational methodologies.[8] Al-Mufīd's very brief treatise on legal methodology was quoted and preserved by his pupil al-Karājikī (d. 440/1048). Of course the Shiʿi community had been acquainted with legal methodology before al-Mufīd, as some earlier Shiʿi jurists[9] had used it; however, only in al-Mufīd's work was it presented as a doctrinal basis for Imāmī thought.

In this treatise, al-Mufīd includes the Imams' narrations among the sources of legal knowledge, along with the Qur'an and the Sunnah, and then explains its authority at great length in Shiʿi *kalām*. He introduces three methods (*ṭuruq*) of arriving at legal knowledge: (1) reason (*ʿaql*), the way to understand the authority (*ḥujjiyyah*) of the Qur'an and the traditions; (2) language (*lisān*), the way to realize the meanings of expressions; and (3) tradition-reports (*akhbār*), the way to indicate the exact text of the Qur'an and Sunnah as well as the Imams' sayings.[10] Within the second context, he briefly deals with the divine commands and prohibitions as well as their semantics. *ʿAql* does not constitute a special faculty here; rather, al-Mufīd uses it to mean "common sense" wherever needed. He also uses the sources of legal knowledge to negate the validity of *qiyās* and accepts *ijmāʿ* only if it includes the Imam's approval.[11]

In his *al-Faṣl*, al-Mufīd proposes that the intellect's (*ʿaql*) judgment be applied where "there is no revealed text exactly applicable to the case."[12] It seems that his emphasis on reason and the validity of the intellect's judgment helped later Shiʿi authors develop the idea of considering *ʿaql* as the fourth source of Shiʿi law, as we shall see below.

Al-Sharīf al-Murtaḍā

ʿAlī ibn al-Ḥusayn, more popularly known as al-Sharīf al-Murtaḍā or Alam al-Hudā (d. 436/1044), studied under al-Mufīd and ʿAbd al-Jabbār and approaches *uṣūl al-fiqh* mostly in its literal context. In the introduction of his *al-Dharīʿah*, he defines the topic of legal methodology as divine addresses (*khiṭāb*), the application and appreciation of which constitute the core of *uṣūl al-fiqh*.[13] He first makes some introductory remarks on the semantics of the words and the definitions of the faculties needed for acquiring religious knowledge (i.e., *ʿilm*, *naẓar*, and *ẓann*), which seems similar to al-Baṣrī's remarks in his introduction.[14] Al-Murtaḍā then deliberates on the "commands and prohibitions," their generality and particularization, and how they can be considered as abrogated. Second, he deals with the evaluation of the traditions (*akhbār*).

Al-Murtaḍā's unconventional position toward the traditions leads him to negate the validity of solitary reports (*āḥād*). He generally divides traditions into two categories: those that convey knowledge (*ʿilm*) and those that do not. The second category is considered void by definition, for conjecture does not convey certainty.[15] Al-Murtaḍā's other topics include consensus, juristic analogy, and ijtihad, all of which, according to him, contribute very little to legal knowledge. Finally, he treats the human discernment of good and evil without the aid of revelation, permissible actions (*ibāḥah*), and the principle of presumed continuity (*istiṣḥāb*) with caution and even skepticism. *Al-Dharīʿah* contains a large number of theological and polemical chapters, despite the fact that the author's intention was to excise the legal methodology of theological issues.[16]

It is noteworthy that al-Murtaḍā preserved and advanced the rise of moderate rational Shiʿism started by al-Mufīd by further expanding reason's scope and making it the starting point for discovering knowledge of God. As such, he positioned himself closer to the Basran Muʿtazilis.[17] In contrast, al-Mufīd's stands were closer to those of the Baghdadi Muʿtazilis when it came to reason's role vis à-vis revelation.

By accepting the office of judge and *naqīb* (supervisor of the descendants of the Prophet's family) offered by the Sunni Caliph of the time and writing a treatise on the legality of working for the government, al-Murtaḍā inaugurated a new peak in Sunni-Shiʿi rapprochement, one that has rarely been surpassed in Shiʿi history. Also, his fellow jurist Sallār b. ʿAbd al-ʿAzīz al-Daylamī (d. 436/1044) reportedly wrote a book entitled *al-Taqrīb fī Uṣūl al-Fiqh*, which has been lost.

Al-Shaykh al-Ṭūsī

As a student of al-Murtaḍā, "Shaykh al-Ṭā'ifah" Muḥammad ibn al-Ḥasan al-Ṭūsī shares many views with him, including the role of reason. However, he presents a more balanced and practical account of legal methodology than does his master by "modify[ing] the radically rationalist and pragmatic positions of al-Murtaḍā,"[18] which largely set the pattern for later Shi'i *uṣūl* writers to follow. Al-Murtaḍā, who lived during the climax of the moderate Shi'i reaction to Imāmī traditionism (*Akhbāriyyah*), was skeptical about the influx of exaggerated traditions. Al-Ṭūsī, on the other hand, initiated a new process that combined Imāmī traditionism with rational *Uṣūlism*, for his proposed synthesis adopted traditions from the exaggerated sources even though he maintained his firm *Uṣūlī* position. Al-Ṭūsī legitimized the solitary reports transmitted by *Akhbārī* reporters because he considered them reliable transmitters of traditions, despite their deviant beliefs.[19]

In addition to adding two new collections to Shi'i tradition sources,[20] al-Ṭūsī also validated solitary traditions with some qualifications in his legal methodology. Thus he is held to have introduced a new conformity between Shi'i traditionism and *uṣūlī* reasoning, which later became Shi'i Ithnā 'Asharī orthodoxy. Apart from his meticulous presentation of Shi'i law, al-Ṭūsī wrote the first comparative intra-Muslim work, *al-Khilāf*, and another detailed work, *al-Mabsūṭ*, both of which contained the viewpoints of most Sunni and Shi'i legal authors and were modelled upon Sunni works.[21] Here, Shi'i legal theory benefitted greatly from the heritage of Sunni legal thought that, in many ways, predates Shi'i legal thought by some 250 years. After all, so long as the infallible Imam was present and considered the sole authority, there was no immediate need to formulate a structured and systematic legal theory.[22] Likewise, the hadiths were not collected until the beginning of his Greater Occultation. Al-Ṭūsī's way of bringing together different views caused British historian and Islamic scholar Norman Calder (d. 1998) to call him the first Shi'i author to establish an area for "doubt" and, consequently, "choice" that "may be interpreted as a desire to incorporate as harmoniously as possible the divergent characters and views which had been gathered into the nascent Shiʿi tradition."[23]

As regards legal methodology, al-Ṭūsī wrote *al-ʿUddah fī Uṣūl al-Fiqh* to explain the rational principles of Islamic jurisprudence. In it, he provides chapters on the principles of presumed continuity (*istiṣḥāb al-ḥāl*) and the human perception of good and evil (*al-ḥaẓr wa al-ibāḥah*).[24] The elaboration of these topics led to the recognition of reason as a source of legal knowledge in later Shiʿi *uṣūlī* works, beginning with Ibn Idrīs al-Ḥillī (d. 598/1201).[25] Al-Ṭūsī nevertheless repudiates the legal effects of analogy and consensus, although he does allocate a chapter to each. Below, we outline his work to see how he treated methodological issues.

Outline of Al-Ṭūsī's Legal Methodology

Al-Ṭūsī defines *uṣūl-fiqh* as the use of *adillah*, by which legal norms are generally discovered from the sources. Like Murtaḍā, he makes the divine addresses (*khiṭāb*) the basis of legal knowledge. He divides his legal methodology into twelve chapters that, according to his categorization, can be further reduced to six.[26]

1. **Introductory remarks**

   a) Semantic remarks on religious knowledge and its indicators. Al-Ṭūsī's traditional definition divides *ʿilm* into necessary and acquired knowledge. Its indicators include reason (*ʿaql*), reflection (*naẓar*), and contextual signs (*imārah*) in addition to the divine addresses.

   b) Theological remarks on human actions, God's attributes, and those of the Prophet and the Imams, for the sake of understanding their addresses.[27]

2. **Tradition-reports:** Al-Ṭūsī relies upon them as a way to indicate the *khiṭāb*, including topics on:

   a) The definition of *khabar* and how to acquire knowledge from it.

b) The division of *khabar* into *āḥād* and *mutawātir*. Here, he presents one of his best arguments to validate solitary reports with some conditions.

c) The commands and prohibitions; their generality and particularization, as well as their lucidity and ambiguity; and the rules of abrogation.[28]

3. **Practices of the Prophet:** Al-Ṭūsī dedicates a separate chapter to this topic.

4. **Consensus, analogy, and ijtihad as annexed methods:** Al-Ṭūsī devotes one chapter to each of these topics, although he attaches real legal value to them only if they include supporting words from the Imams.[29]

5. **Restricted and unrestricted actions (*al-ḥaẓr wa al-ibāḥah*):** Here, al-Ṭūsī presents an interesting account on the human perception of good and evil.

6. **Presumed continuity (*istiṣḥāb al-ḥāl*):** Unlike al-Murtaḍā, al-Ṭūsī's definition of *istiṣḥāb*[30] allows him to conjoin the present with the past.

As mentioned above, al-Ṭūsī validated the Imāmīs' solitary traditions even though he could not ascertain the reliability of some tradition-reporters. He argued that "these reporters," although ignorant in religious matters, were sincere in what they had heard from the Imams or their companions. Moreover, he firmly grounded his argument in Shiʿi precedent, namely, the practice of the righteous sect (*ʿamal al-ṭāʾifah*), an entirely new application of this particular notion. Al-Ṭūsī admitted that most traditions were based on isolated reports, but argued that earlier generations of Shias, particularly the Imams' contemporaries, had practiced them.[31]

The most significant aspect of al-Ṭūsī's work is the opinionated language that he used to substantially raise the mufti's legal authority in relation to that of the tradition-reports. Although al-Mufīd's *al-Muqniʿah* had already started this approach to legal exposition, al-Ṭūsī's achievement surpasses all previous works and actually inaugurated a new era of Shiʿi legal writings. Expanding the law by using a legal methodology (*uṣūl al-fiqh*) and including the author's juridical opinion in the work constituted an implicit acceptance of ijtihad, although he does not use that particular term. Al-Ṭūsī, therefore, was regarded as the one who devised a high level of sound ijtihad without being called *mujtahid*.[32]

After his death Shiʿi jurisprudence stagnated for 150 years, a time when Sunni law underwent a period of great development.

Shiʿi Legal Methodology Adopts Ijtihad

A drastic change appeared in Shiʿi jurisprudence during the seventh/ thirteenth century: The adoption of ijtihad and parts of *qiyās* in *uṣūl al-fiqh* led to the rewriting of Shiʿi law on a wider doctrinal basis. This adjustment occurred after Sunni jurisprudents developed a theoretical approach to legal methodology (see below, chapter 5). Despite their total devotion to the Imams, the new round of Shiʿi *Uṣūlism* (during the Mongol period) incorporated new rational elements into Shiʿi thought. The necessity of theoretical considerations led authors of the Ḥillah school to formally embrace ijtihad and incorporate more rational arguments into their jurisprudence.

Al-Muḥaqqiq al-Ḥillī

Al-Muḥaqqiq al-Ḥillī (d. 676/1277) was the first post-al-Ṭūsī Jaʿfarī author to write a somewhat different treatise on legal methodology. In his *Maʿārij al-Uṣūl*, he opens the discussion with a brief definition of key terms such as *legal norms, knowledge, conjecture, evidence (dalālah), contextual signs (imārah), truth*, and *metaphor*. Nowhere does he include *syllogism*, although he does use some of the terminology of logic.[33] He then proceeds with the legal commands and prohibitions, their characteristics, as well as the role of the traditions and consensus in assessing legal norms. Al-Muḥaqqiq devotes seven chapters to the above topics, all of which Ibn al-Ḥājib had categorized as "revealed indicants."

His ninth chapter, which deals with ijtihad, is divided into two sections: "The Truth of Ijtihad" and "*Qiyās*." Unlike al-Ṭūsī, al-Muḥaqqiq plainly distinguishes ijtihad from *qiyās* and fully legitimizes the former and parts of the latter as derivatives of ijtihad. In the last chapter, under "Miscellaneous," he brings forth several juridical principles, such as "the mufti and commoners" and the presumption of continuity. He legitimizes both of these on the grounds that following the opinions of a mufti who is also entitled to be called a *mujtahid* is the Hidden Imam's indirect deputy and thus equated such a mufti's ruling with "talking with the tongue of [God's] law."[34] He also insisted on the presumption of continuity in the absence of any contrary indication.[35] It is noteworthy that this presumed continuity is the most important rational maxim of the four juridical principles that later Shiʿi authors called "the practical principles" (*al-uṣūl al-ʿamaliyyah*). The other principles include the state of being discharged (*barāʾah*), the observance of prudence (*iḥṭiyāt*), and legal option (*takhyīr*). Interestingly, in the last section of his tenth chapter al-Muḥaqqiq either saw no need to observe *iḥṭiyāṭ* or else regarded it as a juridical principle.[36]

In searching for and legitimizing ijtihad's true meaning, for the first time in Shiʿi jurisprudence al-Muḥaqqiq redefines it as independent from *qiyās*. His argument here is primarily based on the above-mentioned premise that "legal norms are often known from theoretical considerations, and not from the established texts" and that, in practice, Shiʿis also undertake ijtihad.[37] He adds that *qiyās* is not identical with ijtihad, but rather a particular type of ijtihad. Second, he legitimizes the modfication of legal norms (*aḥkām*) according to changing expediencies (*maṣlaḥah*) as judged by a *mujtahid*.[38] On *qiyās*, al-Muḥaqqiq challenges the standard Shiʿi view, previously presented by al-Mufīd, that analogy is void because there is no way to understand the *ratio legis* of legal norms. He therefore concludes that *qiyās* bears some resemblance to legal conjecture, which can be binding in the absence of a better proof.[39]

Ijtihad accommodated a plurality of views on the basis that each qualified jurist exerts himself to the best of his ability by using different sources to derive a legal ruling that would remain a considered opinion subject to error and revision. The transition from certainty to probability was deemed necessary in order to deal with new contingencies and societal changes that were not covered in the texts or had occurred during the Imam's occultation. This prompted Shiʿi jurists from al-Muḥaqqiq onward to accept ijtihad with a clear-cut epistemological distinction between certainty and probability. In other words, no amount of human exertion could ensure that certainty in such matters had been reached. The *Akhbārīs* of the seventeenth century, with Muḥammad Amīn al-Astarābādī as their chief spokesman, sought to return to the earlier practice of rejecting ijtihad because, according to him, certainty could be attained based upon the available material. He argued that even though the *Akhbārīs* were not exhaustive, ijtihad was illegitimate and personal judgment was unnecessary; besides, it could be a source of innovation. After a short period of success, however, the *Uṣūlīs* triumphed and solidified ijtihad's role in addressing new issues and contingencies

Concerning the adoption of ijtihad and the above-mentioned rational principles, Ayatollah Murtada Mutahhari (d. 1979) has suggested that the Ḥillah scholars, under the influence of al-Ghazali's redefinition of ijtihad and *qiyās*, had changed the course of equating ijtihad with *qiyās*, which ended up with their adopting the former and legitimating certain parts of the latter.[40] Wilferd Madelung (b. 1930) offers another explanation for this change of view:

> …the traditional preoccupation of Imāmī thought with the notion of certitude in the law led the Imāmī scholars to view *ijtihād* not simply as a meritorious endeavor to discover the intent of the divine Lawgiver that may either succeed or fail, but rather as an effort to reach the highest degree of probability or the closest approximation to the objective truth possible in the absence of the infallible imam. This effort must constantly be renewed in the hope of coming still closer to objective truth and certainty. *Ijtihād* thus must remain an open process until the return of the imām who alone can offer perfect truth and certainty.[41]

Al-ʿAllāmah al-Ḥillī

The eminent authoritative scholar of Shiʿi theology and jurisprudence Ibn al-Muṭahhar al-Ḥillī (d. 726/1327), usually known as al-ʿAllāmah al-Ḥillī, advanced al-Muḥaqqiq's way of structuring legal methodology, particularly his adoption of ijtihad and parts of *qiyās*. His four works on legal methodology are essentially in line with al-Muḥaqqiq's *uṣūl al-fiqh* framework. In his *Tahdhīb*, al-ʿAllāmah al-Hilli legitimized two kinds of *qiyās*: (1) *al-manṣūṣ al-ʿillah*, in which the *ratio legis* is designated in the Qur'an and/or the Sunnah, and (2) *al-ḥukm fī al-farʿ al-aqwā*, wherein the minor case has more applicability to the law than its premise.[42] Al-ʿAllāmah al-Hilli, as the late Ayatollah Mutahhari suggested, paid careful attention to the changing concept of ijtihad in Sunni law, as well as the exclusion of opinion (*ra'y*) and sometimes of *qiyās* from the sources of the Shariʿah. As a result, he also modified their juridical position and formally incorporated ijtihad and parts of *qiyās* into the Shiʿi legal system.[43]

In his *Mabādi'*, ʿAllāmah al-Hilli summarizes his legal methodology in twelve short chapters. Like al-Muḥaqqiq, he does not concern himself with the hierarchy of sources and formatting the topics of *uṣūl al-fiqh*. Rather, he begins with linguistic questions, such as the appearance of "words" and the grammar,[44] after which he turns his attention to legal norms with a theological approach. He validates the human perception of good and evil, as well as the original permissibility of human acts (*ibāḥat al-aṣl*), prior to receiving directives from the revelations.[45] The chapter of "commands and prohibitions," in which he properly demonstrated his methodological analysis, is followed by "the general and its particularization" and "lucid and ambiguous." Al-ʿAllāmah's treatment of the Sunnah is imbued with a theological discussion of the necessity of following the Prophet's example. He does not include the necessity of following the Imāms in this section.[46]

Al-ʿAllāmah's account of consensus is descriptive and mainly in line with the Sunni understanding of *ijmāʿ*. He validates the consensus of the House of the Prophet, but does not elaborate on its feasibility as did later Imāmī jurists (see below). His conception of *ijmāʿ* appears to be similar to that of the Sunnis, for he generally validates the community's consensus without the qualifying statement that it would be considered valid – but only because the Imam's endorsement of it is assumed.[47] In the section on *qiyās*, al-ʿAllāmah brings to fore the questionability of *qiyās* according to the Shiʿi point of view. However, he endorses any analogy that has had its *ratio legis* established in the text. His elaboration of varieties of *qiyās*, particularly the notion of suitability (*munāsabah*), reveal that he favored the practice of *qiyās* proper.[48] Al-ʿAllāmah undertakes an appreciative inquiry into ijtihad after a brief treatment of the problems concerning the "conflict of laws." He defines *mujtahid* as one who possesses knowledge not only of jurisprudence, but also of formal logic.[49] He upholds al-Ṭūsī's view that the regular *ʿulamāʾ* should follow the opinion of the most learned *mujtahid*.[50]

Both al-Muḥaqqiq and al-ʿAllāmah were clearly impressed by al-Ghazali and Ibn al-Ḥājib's redefinition of ijtihad:[51] "Utmost intellectual endeavor in search for the [most appropriate] legal rule" (*istifrāgh al-wusʿ li ṭalab al-ḥukm al-sharʿī*). This necessitates rational (*uṣūlī*) theoretical considerations, but does not depend upon *qiyās*. Once the distinction between ijtihad and *qiyās* and *raʾy* became clear for the Shiʿis, they embraced the former to the extent that practicing it became one of the most salient characteristics of Shiʿi jurisprudence in the nineteenth century and thereafter.

This trend toward reviving ijtihad was cemented by al-ʿAllāmah, who established its epistemology and legitimacy in his *uṣūl al-fiqh* works by affirming a clear-cut epistemological division of knowledge between certainty (*ʿilm qatʿī*) and probability (*ẓann*) in Shiʿi jurisprudence. The Shiʾis adopted these central Sunni *uṣūl* concepts. He also insisted upon the need for *mujtahid*s. Accordingly, Imāmī scholars from al-Muḥaqqiq al-Ḥilli onward gradually transitioned from the principle of certitude in deriving legal norms to probable opinion and formally embraced it during the fourteenth century by accepting al-ʿAllāmah al-Ḥillī's ijtihad.[52]

Al-ʿAllāmah enhanced the *mujtahid's* position by emphasizing the hierarchical structure of authority that ranked their opinions as "valid conjecture" (*ẓann*) that the community should follow during the Imam's absence.[53] The *mujtahid's* authority arises from his ability to competently apply legal methodology to new cases in order to extricate new legal norms. From the vantage point of jurisprudential knowledge, he divided the Shiʿi community into *mujtahid*s and everyone else; the latter were required to emulate (*taqlīd*) the former's rulings.[54] Al-ʿAllāmah's emphasis on these scholars' position motivated some traditionist Shiʿi ʿulamā (known as *Akhbārī*s) to question the appropriateness of the *uṣūl al-fiqh* discipline itself, which bestowed such exclusive prerogatives upon them.

The Rise of Akhbārism[55]

*Akhbārī*s, who rely exclusively on the Imams' traditions to the exclusion of reason and rationality – as the sources of knowledge, authority, and law – usually do not pay much attention to legal methodology. The only exception in this regard is some semantics of the Qur'an and traditions. Traditionism/Scripturalism, also known as Akhbārism, had existed in the Shiʿi milieu since the second/eighth century but had no distinct doctrinal principle until the midst of the 11th/17th century, when it reemerged as a reaction to the *uṣūlī* rationalism of the Ḥillah school. The founder of neo-Akhbārism, Mullā Muḥammad Amīn al-Astarābādī (d. 1036/1626), was initially a student of *uṣūlī* methodology. He turned the hitherto unarticulated Akhbārism, which called for maintaining one's reliance on the texts, into a juridical school by offering several doctrinal formulas for their legal approach. Among his formulas, the principle of "customary certainty" (*al-yaqīn al-ʿādī*) proposes that Shiʿis should content themselves with "the general certainty" (*al-qatʿ al-ijmālī*) conveyed to them by the contents of the Imams' traditions.[56] According to al-Astarābādī, these traditions were compiled in the four major source books of Shiʿi traditions (i.e. *al-Kāfī, al-Faqīh, al-Istibṣār,* and *Tahdhīb*). He did not elaborate upon the extent or limits of these tradition-reports' "general certainty," but severely refuted the *Uṣūlī*s' reliance upon rational speculation, especially their use of such so-called practical principles as *aṣl al-istiṣḥāb* (the presumption of continuity) and *aṣl al-barā'ah* (original non-liability). In fact, he labeled them borrowings from Sunni methods of jurisprudence that, at best, produced only conjectural knowledge.[57] Etan Kohlberg has a passage that illustrates the *Akhbārīs'* approach to legal methodology:

> The knowledge acquired in this way, while insufficient to lead to absolute certainty (*yaqīn wāqiʿī*) as to God's intent, does establish with certainty that the religious law conforms to the transmitted utterances of the Imams. It is this 'customary' (*ʿādī*) certainty which matters for religious practice, not the preponderant probability (*ẓann*) which, according to the *uṣūlīs*, is the closest one can get to knowing the meaning of the tradition.[58]

The Akhbārī school dominated Shiʿi centers of Iran, Iraq, Lebanon, and Bahrain from the middle of the eleventh/seventeenth century until the end of the twelfth/eighteenth century. The school allowed no scope for reason in matters of religion and rejected the laity's emulation (*taqlīd*) of a jurist. During this period, Mullā Muḥsin Fayḍ Kāshānī (d. 1091/1680), Shaykh al-Ḥurr al-ʿĀmilī (d. 1104/1693), Muḥammad Bāqir Majlisī (d. 1111/1699), and other Akhbārī-oriented authors produced ethico-juridical works based on the Imams' tradition-reports. The *Akhbārīs'* refusal to apply *uṣūl* methodology and accusing those who did so of imitating Aristotelian logic in legal inference does not mean that they rejected all of these instruments.[59] For instance, later *Akhbārīs* practiced *aṣl al-istiṣḥāb*, one of the most popular *uṣūlī* principles, on the grounds that some tradition-reports supported the practice of *istiṣḥāb*.[60] The *Akhbārī* ascendancy was eclipsed by the *Uṣūlīs'* triumphal return toward the end of the eighteenth century.

Shaykh Ḥasan al-ʿĀmilī
Despite *Akhbārī* criticism, Shiʿi *Uṣūlism* continued to prevail after a

short setback. Ironically, one of the best treatises on Islamic legal methodology – it is still used as a textbook in Shiʿi seminaries – was written during the beginning of *Akhbārī* prevalence. Shaykh Ḥasan al-ʿĀmilī (d. 1011/1602),[61] an *uṣūlī* student with *Akhbārī* sympathies, wrote a concise and lucid legal methodology as a prelude to his intended comprehensive work on fiqh. In his brief introduction to legal methodology, he points to the necessity of making some preliminary remarks on "obligation" (*taklīf*) and "argumentation" (*istidlāl*), but does not actually deal with them.[62] His main presentation on the subject begins with semantics, which includes commands and prohibitions of the legal norms; their generality and particularization; and their metaphoric, confined, ambiguous, or lucid meanings.[63]

Hence al-ʿĀmilī concerns himself with two sources of the law, namely, consensus and the traditions, followed by a discussion of abrogation. Although he does not give a title to the Qur'an as a source of the law, he obviously deals with its legal norms in the section on semantics. Despite allocating a chapter to *ijmāʿ*, however, al-ʿĀmilī does not legitimize its use during the Imam's absence due to his heavy reliance upon *akhbār*.[64] He then brings to the fore *qiyās* and *istiṣḥāb* as two other possible sources of the law, but nevertheless tends to discourage their application for validating legal norms in Shiʿi law even though he may attempt to justify the outcome of such arguments in some other way.[65] His last topic concerns ijtihad, *taqlīd*, and preference in the case of conflict – and in all of them he is inclined to reduce the *mujtahid*'s role.[66]

Al-ʿĀmilī's way of arranging the contents of legal methodology seems to be patterned mainly on al-ʿAllāmah's *Mabādi' al-Uṣūl*. Nevertheless, the lucidity of his expositions made his work a model for further elaboration among future generations of Shiʿi students.

CHAPTER 5

The Course of Theorizing Legal Methodology

WE NOW turn to a new era during which Islamic legal methodology adopted certain concepts from Greek logic and set new legal principles as part of its intellectual ancestry. The Muslims' incorporation of Aristotelian epistemological elements into *uṣūl al-fiqh* did not fundamentally change the latter's structure, but rather equipped it with beneficial instruments and, at certain points, added to its methodology's theoretical scope. We already encountered the translation of Aristotelian *Peri hermeneias* by Ibn al-Muqaffaᶜ in the second/eight century. During the following century, the translation of Aristotle's *Categories, Hermeneutica, Analytica Priora,* and *Posteriora* were made available to Muslims mainly through the works of two Abbasid court physicians: Ḥunayn ibn Isḥāq (d. 260/873) and his son Isḥāq ibn Ḥunayn (d. 289/910).[1] Renowned philosophers such as al-Fārābī, Ibn Sīnā, and Ibn Rushd elaborated upon these translations extensively. The former allocated a chapter to juridical analogy in his *Kitāb al-Qiyās al-Ṣaghīr* and tried to explain that "inferences employed in Islamic law can all be shown to comply with rules of Aristotelian assertoric syllogistics."[2] According to Joep Lameer:

… [S]ince Aristotle's theory of the syllogism employs statement-making (i.e. descriptive) sentences only, which are in the *Prior Analytics* called "proposition" (*protasseis*), it was imperative for al-Fārābī, given the objective of his account, to expressly lay down the condition that any legal prescription that is to be part of legal deduction must be of that sort.[3]

Unlike Lameer, K. Gyekye assumed a theological orientation in al-Fārābī's analogy and dismissed the idea that his work is a commentary on Aristotle's *Analytics*.[4] According to Wael Hallaq: "Fārābī places heavy emphasis on the necessity and importance of *ʿillah* in all inferences. For a complete inference, he insists that an *ʿillah* must accompany the judgment. This became the standard view of Sunnism."[5]

John Walbridge considers al-Fārābī's theory of virtuous religion as a system of beliefs and law expressed symbolically by a lawgiver who grasps rational truths intuitively. Al-Fārābī, therefore, necessitates allegorical interpretation by someone capable of philosophical understanding when the expressions of the scripture are not in literal accordance with philosophical truth.[6]

Ibn Ḥazm

A new era of methodological developments was spurred in the fifth/eleventh century by the introduction of logical notions. Among the Muslim *ʿulamāʾ*, Ibn Ḥazm (d. 456/1064) who upheld Zahiri theory (maintaining the literal meaning) was the forerunner of those who would later on bring some epistemological components, clearly from formal logic, into his methodology. He presented an unusual combination of theology, linguistics, and logic in his work on *uṣūl al-fiqh*, namely, *al-Iḥkām*.[7] He begins his account with theories of knowledge: How are things known – by inspiration, through the guidance of an Imam, by a tradition (*khabar*) of the Prophet, by imitation (*taqlīd*), or by human reason. He favored reason because all channels, even "the traditions should be verified by reason."[8] He adds that logical principles help us "to understand God's intention as conveyed to us through His speech."[9] Ibn Ḥazm then poses the question: Do the words (*kalām*) bestowed upon man emanate from God, or are they conventional?" He favored the former, although he acknowledged the role of people in promoting and polishing the language after having received it. He then defines a certain number of technical terms,[10] among them logical terms such as *ḥadd* (definition), *rasm* (description), and *burhān* (demonstration), thereby showing that he was one of the foremost jurists who began to incorporate logic into his legal methodology.

After making other introductory remarks on theological questions, Ibn Ḥazm turned his attention to methodological topics beginning with [God's] speech (*bayān*) and the Qur'an; however, he focused mainly on evaluating the traditions. In the third and fourth parts, he dealt with commands and prohibitions, the semantic rules of interpretation, and finished his discussion with the subject of consensus. From the fifth to the eighth part, he concerned himself with aspects of individual reasoning, either accepting or refuting them. This included the presumption of continuity (*istiṣḥāb*), the principle of precision (*iḥtiyāṭ*), imitation, the indicator of God's addresses (*dalīl al-khiṭāb*), juridical analogy and preferences, and, finally, ijtihad. In the course of discussing these topics, Ibn Ḥazm explores a number of maxims (*qawāᶜid al-fiqh*).

Imām al-Ḥaramayn al-Juwaynī

This new phase of methodological development reaches its zenith in the works of al-Juwaynī and al-Ghazālī, both of whom welcomed the inclusion of logic in legal methodology. Imām al-Ḥaramayn al-Juwaynī (d. 478/1085), the Ashᶜarī theologian, wrote four books on legal methodology. Of the four, it is in *al-Burhān* that he marshals the most relevant elements to epitomize the knowledge of his time. The influence of logic and epistemology is visible in his introduction, although he ultimately emphasized rational theology, Arabic grammar and jurisprudence.[11] His book is divided into seven parts, each one comprising several chapters. In the introduction, al-Juwaynī defines the methodology of *uṣūl* as the science of proofs for legal norms (*aḥkām*). He then deals with theological conceptions of good and evil actions, reviews the Muʿtazilī theory of basing the evaluation of "commands and prohibitions" on human perception of good and evil, and rejects the Ashʿarī thought of his teachers, especially that of Abū Bakr al-Bāqillānī (d. 403/1013).[12]

Al-Juwaynī presents an interesting account of "knowledge, its bases and indicators" in this work's introduction. He gives the definitions of *ʿilm* according to various theological schools and divides knowledge into ten categories, among which the knowledge of scripture and the traditions (*samʿiyyāt*) are ranked last.[13] Concerning the basis of knowledge of religion, he ranks *ʿaql* (reason) first but confines its role to the necessary understanding of fundamental religious premises. After these introductory remarks, al-Juwaynī devotes the first part of his book to the exposition (*bayān*) [of truth], its meaning, hierarchy, and means of expression. In the same part he discusses commands and prohibitions, their semantic interpretations, the traditions of the Prophet, and the evaluation of hadith. The second part comprises consensus, variation, and qualifications. The third part is allotted to juristic analogy (*qiyās*), which al-Juwaynī considers as the groundwork of ijtihad and the foundation of *ra'y*. He therefore devotes ample attention to its applicability. He maintains that the Companions practiced analogy and, as such, it should be regarded as one of the sources, as opposed to merely a method of individual reasoning, of legal knowledge.

Al-Juwaynī deals with individual reasoning (*istidlāl*) in the fourth part. He barely allows any scope for it on the grounds that there is no precedent for it in Shariʿah. He marshals Imām Mālik's idea of considering the public interest (*istiṣlāḥ*) and al-Shāfiʿī's proposal for justifying the sound opinion that nearly corresponds to the text (*istiṣwāb min qurb*), but endorses them only if they have enough links to the established texts and precedents. Al-Juwaynī likewise implies his discomfort with the principle of the presumption of continuity (*istiṣḥāb*).[14] The fifth part is on juristic preferences, in which he finds precedents in the Companions' practice.[15] He considers abrogation a "preference" by including it among the topics of juristic preferences. Part six is allocated to ijtihad, where he again tends to justify it on the basis of precaution. The last topic is *fatāwā* (pl. of fatwa).

To sum up, Juwaynī opens his discussion with an epistemological approach by defining *ʿilm* and *bayān*; however, he embodies them in scripture and the traditions followed by consensus and analogy. Subsequently, he turns toward individual reasoning and juristic preferences and concludes with the position of muftis and *mujtahid*s.

Abū Ḥāmid al-Ghazālī

Abū Ḥāmid Muḥammad al-Ghazālī (d. 505/1111) is the legal thinker who greatly advanced the theoretical dimension of *uṣūl al-fiqh* and gave a new structure to Islamic legal methodology. He wrote four books on the subject, three of which have reached us. In his first work *al-Mankhūl*, he presents the methodological topics of Islamic jurisprudence on the same pattern established by al-Juwaynī, but gives greater prominence to epistemological and theological issues.[16] His second book, *Shifāʾ*, is dedicated to the analysis of varieties of *qiyās* and expressly excludes problems discussed in *al-Mankhūl*.[17] In his later work *al-Mustaṣfā*, he sets out a new arrangement for the topics of legal methodology and delicately incorporates some of the epistemological parts of formal logic into his methodology. In the introduction, he states that he provided a new and wondrous (*ʿajīb*) articulation of *uṣūl al-fiqh* in which he combined investigation with innovation.[18]

It was al-Ghazālī who provided new definitions for *qiyās* and ijtihad by placing them in two theoretically separate spheres. He characterized *qiyās* as part of "the method of inference" (*kayfiyyat al-iqtibās min maʿqūl al-alfāẓ*) and placed ijtihad in the category of "qualification of indicants of legal rules,"[19] which is required in all spheres of legal inquiry. Unlike most of the preceding jurists, he did not include *qiyās* among the specific sources of law, for he considered it as nothing more than a method of inference that would prove to be effective with newly arising similar cases. The following schematic summary reveals how he replaced the hierarchical classification of the topics of *uṣūl al-fiqh* with a horizontal one.

The Structure of al-Ghazālī's Legal Methodology
Al-Ghazālī begins by defining legal methodology as knowledge of the sources of legal norms and subsequently articulates the meaning of every term that appears in this definition, starting with knowledge. This leads to an extensive epistemological introduction to determine criteria for man's understanding. He restricts them to definition (*ḥadd*) and demonstration (*burhān*), which are applicable to all theoretical sciences.[20]

1. The first quarter deals with legal norms and encompasses:
   a. The nature of legal norms, whether they are based on a rational understanding of good and evil.
   b. Varieties of legal norms: obligatory, forbidden, permissible, etc.
   c. Constituent elements (*arkān*) of legal norms (i.e., God-human relations).
   d. Causes that necessitate the application of a norm. He sets forth the problems encountered in determining the validity of actions (*ṣiḥḥah*) and concessionary laws (*rukhṣah*).[21]

2. The second quarter covers the sources of Islamic law, which include:
   a. The book of God (the Qur'an) followed by these issues:
      i) Facts and metaphors,
      ii) explicit and symbolic verses, and
      iii) abrogation.[22]
   b. The traditions of the Prophet, including discussions on:
      i) the validity of reports,
      ii) solitary reports (*āḥād*).
   c. Consensus, including:
      i) the proof for its being the source of law,

    ii) its constituent parts, and

    iii) rules of consensus, including *istiṣḥāb*.

3.   The third quarter deals with the method of setting rules based on the sources. Describing this as the discipline's essential part, it begins with introductory remarks on semantics. This quarter is basically divided into three parts that encompass several chapters and sections.

    a. The expressed speech of God:

        i) General and lucid words (*mujmal wa mubayyan*).

        ii) Apparent and divergent meanings (*ẓāhir wa mu'aw-wal*).

        iii) Commands and prohibitions, and their meanings and application.

        iv) The generals and particulars on which he allots five sections.

    b. The implied and alluded meanings, including the Prophet's actions.

    c. The method of deriving legal norms (*aḥkām*) from the sources:

        i) On the validity of juridical analogy (*qiyās*).

        ii) Validating the cause (*ratio legis*).

        iii) On the analogy of resemblance (*qiyās al-shabah*).

        iv) The constituent parts of *qiyās*.[23]

4.   The fourth quarter is dedicated to the methodology's end users and comprises three chapters:

    a. Ijtihad: Al-Ghazālī presents one of the best definitions, namely, the exertion of maximum mental energy to deduce the law from the sources.

    b. Imitation and seeking the opinion of *mujtahid*s.

    c. Juridical preferences (*tarjīḥ*).[24]

As shown above, al-Ghazālī's division of legal methodology into four parts encompasses all topics that arise under *uṣūl al-fiqh* in accordance with the pattern he set out in his famous book, *Iḥyā'*: 1) legal norms (*aḥkām*), 2) sources or indicators (*adillah*) of the legal norms, 3) the methodology of deriving these norms from the sources, and iv) the necessary qualifications of the one who deduces the law (i.e., the *mujtahid*). He likens this structure to a tree: Its fruits are the legal norms, its roots are the sources, its manner of bearing fruits is the legal methodology, and its end users are the *mujtahids*.[25]

Al-Ghazālī attempts to exhibit a coherent and strong relationship among the various topics of his methodology by frequently explaining the logic behind his arrangement. On several points, as we saw in the above outline, he tended to engage in logical and theological issues but contented himself with brief introductory remarks only and referred readers to his other books for details. We know that due to epistemological connections, *ʿilm al-uṣūl* thematically overlaps with both theology and logic. But these connections unwind due to the heavy reliance of *uṣūl* on scripture and traditions. Al-Ghazālī alludes to this point at the beginning of *al-Mustaṣfā*, where he praises human reason and likens it to a judge who may never be dismissed or replaced. Nevertheless, he adds that *ʿaql* is a witness (*shāhid*) for the Shariʿah, a spectator that refines and accommodates.

He then divides knowledge into three kinds: rational, religious, and the combination of these two, and considers the proper methodology to be one that combines both of them.[26] He had already ranked the legal issues as "worldly science" in contrast to the spiritual knowledge of the mystics.[27] Thus, the aforesaid way of characterizing Islamic law should be regarded as al-Ghazālī's later position on the matter. He proposes that knowledge is a "conceptual existence" and divides it into four stages: 1) substantial; 2) conceptual (*dhihnī*), which is called *ʿilm*; 3) literal, which portrays human concepts; and iv) written.[28] He warns that ideas should not be explored through words alone because ideas occur in the mind first and words just follow them.[29]

Apart from his introductory remarks on "knowledge" and "definition," al-Ghazālī's point of departure in *al-Mustaṣfā* is the legal norm (*ḥukm*), after which he proceeds to deliberate on the sources and the method of understanding legal norms from them. This point of departure should have engaged him in matters of positive law; however, he turns the discussion toward either theology (such as "the determination of good and evil") or to the general principles of jurisprudence. Beginning the discussion with legal norms gives his account a horizontal scope, one that differs from the hierarchical classification of the sources of legal knowledge as understood from al-Shāfiʿī's *al-Risālah*, whose template became deeply ingrained in later works. In the second quarter, concerning the sources, al-Ghazālī elaborates on the indicants (*adillah*) of the law: the Qur'an, the traditions and consensus. He reserves *qiyās* for the third quarter, which presents the method of acquiring legal norms. This does not necessarily imply that *qiyās* was excluded from the sources, but rather that he considered the role of human reasoning in the case of *qiyās* strong enough to transfer it to the third quarter. In a similar manner, he separates ijtihad from *qiyās* and delays the discussion on the former to the quarter dealing with the *mujtahid*s, which had gained fame since the fourth/tenth century.

Besides his innovative introduction, al-Ghazālī's accounts on *qiyās* and ijtihad contain seminal and groundbreaking elements. In the case of the former, he elaborates upon the question of *munāsabah*, the suitability of *ratio legis* to the case, in a way that provides more room for intellectual argument to supply rational causes for the practice of *qiyās*. If the efficacious cause (*ʿillah*) has been fixed through the text or consensus, he considers it as *mu'aththir* (effective); otherwise, the underlying cause would be discerned by rational reasoning as suitable (*munāsib*) or compatible (*mulā'im*). This distinction, according to the contemporary author Imran Nyazee, "lies in the way the law has acknowledged the attribute that serves as the *ʿillah*."[30] For instance, wine has the attribute of intoxication, which leads one to neglect religious duties. Because it has a similar effect, the prohibition of beer can rationally be placed in the same category, even though it was not specified in the Qur'an and the Prophet's traditions.[31]

Al-Ghazālī eventually links the practice of suitability to *maṣlaḥah* for serving the law's end goals. This is particularly relevant when a remote suitability overrules other textual or contextual signs due to the underlying *maṣlaḥah*, based on the main objectives of the law (*maqṣūd al-sharᶜ*).³² It is noteworthy that he invokes *maṣlaḥah* in an attempt to protect the law's end goals (i.e., life, religion, intellect, property, and the family).³³ The authority of this *maṣlaḥah* is divided into three levels: *ḍarūrāt* (lit. necessities), *ḥājāt* (lit. needs), and *taḥsīnāt* or *tazyīnāt* (lit. embellishments).³⁴ It is striking that he allows only *qiyās* and suitability to serve as a yardstick when considering the *maṣlaḥah*. He had already excluded *istiṣlāḥ* (seeking *maṣlaḥah*) from the *adillah* because of its wide and undefined application.³⁵ Other juridical formulas that he excludes from the *adillah* are *istiḥsān* (juristic preference), the Companion's words, and the status of acts before the Qur'an was revealed. This demonstrates that he readopted *maṣlaḥah* within the context of *qiyās* because it conformed with the law's end goals (*maqāṣid*), which, in his view, can be better devised by the principles of *qiyās*.

On the issue of ijtihad and its corollary *taqlīd*, al-Ghazālī offers one of the best definitions. The lucidity of his expression in defining the former as one's "utmost exertion to infer the law" and "following the opinion of others without reasoning" for there was a tendency to embrace *taqlīd*, as evidenced in the works of succeeding authors.³⁶ His exposition upon conflicting laws under *tarjīḥ* also seems impressive. To solve these conflicting laws, he briefly propounds a number of practical formulas like *takhyīr* (lit. choice of law) and *istiṣḥāb* (then presumption of continuity) and notes that they should all be governed under the rubric of *maṣlaḥah*.³⁷ These formulas were elaborated by later authors, as we will see in the succeeding chapters.

Fakhr al-Dīn al-Rāzī

Almost a century after al-Ghazālī, the Shāfiᶜī jurisprudent Fakhr al-Dīn al-Rāzī (d. 606/1209) tried, among other things, to explain the logic of legal methodology and the sequences of its various subjects. In his famous book *al-Maḥṣūl*, he defines *uṣūl al-fiqh* as a compound method by which legal norms are generally known and also discusses the method of reasoning and who is qualified to perform it.[38] This definition reflects the complex and sophisticated nature of legal methodology at that time. In fact, the next problem that al-Rāzī takes up is epistemological, as he offers definitions of knowledge (*ʿilm*), speculation (*ẓann*), and conception (*naẓar*) as the first necessary steps to understanding key methodological notions such as legal proofs and contextual indicators (*al-dalīl wa al-imārah*).[39]

Yet, Rāzī's introductory remarks seem condensed and rather brief when compared to those of Ghazālī, Juwaynī, and Ibn Ḥazm. By naming his chapter "Some introductory remarks required by the science of legal methodology," Rāzī alludes to his intention to remove the logical and theological accounts from *uṣūl al-fiqh*.[40] Generally speaking, he prefers to see legal methodology in its "Islamized" or "unadulterated" fashion, rather than with a direct incorporation of elements of formal logic. His brief introduction gives enough insight into logical notions for the reader to understand legal methodology. Moreover, he often takes into consideration the theological basis while dealing with the relevant topics of legal methodology.

Like al-Ghazālī, al-Rāzī felt it necessary to deal with legal norms first, thereby preparing the ground for dividing actions into inherently good or evil. Legal norms, he says, concern one's actions, which are subjects of the divine speech. Instead of looking variably at the divine address (*khiṭāb*), as the authors before al-Ghazālī did, al-Rāzī focuses directly on characterizing the legal values to which God's addresses apply.[41] Unlike al-Ghazālī, al-Rāzī's account here appears as an introduction to the methodology that actually opens with linguistics.

The main topics of al-Rāzī's work, as he enumerates in his introduction, comprise thirteen parts: 1) linguistics, 2) commands and prohibitions, 3) the general and the particular, 4) the ambiguous and the lucid, 5) actions, 6) abrogation, 7) consensus, 8) traditions, 9) analogy, 10) juristic preferences, 11) ijtihad, 12) asking the juridical opinion, and 13) discrepancy among *mujtahid*s.[42] These topics can be reduced to three major subjects: 1) linguistics (comprising the first seven topics); 2) consensus and validity of the traditions; and 3) discursive reasoning, including analogy, ijtihad, and preferences.

His account of the various ways of rational reasoning cover more ground than what he describes in his summary. In the section on analogy, following in the footsteps of Ghazālī, Rāzī brings forth the doctrine of the suitability (*munāsabah*) of a legal norm with the law's basic objectives. From this point, he then moves on to the justification (*ta'līl*) of God's commands and ends with the principle of considering the public welfare based on textually unattested evidence (*al-maṣāliḥ al-mursalah*).[43] He also adds a novel chapter, "The legal proofs on which *mujtahids* disagreed,"[44] to the last part of the section on ijtihad. Here, he sets forth a number of "principles of jurisprudence," among which are the presumption of the past situation's continuity (*istiṣḥāb*), juristic preference (*istiḥsān*), the presumption of disengagement (*aṣl al-'adam*) when the case is not subjected to any ruling, and, more importantly, the principle of the induction of conjecture (*al-istiqrā' al-maznūn*).[45] He briefly defines the latter as akin to a syllogism of formal logic, which may rise to the level of conjecture (*zann*). As such, he appears to be one of the foremost authors who shifted the emphasis from theological to methodological problems without changing the structure of *uṣūl al-fiqh*. As we will see, this way of restricting the scope of legal methodology became a model for later jurists.

Sayf al-Dīn al-Āmidī

The course of segregating *uṣūl al-fiqh* from theology while incorporating elements of logic and *kalām* finds another exponent in Sayf al-Dīn al-Āmidī (d. 631/1233), who condenses an epistemo-theological introduction into three and half pages and refers readers to his *Abkār al-Afkār* for greater elaboration. However, under the title of *istidlāl*, by which he means logical inference, he dedicates a chapter to syllogism.[46] Nonetheless, he employs a theological approach when dealing with some of the topics listed under *uṣūl al-fiqh*, as evident in the outline below. He enriched his language with terms borrowed from formal logic and with insights derived from his theological background.

Outline of al-Āmidī's Legal Methodology
He divides his account into four sections:

I. The definition of *uṣūl al-fiqh*, description of its contents and end goals (*al-ghāyah*), and introductory remarks on:
   1. The epistemological premise: definitions of *dalīl*, *ʿilm*, *ẓann*, and *naẓar*.
   2. The function and semantics of words.
   3. The fundamental concepts of fiqh and legal norms (*aḥkām*).[47]

II. The legal indicant (*al-dalīl al-sharʿī*), primarily divided into two types:
   First: Valid in their essence and obligatory (*wājib*) in practice.
   1. The scripture, which is the first and prime source of Islamic law.
   2. The traditions of the Prophet and their infallibility.
   3. Consensus: its validity and varieties.[48]
   4. The *khabar* character of the transmission of legal norms that are shared in the Qur'an, Sunnah, and *ijmāʿ*.[49]
      Al-Āmidī studies *khabar* from two points of view:
      a. According to its basis of transmission (*sanad*), which is either *mutawātir* or *āḥād*, and their validity and varieties.
      b. According to their text (*matn*), which he divides into:
         i. Explicit indication, which includes:
         a) Commands and prohibitions,
         b) General expressions and their particularization,
         c) Absolute and qualified expressions, and
         d) Ambiguity, lucidity, and diversion to non-apparent meaning.
         ii. Implicit indication and its varieties.
         iii. Abrogation: applicable only to the Qur'an and the Sunnah.

5. *Qiyās*: its definition and constituents: i) conditions of the
   principle case (*aṣl*), ii) cause (*ʿillah*), and iii) the novel case
   (*farʿ*).[50]
6. *Istidlāl* (inference) and its varieties. Under this rubric, al-Āmidī
   a. first forwards the basic type of syllogisms known in
      formal logic
   b. then deals with presumption of continuity (*istiṣḥāb*).[51]

Second: Indicants that are deemed correct but are not:
1. Scriptures that came through earlier prophets.
2. The practice of a single Companion.
3. Juristic preference (*istiḥsān*) based on general observations.
4. Consideration of public interest.[52]

III. Ijtihad and *mujtahid*s:
1. The qualification of *mujtahid*s.
2. Imitation (*taqlīd*) of the opinions of *mujtahid*s and muftis.

IV. Preferences in case of conflicting laws (*tarjiḥāt*):[53]
1. When the means to arrive at judgment is subject of the
   preference.
2. When the definitions of conceptual ideas are subjected to the
   preference criterion.

From the above outline, we can discern that classifying the sources of
legal knowledge constitutes the nucleus of al-Āmidī's legal methodology, around which he elaborates most of the related topics. He deals
with legal indicant (*al-dalīl al-sharʿī*) in its general sense and includes
istidlāl (inference) in this classification, although most authors in the
field did not consider a "revealed indicant." Nevertheless, he excludes
istiḥsān and *al-maṣāliḥ al-mursalah*, two popular concepts at least
among the Ḥanafīs, because they allow non-juridical considerations
to factor in juristic issues.[54]

Compared to al-Ghazālī's and al-Rāzī's accounts, al-Āmidī brings forth two significant changes in categorizing the legal proofs (*adillah*), including the four traditional sources (i.e., the Qur'an, Sunnah, consensus, and analogy). Firstly, he uses the *khabar* character of the transmission of legal norms, shared in the Qur'an, Sunnah, and *ijmāʿ*, as his point of departure to approach the explicit or implicit text commands and their varieties, which are the fundamental basis of *uṣūl al-fiqh*. This approach, which can be traced back to the theological accounts of the early period, delineates the influence of theology in his methodology. Here, he not only presents a new definition for *khabar*, but also provides four contexts, namely *sanad* (reference), *matn* (text), and "explicit and implicit indicators," to exhibit the logic behind his classification of the sources of legal knowledge.[55]

Secondly, al-Āmidī tries to associate the rational principle of *istiṣḥāb* with syllogistical premises in an effort to make an independent category of reasoning under the rubric of *istidlāl* an auxiliary to *qiyās*. He defines the former in its specific sense as a rational proof that is not necessarily based on the four above-mentioned religious sources. He then exemplifies this kind of inference in logical concepts of "causality" (*sababiyyah*), "impediment" (*manʿiyyah*), "vicious circle" (*dawr*), and the presumption of the nonexistence of a *ḥukm* when there is no proof for it (*aṣl al-ʿadam*), and so on. However, his main topic is the conjunctive syllogism (*iqtirānī*), which he divides into two forms each constituting four kinds.[56] The next important case of *istidlāl*, according to him, is the presumption of continuity (*istiṣḥāb*) of a situation initiated in the past when there is no reason to conclude that it had come to an end. He corroborates the rationality of both positive and negative *istiṣḥāb*, despite the opposition of most Ḥanafīs and some Shāfiʿīs.[57]

Ibn al-Ḥājib

The process of summarizing *uṣūl al-fiqh* reached its peak with the Mālikī jurist Jamāl al-Dīn Ibn al-Ḥājib (d. 646/1248), whose abridgment of legal methodology attracted Muslim commentators (including Shiʿis) for the next four centuries. He first wrote *Muntaha al-Wuṣūl*, which he later shortened in his *Mukhtaṣar*. This abridgment was commented upon by the famous Shāfiʿī jurist Qāḍī ʿAḍudī (d. 756/1355), then annotated by his theologian disciple Saʿd al-Dīn al-Taftāzānī (d. 791/1388), and the philosopher/jurist Sayyid Sharīf al-Jurjānī (d. 816/1413), as well as other important Sunni jurists.[58] Among Shiʿi *ʿulamā*ʾ, the renowned al-ʿAllāmah al-Ḥillī (d. 726/1327) and the Safavid court jurist Shaykh Bahāʾī (d. 1030/1631) incorporated the above-mentioned *Mukhtaṣar* in their works.[59]

Ibn al-Ḥājib divides his legal methodology into four parts: 1) elementaries (*al-mabādī*), 2) revelational indicants (*al-adillah al-samʿiyyah*), 3) preference (*al-tarjīḥ*) and, 4) ijtihad.[60] The elementary section includes rules on definition and syllogism borrowed originally from formal logic. As such, Ibn al-Ḥājib, makes epistemological topics an essential part of *uṣūl al-fiqh* and far more important than the introductory remarks by al-Ghazālī, al-Juwaynī, and Ibn Ḥazm. Qāḍī ʿAḍudī comments that this account is not really part and parcel of *uṣūl al-fiqh*, and Taftāzānī adds that authors used to include this part under legal methodology only because it had become commonplace (*bi ṭarīq al-taghlīb*) to do so, not because it was a constituent part of the discipline.[61] However, Ibn al-Ḥājib's adoption of syllogism as one of the "elementaries" brought both syllogistical definitions into focus again, a clear departure from the early path of legal methodology when either the hierarchy of the sources of the law or their semantics were of prime focus, whereas the authority of revelational indicants appears to be a routinized argument in Ibn al-Ḥājib's account.

By giving separate sections to preference (*tarjīḥ*) and ijtihad, Ibn al-Ḥājib clearly demarcates non-revelational sources from routinized sources. Although Muslim authors originally applied "preference" to those traditions that had discrepancies, it nevertheless came to include other legal evidences. This topic provided a necessary context for Muslim jurists to employ their individual observation in choosing between equally balanced traditions and indicants (*adillah*). By definition, ijtihad requires the independent use of intellectual energy to deduce law from the sources. These two topics had been deliberated by some of the previous authors,[62] but Ibn al-Ḥajib laid more emphasis on their distinct nature by dedicating a section to each of them. His way of setting the topics of legal methodology caught the attention of his contemporaries, who either accepted or challenged his methodology. A century later, as we will see below, the focus shifted to the law's social function, in which juridical ijtihad and the preferences were employed regularly.

Tāj al-Dīn al-Subkī

Impressed by the logical method of defining legal terms, Tāj al-Dīn al-Subkī (d. 771/1369) recapitulates some legal and theological concepts along with *uṣūl al-fiqh* in his *Jamʿ al-Jawāmiʿ*. His introduction redefines a number of key methodological terms such as *ḥukm* (legal norm), *sabab* (cause), *sharṭ* (condition), *dalīl* (indicant), and *naẓar* (reflection), along with a few legal and theological principles like *ʿazīmah* and *rukhṣah* (strict and concessionary laws) and "expressing thanks to God's benevolence is obligatory by the law."[63] The bulk of his legal methodology centers on the authority of the law's four sources (i.e., the Qur'an, sunnah, consensus, and *qiyās*) followed by a chapter on rational reasoning under the rubric of *istidlāl*. Topics of literal interpretation (*mabāḥith al-alfāẓ*), including grammar and abrogation (*naskh*), are discussed here on the first source of the law, the Qur'an. His chapter on *istidlāl* briefly deals with the two kinds of *qiyās*: conjunctive and exceptional analogy (*al-qiyās al-iqtarānī* and *al-qiyās al-istithnā'ī*) and topics such as induction (*istiqrā'*), the presumption of continuity (*istiṣḥāb*), and juristic preference (*istiḥsān*).[64] He closes his account with a chapter on the problems associated with conflicting laws, ijtihad, and *taqlīd*.[65] One may detect the influence of Ibn al-Ḥajib's work, for Subkī frequently refers to him. Nevertheless, Subkī's brief account on *uṣūl al-fiqh* appeals to a number of later scholars and commentators.

The conventional course of theoretical writings on *uṣūl al-fiqh* continued during the seventh/thirteenth century and thereafter. Among those authors whose works must be mentioned are the

70

Ḥanafīs Muẓaffar al-Dīn al-Sāʿātī (d. 694/1295) and Ṣadr al-Sharīʿah (d. 747/1346), the Shāfiʿī Badr al-Dīn al-Zarkashī (d. 794/1348), and the Mālikī al-Qarrāfī (d. 684/1285).[66]

CHAPTER 6

Remolding Legal Methodology to Respond to Social Reality

A NEW tendency appeared among some of the legal scholars from the eighth/fourteenth century onward, one that shifted the emphasis from the theoretical, which emphasized the Qur'an and the Sunnah, to the social and practical aspects of Islamic legal methodology. Two towering juridical figures of this period were al-Ṭūfī and al-Shāṭibī, who turned their attention to practical problems of Islamic jurisprudence and sought to lessen the grip of literal hermeneutics. In fact, the theoretical culmination of Islamic legal methodology in the works of al-Ghazālī and Ibn al-Ḥājib paved the way for widening its scope to include new juridical devices such as the "presumption of continuity" and the "higher objectives of law." These devices can practically transcend the limits of text-based reading of the Sharīʿah and thus act as a bridge between the methodological theories and social realities of the time.

Najm al-Dīn Sulaymān al-Ṭūfī

Najm al-Dīn Sulaymān al-Ṭūfī (d. 716/1316), a Hanbali jurist of Baghdad, modified the legal methodology to respond to the existing social context by rearranging the contents of Islamic legal methodology according to pragmatism. He wrote several abridgements on the *uṣūl* works of earlier authors, including Ibn Qudāmah (d. 620/1223).

In a detailed commentary on his own abridgment of Ibn Qudāmah's *Rawḍat al-Nāẓir*, al-Ṭūfī says Ibn Qudāmah first followed al-Ghazālī's pattern of incorporating logic into his legal methodology, but later on dropped it due to the protest of his companions.[1] Al-Ṭūfī has apparently chosen the latter version for his commentary, for he claimed that only Ibn al-Ḥājib had really followed al-Ghazālī's method of presenting *uṣūl al-fiqh*.[2]

Al-Ṭūfī considers his approach to legal methodology as moderate and comprehensive, one that does not exceed the acceptable boundaries of pre-modern understandings of *uṣūl al-fiqh*. Following the pattern set by Ibn Qudāmah, he opens his account with a brief explanation of the importance of the hierarchy of the law's sources, followed by a detailed definition of *uṣūl al-fiqh*. His first concern is the qualifications of the *mukallaf*, namely, what conditions must be fulfilled for one to be considered competent in the eyes of Islamic law and therefore worthy to shoulder the religious responsibilities associated with carrying out the legal obligations. After dealing with the five categories of *aḥkām* (i.e., obligatory, recommended, permissible reprehensible, and forbidden), he discusses the theological question of whether human beings can determine good and evil and asks "is it necessary for God to consider human good (*maṣlaḥah*), or not?" Despite Ashʿarī theology's tenacious grip and prevalence on that time's juristic milieu, he responds that "yes, it is necessary upon God," for otherwise applying rules to people's actions would be irrational.[3]

The next topic is the four sources of Islamic law. Following the template adopted by Ibn Qudāmah, al-Ṭūfī labels them *al-uṣūl*: the Qur'an, the Sunnah, consensus, and the principle of presumption of continuity (*istiṣḥāb*).[4] Although he adds that these are indicants (*adillah*) of the law as well, in this book he nevertheless prefers to apply the latter designation to other indicants such as *qiyās*, the legality of the past religions, the traditions of the Companions, preference, and consideration of the public welfare.[5] In his *Sharḥ al-Arbaʿīn*, he claims, based upon personal research, that the number of the law's indicants (*adillat al-sharʿ*) reaches nineteen: the consensus of Madinah, the principle of being discharged of any obligation (*barā'ah*), customs, induction, *sadd al-dharā'iʿ*, infallibility (*ʿiṣmah*), the consensus of the people of Kufah, the consensus of the Prophet's family according to the Shiʿis, and the consensus of the four pious Caliphs, along with the nine above-mentioned primary sources and indicants.[6] This way of looking at the law's sources and indicants points to the fact that practical juridical techniques, such as *istiṣlāḥ* and *sadd al-dharā'iʿ*, had acquired enough legitimacy to be integrated among the legal indicants.

In *Sharḥ Mukhtaṣar al-Rawḍah*, al-Ṭūfī elaborates on the Qur'an, Sunnah, and *ijmāʿ* in a conventional manner and then adds *istiṣḥāb* as a fourth source of law. He, therefore, tries first to establish this new principle's authority.[7] *Qiyās* occupies a large portion of his work, but instead of including it among the sources or the specific indicants, he separates it as an independent rational reasoning added to the sources and indicants.[8] As such, the influence of Ghazālī's method of excluding *qiyās* from the sources and placing it under rational reasoning can be seen in his and Ibn Qudāmah's works. Ṭūfī's concluding topics center on ijtihad, following the opinions of others (*taqlīd*), and the problems associated with the conflict of laws, which are dealt with under the rubric of *tarjīḥ* (preference).[9]

Al-Ṭūfī placed special emphasis on socio-legal issues. In fact, he dedicates two chapters of his *Sharḥ Mukhtaṣar al-Rawḍah* to the principles of *istiṣḥāb* and *istiṣlāḥ*, both of which are of practical import. The juridical principle of *istiṣḥāb* was first brought into Muslim juridical discourses by Mālik ibn Anas (d. 179/ 795) and followed by Aḥmad ibn Ḥanbal (d. 241/855), al-Muzanī (d. 264/878), the prominent student of al-Shāfiʿī and Abū Bakr al-Ṣayrafī (d. 330/942) who wrote a commentary on al-Shāfiʿī's *al-Risālah*. Al-Juwaynī and al-Ghazālī[10] later elaborated upon this principle, which was considered a source of law despite Ibn Qudāmah and al-Ṭūfī's proposal. The latter employs *istiṣḥāb* not only to establish continuity in the state of legal premises, but also to secure the authority of other legal principles. For instance, the presumption of innocence or the state of being discharged (*al-barā'ah al-aṣliyyah*) in cases of individual rights is a rational principle. An example given by al-Ṭūfī reads "the claimant bears the burden of proof" (*al-bayyinah ʿalā al-muddāʿī*), because presuming that "nothing has changed the status quo" requires that the defendant, by definition, should be considered discharged from bearing proof.[11]

Al-Ṭūfī presents the presumption of being discharged as a corollary to the principle of *istiṣḥāb*, but, as mentioned earlier, also reckons it to be an independent indicant in his *Sharḥ al-Arbaʿīn*. In contrast, *aṣālat al-ishtighāl* (the principle of being engaged) applies to cases of duty toward God. Its authority can also be established via *istiṣḥāb* (i.e., the presumed continuity of the primordial pledge of obedience that human beings gave to God on the Day of the Covenant [*Yawm al-Mīthāq*]).[12]

The next juridical tool invoked to deal with contemporary socio-legal issues is *maṣlaḥah*. Al-Ṭūfī discusses it in a conventional manner in his *Muktaṣar*,[13] but then presents it as a theory in *Sharḥ al-Arbaʿīn*, where he begins with the claim that considering the public good is one of religion's foundations (*uṣūl al-sharʿ*). He bases his argument mainly upon the Prophetic tradition that "no harm shall be inflicted or reciprocated" (*lā ḍarar wa lā ḍirār fī al-Islām*).[14] As such, considering the public good in all aspects remains a top priority. The law's strongest indicants, he adds, are "the fixed texts (*naṣṣ*) and consensus." However, he notes that considering the public welfare must overrule them if expediency so requires, which is to be done by introducing the principle of particularization (*takhṣīṣ*) under the rules of interpretation (*bayān*) in the same manner that the Sunnah occasionally overrules the Qur'an.[15]

Al-Ṭūfī divides the application of *maṣlaḥah* into two domains: rituals and customary practices (*ʿādāt*) governed by the Shariʿah's higher objectives. He categorizes human actions as belonging either in the realm of divine right (*ḥaqq Allāh*) or individual right (*ḥaqq al-nās*). As a proof, he advances such recurring Qur'anic concepts as mercy (*raḥmah*), guidance (*hudā*), and healing (*shifāʾ*), all of which are aimed at the public good in general.[16] Finally, he engages in polemics to argue that prioritizing the principle of public welfare does not curtail the application of other legal principles and norms. Rather, the law advises it so that the legal norms can be better implemented.[17]

Al-Tufi's most significant innovation to the legal theory was his extending the scope of the sources of Islamic law beyond the four conventional legal indicants (*adillat al-shar*). While recognizing the supremacy of the Qur'an and Sunnah, he gives functional authority to the principles of *istiṣḥāb*, *maṣlaḥah*, the legality of past religions, the traditions of the Companions, and juristic preference in addition to *ijmāʿ* and *qiyās*.

The idea of correlating the law's higher objectives with the public welfare was further developed by another prominent jurist of the eighth/fourteenth century, to whom we now turn.

Abū Isḥāq al-Shāṭibī

Abū Isḥāq Ibrāhīm al-Shāṭibī (d. 790/1388) offered the most impactful changes to the legal theory so that it could address that time's socio-legal challenges. He wrote one of the most inspiring works on legal methodology and its relation to the philosophy of law with a new arrangement based mainly upon the practical context of jurisprudence. In his *al-Muwāfaqāt* (lit. the Concordances), al-Shāṭibī presents *uṣūl al-fiqh* not only as a method to extrapolate rules from the sources, but also to serve the law's aims and objectives – what he calls *maqāṣid al-sharīʿah*. By offering twelve theoretical premises (*al-muqaddimāt al-ʿilmiyyah*) as an introduction, he elaborates upon methods and theories of harmonizing the legal norms (*aḥkām*) with the philosophy of law within the context of the public welfare (*maṣlaḥah*).[18] This approach led him to either propose or maintain several additional postulates as the key methodological premises for understanding the law according to its objective.

The first premise he sets out is that the law's methodological principles are *qaṭʿī* (lit. decisive) not *ẓannī* (lit. probable), because they are concerned with its universal principles (i.e., *ḍarūriyyāt* [lit. necessities], *ḥājiyyāt* [lit. needs], and *taḥsīniyyāt* [lit. improvements]).[19] By presenting this premise, al-Shāṭibī indicates his novel approach to legal knowledge, one that Wael Hallaq considers as "epistemology refashioned."[20] Methodological principles may be drawn from the revelation, reason (*ʿaql*), or convention (*ʿādah*); their certitude can be established by inductive search (*istiqrāʾ*).[21] Al-Shāṭibī lays special emphasis on the inductive method of reasoning and opposes the deductive or analogical reasoning practiced by the traditional jurists. The latter practice, he adds, allows a jurist to select the text that suits only his purpose, something that is incompatible with the Lawgiver's overall aims and intentions. Khalid Masoud considers *istiqrāʾ* as al-Shāṭibī's normative basis of Shariʿah, which is deeply rooted in human welfare and social practices.[22] This assertion can be endorsed by looking at how al-Shāṭibī stresses the notion of *ʿādah* as a valid practice and the method of *istiqrāʾ* as the best way to reach the truth. They evidently point to his conception of a normative basis for the Shariʿah, which in contemporary society can only be expected.

After an extraordinary introduction, al-Shāṭibī divides his account of legal methodology into four parts: *aḥkām*, *maqāṣid*, *adillah*, and ijtihad. The part on *maqāṣid* seems innovative in Islamic legal methodology both in terms of the title and substance, as we will briefly examine below.

Al-Shāṭibī's treatment of *aḥkām* is notably different from the standard *uṣūlī* methods of dealing with Islamic legal norms. He opens his account with the category of *mubāḥāt*, permissible acts whose commission or omission is equally legal. Within a socio-philosophical elaboration of *mubāḥ*, he refers to other categories (*ḥarām*, *ḥalāl*, *mandūb*, and *makrūh*); nevertheless, his main focus is on explaining *mubāḥ* and its juridical and social variants in light of their end goals for the human good. Legal topics such as *ʿazīmah* and *rukhṣah* (strict and concessionary laws, respectively) and *tarājīḥ* (preferences) are discussed in this part.[23] In his introduction, al-Shāṭibī had already underlined the concept that according to Qurʾan 5:101 and several traditions, the Prophet did not allow his Companions to engage in inquisitiveness and unnecessary questioning that may lead to the prohibition of what otherwise would be allowed.[24] Reacting to the over-zealous attitude of some Sufis and legists of his time, he argues that leniency in the interpretation of the law is God's grace prescribed by the Scripture.[25]

The second part of his legal methodology is dedicated to the *maqāṣid*, which is the attempt to understand the Lawgiver's intention and to bring the legal norms into line with His ultimate objectives. According to him, the Lawgiver's primary intention is to preserve the people's welfare. He divides the *maṣlaḥah* into the three categories of necessity (i.e., protecting religion, self [*nafs*], family, property, and intellect), needs, (i.e., rituals and transactions designed to mitigate hardship), and improvements (i.e., the best conduct and customs [*ʿādāt*]), which may be in harmony with the typology of the respective legal norms, depending upon the circumstances.[26] Before al-Shāṭibī, such jurists as al-Juwaynī, al-Ghazālī, al-Qarafī, and others placed this categorization in the chapter on *qiyās* mainly to justify the appropriate application of *ratio legis* (*ʿillah*) to new legal cases. By commensuration of this category with the public good (*maṣlaḥah*), al-Shāṭibī introduced a new rational approach to the sources of law, one that considers social realities while formulating suitable legal norms. As a result, he held that one's adherence to the law's text must not be so rigid that it alienates the Shariʿah's rationale and purpose.[27]

The third part of al-Shāṭibī's work concerns the law's sources (*adillah* [lit. indicants]), in which he subsumes the Qurʾan, the Prophet's traditions, the community's consensus, and *ra'y* (the opinion of Muslim scholars). In this part he deals with the first two sources as textual evidences and leaves the rational evidences to the section on ijtihad. Before treating the *adillah*, he offers another socio-legal introduction to explain the characteristics and applicability of legal *adillah* vis-à-vis the social requirements of the time. Here, he attempts to analyze the Shariʿah's content and structure. In his view, the Makkan phase of revelation was the basis of religion during which the universal principles (e.g., *ḍarūriyyāt* and *ʿibādāt* [matters of worship and rituals]) were laid down, whereas the Madinan verses either elaborate or complement the Makkan verses' basic norms.[28] Al-Shāṭibī, who had already distinguished rituals (*ʿibādāt*) from customary practices (*ʿādāt*),[29] assigns the former to the Makkan phase and the latter to the Madinan phase. The former are acts of devotion that require uncritical acceptance (*taʿabbudī*) and are immutable, whereas the latter (e.g., sale, rent, and marriage) are variable and subject to choice. This kind of dichotomous treatment of concepts, as well as their division into Makkan and Madinan phases of revelations, is typical of his approach to legal theory in *al-Muwāfaqāt*[30] and influenced some later legists and Muslim scholars.

Al-Shāṭibī subsequently deals with the problem of abrogation by launching an inductive search for the Qur'an's abrogated verses. He evaluates most of them as cases of particularization, for he contends that true cases of abrogation involve mainly those Madinan verses that are unrelated to the three categories of *ḍarūriyyāt*, *ḥājiyyāt*, and *taḥsīniyyāt*.[31] The discourse encompasses the varieties of commands and prohibitions, as well as issues dealing with how to characterize them.[32] Problems emanating due to the particularization and ambiguity of legal norms are discussed in the following chapter.[33]

The authority of the Qur'an and the Sunnah, along with the necessity of learning the related disciplines (e.g., *tafsīr* and *ḥadīth*), are tackled in the next two chapters of his work. He corroborates that knowledge of the causes of the revelation and of pre-Islamic Arab customs, in addition to Arabic semantics, are necessary to understand the totality of the Qur'anic message's aims and objectives.[34] Concerning the Qur'an's inclusiveness, he admits that the specifics of most legal norms (*aḥkām*) on rituals and contracts are not found in it. Nevertheless, he adds, the above-mentioned generalities of the legal norms are so well expressed in the Qur'an that it allows insight into how they should be drawn from the general ones. Moreover, the Qur'an is the basis of all other legal sources (i.e., Sunnah, *ijmāʿ*, and *qiyās*).[35] In his conclusion, he discusses the hermeneutic question of exoteric and esoteric meanings of some of its verses.[36]

The tradition of the Prophet occupies the second place as a source of the law. Al-Shāṭibī considers it to be a practical elaboration of the Qur'an, a secondary source that can be in apparent conflict with it only to explain or to particularize its verses.[37] He closes his account of *adillah* with the Sunnah and does not deal with the law's other indicants (i.e., consensus and *ra'y*) that he had previously included among its sources. Similarly, *qiyās* seems to have been excluded as well, even though he mentions it among the *adillah* once only. Nevertheless, parts of the above-mentioned rational indicants, particularly *ra'y*, can be found in the section on ijtihad.

The last part of al-Shāṭibī's legal methodology is on ijtihad. The first section focuses on the qualifications of a *mujtahid* from the viewpoint of his ijtihad. Instead of defining his conception of ijtihad, al-Shāṭibī elaborates upon the avenues of interpreting and applying the legal norms. Instead of stressing knowledge of Arabic or semantics, he either proposes or refashions a number of interpretive avenues to find a more meaningful application for ijtihad. His opening argument centers on the types of ijtihad. First is *taḥqīq al-manāṭ*, which means to determine if a case and the involved parties are true subjects of a specific law (e.g., if they qualify for legal maintenance based on their financial situation). He considers the process to be perpetually relevant because this category of ijtihad and, as such, the notion of *taqlīd* (lit. emulation or following past precedents) does not apply.[38] He divides the second type of ijtihad, one that can be terminated, into two categories: *tanqīḥ al-manāṭ*, "the identification of the *ratio legis* insofar as it can be isolated from attributes that are co-joined with it in the texts,"[39] and *takhrīj al-manāṭ*, "investigating the texts in order to extract what is otherwise an unspecified *ratio legis*."[40] The degree of one's proficiency in ijtihad is determined by two components: understanding the law's aims and one's ability to extract rules from the sources. Al-Shāṭibī contends that the second one serves the first one, since the Lawgiver's main objective is to consider the public interest, and needs a superior intellectual capacity to determine the law according to *maṣlaḥah*.[41]

Al-Shāṭibī stresses the significance of interpretation when it comes to applying the legal norms for, according to him, this is just as important as introducing a new law. The *mujtahid* or mufti occupies the office of the Prophet in respect to what reaches him from the Shariʿah; either by means of transmitting the Sunnah or what he understands from the Shariʿah. In the first case he is no more than the one who conveys the Shariʿah's commands, whereas in the second case the mufti stands in the position of the Prophet as regards setting up legal norms.[42] It is noteworthy that his account here does not seek to prove a new position for the exponents of the Shariʿah, namely, the *ʿulamāʾ*, because he aspires to achieve a better understanding of the importance of the law's interpretation and application.[43]

His last concern as regards legal methodology centers on *taqlīd*, how to follow the commonly established Islamic practices, seek out a mufti to solicit his opinion, and implement his fatwa. The limits of questions and the scope of the mufti's involvement in the people's affairs, particularly while determining the law's applicability to a case (*taḥqīq al-manāṭ*), are discussed in this section.[44]

Given the above, al-Shāṭibī's framework does not fit the conventional structure of legal methodology. Instead of beginning with the hierarchy of the law's four sources followed by the semantics of the Qur'an and traditions, the authority of *ijmāʿ* and *qiyās*, and concluding with the office of *mujtahid* and his preferences, he opens with a socio-historical evaluation of legal norms followed by the philosophy of the law, by another socio-legal assessment of the sources, and finally closes by relocating ijtihad's place in Islamic jurisprudence. By doing so, he instrumentalizes legal methodology so that it can address socio-legal theories and thereby provide a wider scope that was not employed (or even noticed) until the contemporary era.

The Reorientation of Legal Methodology in the Recent Era: From Shāh Walīyullāh to al-Zuḥaylī

MUSLIMS DIVIDE Islamic legal history into three eras: the early (*al-mutaqaddim*), the middle (*al-mutawassiṭ*), and the moderns or later scholars (*al-muta'akhkhir*). Although the precise beginning of the recent era is not clearly defined, the period after the Ḥanbalī theologian Ibn al-Qayyim al-Jawziyyah (d. 751/1350) is commonly regarded as "the recent era." Each period, of course, has its own characteristics and figures, but they hardly define an epoch in its totality. This is particularly true with the recent era, which often appears to Muslims as devoid of any outstanding luminaries who are on the same level as their predecessors. As regards legal methodology, a significant feature of the post Ibn al-Qayyim era is the reorientation of al-Ghazālī's method of structuring *uṣūl al-fiqh*, as seen below in the works of some leading Sunni authors. The recent changes in Shiʿi methodology, which mainly highlight the development of literal and rational reasoning, will be dealt with in the succeeding chapter. All of the above changes are considered to have occurred within the conventional parameters of *uṣūl al-fiqh*. Modern approaches to the Shariʿah that, among other things, brought forth a range of methodological arguments will be discussed in the last chapter.

The Reorientation of Legal Methodology in the Recent Era

The Ḥanafī Elaboration of Legal Maxims
One of the recent era's first juridical developments is the elaboration of legal maxims (*qawāʿid al-fiqh*) by the Ḥanafī scholars Ibn Nujaym (d. 970/1562) and Ibn ʿĀbidīn (d. 1252/1836). The former was an Egyptian author who wrote one work on *uṣūl* and five books on fiqh and legal maxims. The significance of his contribution lies in how he elaborated on a number of legal maxims, such as "the role of intention (*niyyah*) in contracts and rituals" and particularly "habit and custom" (*al-ʿādah wa al-ʿurf*), which indicates the *ʿulamā's* interest in time-honored public practices and merits our attention. Basing the legality of *ʿādah* on the prophetic tradition "Whatever the Muslims deem to be good is good in the eyes of God," he claims that the scope of *ʿādah* is so widespread in jurisprudence that scholars consider it an established principle (*aṣl*). By quoting al-Bazdawī, an early-period Ḥanafī scholar, he attempts to redefine the close connection of habit and "practice" (*istiʿmāl*).[1]

The Syrian jurist Ibn ʿĀbidīn wrote a special treatise on *ʿurf*, which he divides into "practical" and "literal," both of which may lack juridical evidence but are still considered legitimate if they do not contradict the revealed texts of the law. He stipulates this with a condition: *ʿUrf* should be general and time-honored, as opposed to confined to a particular application.[2] In furthering the ongoing discussion, he claims that customs may change with time and, as such, knowledge of the people's current customs ought to be made a requirement of an aspiring *mujtahid*. He presents the example of levying fees for teaching the Qur'an, which Abū Ḥanīfah and Shaybānī prohibited but later scholars allowed because they were confident that Abū Ḥanīfah would have reversed his ruling in light of the new context and time.[3] As such, the emphasis on *ʿādah* and *ʿurf* is a throwback to Shāṭibī's method of incorporating social realities into jurisprudence.

Shāh Walīyullāh Dehlawi
Shāh Walīyullāh of Delhi (d. 1176/1762), whose writings have had a

lasting impression upon Muslims living in the Indian Subcontinent and Southeast Asia, did not write a specific work on legal methodology. However, he did elaborate on several key notions of the *uṣūl* in an attempt to explain his new approach to the Shariʿah. His 32 books emphasize the role of both hadith and history in understanding the Qur'an and Islam in practice. Underlining the critical role of ijtihad ranked next in importance, for he considered it "the only instrument left with us for solving the problems emerging in the swiftly changing condition of modern times."[4] In his Persian-language *Muṣaffā*, he unequivocally states that the ijtihad undertaken by contemporary Muslims should be independent, like that of Shāfiʿī's, because the existing hadith texts cannot adequately cover newly occurring cases.[5] The following outline shows the scope and various types of ijtihad that he had in mind:

1. When the truth is decisively determined, then its necessity in such cases is due to its opposite being contradicted, for it is false.
2. When the truth is determined by common consensus, its opposite is therefore false.
3. When a definite choice has been provided between adopting either one or another of the two alternatives.
4. When the above choice is given by the dominant opinion.[6]

In his *magnum opus Ḥujjat Allāh al-Bālighah*, which deals with Islamic jurisprudence (fiqh) and its philosophy, Shāh Walīyullāh deliberates on the history of the rise and development of several socio-juridical notions and their social objectives. Its remarkable part is the chapter on human development (*irtifāq*), which he contends is based on divine inspiration. This eventually turns into a process of social development. He includes the following items among the *irtifāqāt*: language, management of the household, the art of economic transactions, and the necessity of assigning a leader to govern.[7] Moreover, he attempts to find a natural context for a new esoteric spiritual interpretation of the Shariʿah's rules and extends ijtihad's scope to allow a *mujtahid* to adopt such an approach. Due to this creative and novel reinterpretation, Shāh Walīyullāh's followers regarded him as a restorer (*mujaddid*) of the religion, one whose thought contributed to an Islamic renaissance in South Asia.[8]

Al-Shawkānī

The renowned Yemeni jurist and judge Muḥammad ibn ʿAlī al-Shawkānī (d. 1255/1839), one of the prominent and authoritative representatives of restructuring legal methodology in the thirteenth nineteenth century wrote several books on Islamic theology and fiqh. His work on legal methodology remains a highly referenced textbook. He expounds *uṣūl al-fiqh* in its horizontal structure by abandoning the hierarchical arrangement of legal methodology that had prevailed since the time of Ibn al-Ḥājib.[9] Instead he adopted, with some adjustments, al-Ghazālī's method of commencing with *ḥukm* (legal norm) and then turning to *ḥākim* (juridical governance [i.e., revealed and non-revealed indicants, or *adillah*]), *al-maḥkūm bihi* (the subject of legal ordinances [i.e., the obligation]), and finally to *al-maḥkūm ʿalayhi* (what has been ordained by the law [i.e., "the capacitated person," or *mukallaf*]).[10] Given the diverse topics amassed in *uṣūl al-fiqh*, he treated several issues independently because they did not fit into the aforesaid format. The significance of his work, however, lies in its well-balanced judgments on many controversial issues, some of which are presented below.

Al-Shawkānī initiates his discourse with introductory remarks on *aḥkām* (legal norms) before focusing on the *adillah* as the sources of the law. After elaborating on the Qur'an, the Sunnah, and *ijmāʿ*, he turns to the literal interpretation of the source-texts under the heading "commands and prohibitions." He does not include *qiyās* (the fourth source of Sunni law) among the *adillah*, but rather discusses it in a distinct chapter along with such non-text-based indicants as *istiṣḥāb* (the presumption of continuity) and *maṣlaḥah* (considering the public welfare). He gives the rubric of *istidlāl* (reasoning) to this kind of legal analysis. It is evident that he intended to separate "the text-based indicants" from the rational or "non-text-based indicants."[11] The last chapter is allocated to ijtihad, *taqlīd* (unquestioned emulation), and the problem of conflicts among the laws.

His account on legal indicants appears clear and solid, although he sets forth several scholarly views for discussion. In sorting out the legality of various kinds of revealed texts, he assigns no legal authority to the Qur'an's symbolic or allegorical verses (*mutashābihāt*) or ambivalent tradition-reports (*mubhamāt*).[12] After elaborating on *qiyās* he sets forth the novel heading of *istidlāl*, in which he incorporates a number of rational arguments not directly based on the revealed texts. He terms the first topic in this vein *talāzum* (lit. concomitance), although it is a discussion of "the co-presence and co-absence" (*ṭard wa ʿaks*) of the *ratio legis* (*ʿillah*), which is actually an extension of *qiyās*. The second is the principle of the presumption of continuity, parts of which he endorsed. The third is the theological question of the legal status of pre-revelation societies, an issue that he sidesteps by quoting Imām al-Ḥaramayn al-Juwaynī that there is no legal benefit in discussing it.[13] The fourth is *istiḥsān* (juristic preference), a principle to which al-Shawkānī gives no legal authority.[14] The fifth concerns a brief examination of the principle of considering the public welfare (*al-maṣāliḥ al-mursalah*). He justifies them and notes that al-Juwaynī categorized them as *istidlāl*.[15]

His closing chapter is on ijtihad, *taqlīd*, and the problems resulting from conflicting laws – all of which he treats in their conventional forms and, in most cases, mentions the viewpoints of early and later authors. His own opinion, which is not clearly stated, is often understood between the lines of those belonging to earlier writers. On the question of the "absence of a *mujtahid* in a given time" (*khuluw al-ʿaṣr*), which necessitates *taqlīd*, al-Shawkānī goes out of his way to state that God never deprives any Muslim generation of His benevolence and mercy.[16] In the epilogue, he again brings to the fore some rational issues, among which the question of original permissibility (*aṣl al-ibāḥah*) in legal matters is worthy of note. He deliberates on the opinions of various scholars who either support or negate the above principle or believe that it has been suspended (*waqf*). Al-Shawkānī appears to have held the last position.[17]

Shaykh Muhammad Abu Zahrah

Although affected somewhat by modern approaches to the law, contemporary Islamic legal methodology continues to flourish in its conventional fashion. In this vein, the Egyptian scholar Shaykh Muhammad Abu Zahrah (d. 1974) of al-Azhar University wrote an up-to-date exposition of *uṣūl al-fiqh*. His work is significant because he takes a historical look at a number of important *uṣūlī* questions and also presents a timely re-orientation of notions such as considering the public welfare, objectives of the law, and social justice. Abu Zahrah follows al-Shawkānī's (and to some extent al-Ghazālī's) formula of presenting legal methodology in four quarters.[18] His mature arrangement of the diverse *uṣūl* topics shows how deeply he had read and benefited from more than eleven centuries of *uṣūl* writings.

Abu Zahrah opens his work with a brief review of the birth and rise of legal methodology, particularly the emergence of the two main trends of the *uṣūlī* development (i.e., the Ḥanafī and Muʿtazilī) trends (see Chapters 2 and 3). His first chapter deals with legal norm (*al-ḥukm al-sharʿī*), its variety, hierarchy, and intensity. A corollary of the legal norm is declaratory law (*al-ḥukm al-waḍʿī*), whereby Abu Zahrah elaborates upon "legal cause" (*sabab*), "legal condition" (*sharṭ*) and "legal impediment" (*māniʿ*).[19]

The second chapter focuses on both the revealed and rational indicants under the rubric of *ḥākim* (the juridical sources of law). This constitutes the core of the *uṣūl* with which he deals, not only with the authority of the Qur'an, the Sunnah, *ijmāʿ*, and *qiyās*, but also with their literal interpretations and implications. In addition, this quarter deals with rational (*ʿaqlī*) indicants such as human perceptions of good and evil, custom (*ʿurf*), considering the public welfare (*maṣlaḥah*), the presumption of continuity (*istiṣḥāb*), and their conflicts and preferences.[20] Abu Zahrah does not separate practical principles such as *istiṣḥāb* and *maṣlaḥah* from the revealed indicants, as most traditional authors did. Readers will recall that even al-Ghazālī, in his quartet arrangement of *uṣūl al-fiqh*, distinguished the method of setting legal norms from the legal indicants (see Chapter 5). Abu Zahrah's all-inclusive treatment of all *adillah* and their applied functions seems directed toward simplification and gaining greater control over the diverse *uṣūlī* subjects.

At the beginning of his chapter on *ḥākim*, Abu Zahrah reflects on the part played by the human intellect in the absence of revealed indicants. After deliberating on the Shiʿi and Muʿtazilī conceptions of *ʿaql*, he concludes that it can be reduced to "the human perception of good and evil" (*al-taḥsīn wa al-taqbīḥ*). He eventually tends to embrace the Ashʿarī view that *ʿaql* has no role other than understanding and interpreting the revealed indicants. In enumerating the *adillah*, he mentions that, save for the Qur'an and the Sunnah, the rest of them are definitely not accepted by all Islamic schools and, moreover, that some of them are quite controversial.[21]

In the third chapter, Abu Zahrah turns to such theological concepts as the limits of human acts and people's rights versus divine rights under the heading of *al-maḥkam fīhi* (the subject of legal ordinances). The fourth quarter is mainly concerned with jurisprudential issues such as eligibility and compulsion under the rubric of *al-maḥkūm ʿalayhi* (what has been ordained by law). In the last two independent chapters, he touches upon the important *uṣūlī* subjects of the objectives (*maqāṣid*) of the law and ijtihad. He explores three specific applications for the objectives of the law: 1) to educate humans on the path to take so that they will do well and become benevolent members of their societies, 2) to ensure that social justice and equality reign in a Muslim society, and 3) to consider the public welfare. Abu Zahrah's elaboration on various kinds of valid *maṣlaḥah* and its hierarchy are similar to what the preceding *ʿulamā'*, especially al-Ghazālī, had presented.[22] In the chapter of ijtihad, Abu Zahrah once more focuses on knowledge of the *maqāṣid* as a necessary prerequisite to being a bona fide *mujtahid*.[23]

In reviewing his exposition of *uṣūl al-fiqh*, we notice a shift of emphasis from the law's literal interpretation to its social objectives. This development marks the beginning of a timely trend of searching for a new vitality in Islamic legal methodology. As noted above, Abu Zahrah maintained his traditional approach to Islamic law in general, but at the same time managed to incorporate some new concepts into his legal methodology. This trend made significant headway and became accentuated in the contemporary era, as we will have occasion to see in Chapter 9.

Wahbah al-Zuhayli

Wahbah al-Zuhayli (d. 2015) is a traditional mufti and university professor who has written voluminous works on Islamic jurisprudence and Qur'anic exegesis. His book on legal methodology is one of the most referenced works in the field, after that of his teacher Abu Zahrah.

Like Abu Zahrah, Zuhayli approaches legal methodology by first appraising the legal norms (*aḥkām*) and then turning to the method of deducing *aḥkām* by evaluating their sources, executors, and beneficiaries. We know that this way of formatting *uṣūl al-fiqh* commenced with al-Ghazālī's horizontal approach to legal methodology (see Chapter 5). "The main purpose of legal methodology," al-Zuhayli adds, "is to distinguish legal norms."[24] Similar to Abu Zahrah, he divides the topic of legal norms into four sections: 1) types of legal rules (*ḥukm*), 2) the lawgiver (*ḥākim*), 3) the subject of the law (*maḥkūm fīhi*), and 4) what the law has ordained (*maḥkūm ʿalayhi*). But unlike his teacher, he does not discuss the sources of the law under the rubric of *ḥākim*, but contents himself with presenting a theological argument on reason's role vis-à-vis the revelation.[25]

The second topic is "the method of deducing legal norms," in which he includes varieties of literal interpretations and contextual implications.[26] The third topic centers on the sources of Islamic law under the rubric of *maṣādir* (i.e., the Qur'an, the Sunnah, consensus, and *qiyās*). We know that most authors, among them al-Ghazālī, regarded these two topics as the core of *uṣūl al-fiqh*. As a corollary to the sources, Zuhayli adds some practical principles such as juridical preference (*istiḥsān*), considering the public interest (*istiṣlāḥ*), custom and habits (*ʿurf wa ʿādah*), and blocking the means (*sadd al-dharāʾiʿ*); such theoretical principles as the legal state prior to revelation and the presumption of continuity (*istiṣḥāb*); and some rational maxims such as induction (*istiqrāʾ*).[27] Zuhayli's fourth topic on legal methodology deals with the abrogation of the law (*naskh*), which is the result of an ongoing re-evaluation of textual sources.

He presents a chapter each on *taʿlīl al-nuṣūṣ* (textual analysis) and *maqāṣid al-sharīʿah* (the end goals of the law) to secure the traditional method of understanding the sources. Instead of providing a broad context for the *maqāṣid* theory as al-Shāṭibī did (see Chapter 6), he tries to confine them to already well-defined juridical concepts.[28] The two interrelated topics of ijtihad and *taqlīd* are, in fact, two socio-religious questions on the process to gain the credentials of a *mujtahid* in order to be able to adjudicate cases properly, discern the law theoretically, and determine at which stage one is religiously duty-bound to fulfill the religious tasks. Despite their methodological nature, these topics are among the most debated parts of jurisprudence and became part of the applied law in Shiʿi fiqh (see Chapter 8). Zuhayli's last chapter deals with the problem of conflicting laws, in which he includes cases of abrogation and juristic preferences.[29]

Revival of the Shiʿi *Uṣūlī* Doctrine: The Elaboration of Literal-Rational Principles

THE *UṢŪL* methodology found a new momentum in the Shiʿi seminaries during the second half of the eighteenth century when the leading jurisprudents of the shrine cities of *al-ʿAtabāt* inaugurated an extended form of ijtihad to widen the scope of the *uṣūl* in order to deal with newly occurring issues. This trend, which has continued, gave a distinct identity to a host of rational principles by separating them from semantics and literal interpretations. A significant number of works were produced to elaborate the new *uṣūlī* methodology among which, the following four renowned figures represent this trend: al-Qummī, Anṣārī, Khurasani and al-Muẓaffar. They were instrumental in solidifying the triumph of the *Uṣūlīs* over the *Akhbārīs*. The latter repudiated the discipline of *uṣūl al-fiqh* and argued in favor of espousing the literal meaning of the hadiths.

During the *Akhbārī's* dominance on the Shiʿi centers of Iran, Iraq, Lebanon and Bahrain, the jurists produced a number of ethico-juridical works based mainly on the tradition-reports compiled by authors such as Mullā Muḥsin Fayḍ Kāshānī (d. 1091/1680) and Mullā Muḥammad Bāqir Majlisī (d. 1111/1699). These works, nevertheless, were not considered typical legal works to meet the growing demands of time-honored questions. By the late twelfth/

eighteenth century the *Akhbārī* trend lost much of its appeal among the Shiʿi school of the shrine cities of *al-ʿAtabāt*, and gave way to the application of *uṣūlī* principles.

The catalyst for the downward trend of *Akhbārism* was the chief jurist of the time Shaykh Yūsuf al-Baḥrānī (d. 1186/1772) who set out to write a comprehensive book on Shiʿi fiqh. To write a full-fledged work of such kind, he had to invoke ijtihad and some *uṣūlī* principles such as *istiṣḥāb* although he theoretically rejected the role of ʿaql (intellect) and *ijmāʿ* (consensus) in deriving legal rulings.[1] In fact, he posed the question: how is one to derive law when the possibility of acquiring knowledge no longer existed with the onset of the Imam's occultation? He suggested that the community had no choice but to seek recourse to ijtihad to derive new legal norms.[2] The modern scholar W. Madelung opines that al-Baḥrānī later espoused an intermediate position between *Akhbārism* and *Uṣūlism*.[3] The contemporary author Ayatollah Jannaati has even suggested that al-Baḥrānī had later changed his position and adopted the *uṣūl* methodology and the practice of ijtihad but had kept this hidden from the public.[4]

Al-Baḥrānī exhibited respect and reverence for his *uṣūlī* opponents to the extent that he allowed his chief adversary Muḥammad Bāqir Bihbahānī (d. 1205/1791) to flourish in seminaries by encouraging his students to attend his lectures, and still more, by assigning him the task of leading his funeral prayer upon his death.[5] The efforts made by al-Baḥrānī to reduce the tension between the two factions were misinterpreted by later *Uṣūlīs* as a sign of weakness and, as such, they credited Bihbahānī with victory over the *Akhbārīs*. Despite al-Baḥrānī's aspiration for respect and civility, the *Uṣūlī–Akhbārī* conflict continued and eventually turned into personal refutations and even bloody clashes between the supporters of two sides during the nineteenth century. Bihbahānī succeeded in re-establishing *uṣūl* methodology in the shrine cities, however he digressed to writing polemical treatises rather than *uṣūl* works.[6] Yet, his direct and indirect students fulfilled the function to which we now turn.

Al-Qummī

Al-Mīrzā Abū al-Qāsim al-Qummī (d. 1231/1815), one of the most renowned students of Bihbahānī, vehemently espoused the method and principles of *uṣūl al-fiqh* and wrote a detailed textbook on this subject. It is worthy to note that following the model set by Shaykh Ḥasan al-'Āmilī in his *Ma'ālam al-Uṣūl*,[7] al-Qummī focused on semantics and literal interpretation, and presented strong arguments which had often been equipped with terms borrowed from formal logic. However, because of the remnant effects of *Akhbārī* influence, the parts on "discursive reasoning" (*al-mabāḥith al-'aqliyyah*) could not yet be developed in their own right in Shi'i *uṣūlī* writings of the time.

In the introduction of his work, al-Qummī deals with the definition of *uṣūl al-fiqh* as well as the connotation of a word, its varieties and true meanings: real or metaphor, homonym (*mushtarak*) and derived (*mushtaqq*). He does not hesitate to employ terms borrowed from grammar and logic (such as definition, differentia and genus) to illustrate his arguments.[8] He divides his work into six chapters of which five are allocated to either semantics or literal interpretation of legal norms, and the last chapter covers sources of the law and who should be in charge of implementing it.

The first chapter bears the title of "Commands and Prohibitions" wherein al-Qummī elaborates on both semantics and literal interpretation of legal norms, their applicability and prerequisites. It is remarkable that semantical topics such as *tabādur* (lit. to appear at first glance), *taqdīm* (lit. to advance prerequisites) and *iqtiḍā'* (lit. requirement) appear to be of central importance in this part of his work[9] and this also becomes a pattern for succeeding Shi'i authors. The second chapter also concentrates on literal interpretation under the rubric of "perspicuous and intricate" and "apparent and divergent meanings." In the first section of this chapter, he seems concerned with the literal interpretation only; whereas in the second, he is more focused on semantics.[10] He focuses on "general and its particularization" in the third chapter where he presents an extensive elaboration on the method of finding the true legal norms from amongst conflicting and sometimes contradicting or abrogating rulings derived from the revealed texts. With a lesser scope, he then deals with "the clear and metaphorical" in Chapter 4, and "absolute and qualified" in Chapter 5.[11]

After dealing with literal analysis and semantics in five chapters, al-Qummī turns to legal indicants or sources of the law (*al-adillah al-sharʿiyyah*) beginning with *ijmāʿ*. He does not explain why he commenced his account on the *adillah* with the controversial authority of *ijmāʿ*, which implies that he dismissed the hierarchy of the sources of the law. He, like most of the Shiʿi authors, invalidates *ijmāʿ* in the absence of the Twelfth Imam. Nevertheless, he upholds the validity of *shuhrah* (lit. fame) and the practice of conscious following of a prevalent view (*mutābaʿat al-qawl al-mashhūr*). He introduces the new concept of *mutābaʿah* as a supplement to *ijmāʿ* and in this context it means compliance of a number of the ʿulamāʾ on a fatwa by a *mujtahid* in specific cases which would overrule opinions of others. Al-Qummī considers *mutābaʿah* as a concomitant component of *ijmāʿ* and bases its validity on the Qurʾanic verse: "As for the one who opposes the messenger, after the guidance has become clear to him, and follows other than the believers' way, we will direct him in the direction he has chosen, and commit him to Hell; what a miserable destiny" (4:115). He concludes that "believers' way" (*sabīl al-muʾminīn*) by itself constitutes a positive practice, and conveys the idea of *mutābaʿah* from which no learned jurist should deviate.[12] His emphasis on *shuhrah* and "believers' way" may explain why he prioritized the topic of *ijmāʿ* over the Qurʾan and the Sunnah. However, discussion on the Qurʾan and the Sunnah do appear in the same chapter that was initially dedicated to *ijmāʿ*.

Al-Qummī's discussion of the Qurʾan has a polemical character and focuses on refuting *Akhbārī* views and their way of approaching the Scripture. He opens his debate with the legal value and the practices adopted with reference to the perspicuous (*muḥkamāt*) verses of the Qurʾan as a point of departure to repudiate the *Akhbārī* claim that the Qurʾan is generally metaphorical or symbolic (*mutashābih*). This is to deflect the *Akhbārī* claim that only the Imams can be deemed to be true interpreters of the Book. This argument eventually ends up pervading the entire discussion on the Book,[13] and does not allow him to remind his readers that semantics and literal elaborations would solve much of the implications of the Qur'anic verses which are not considered appropriate for direct application. His discussion of the Sunnah begins with a definition of *khabar* (statements), and it extends to varieties and qualifications of tradition-reports. He, indeed, uses "tradition" in the sense of "utterances of an infallible person" (*qawl al-maʿṣūm*) by which is meant the traditions on the authority of the Prophet and the Imams either combined or separate.[14]

The importance of the idea of *mutābaʿah* in his thought is reflected in one of his juridical letters recorded in a contemporaneous work. In this letter, he speaks about the necessity of choosing the most distinguished and supreme *mujtahid* as a *marjaʿ* (a source of emulation by others). In addressing a juridical question raised by one of his colleagues, he wrote:

>...In your case, I think you could be excused if you had no idea of having possible access to a superior *mujtahid*. Your shortcoming is not in performance of prayer, rather it is in your choice of *marjaʿ*. If you generalize this case and include the public interest, you would see that the problem rests in finding a true and superior *mujtahid*.[15]

Concerning the position of *marjaʿ* in the Shiʿi community, the language used in the above letter has no precedent in the history of Shiʿism. The content of this letter shows that the rise of the clerical authority of *Uṣūlī* *ʿulamā'* had come of age and burgeoned enough to engender the centralized position of *marjaʿ al-taqlīd* for the Shiʿi community of this period. In fact, al-Qummī's aspiration as echoed in the above letter was realized in the person of one of his students – namely Muḥammad Ḥasan Najafī-Isfahānī (d. 1266/1849), who was acclaimed as the sole *marjaʿ* three decades later.

Anṣārī

A new strand of rational maxims developed in the Shiʿi seminaries in the second half of the thirteenth/nineteenth century when the *uṣūlī* trend of jurisprudence became recognized as conventional and mainstream in the Shiʿi community. In constructing and rehabilitating the legal methodology, emphasis on semantics and literal interpretation remained the same, but had been supplemented with a new series of rational argumentations whose essence laid in meticulous interplay between conflicting rules of the law. The towering figure in this regard was Shaykh Murtaḍā Anṣārī (d. 1281/ 1864) who developed this trend of *Usūlism* in the shrine seminary of Najaf. He presented *uṣūl al-fiqh* in two parts: 1) the literal subject matters (*al-mabāḥith al-lafẓiyyah*), and 2) the rational subject matters (*al-mabāḥith al-ʿaqliyyah*). The first discourse was recorded by one of his students in a book named *Maṭāriḥ al-Anẓār*.[16] The second discourse was contained in several treatises signed and titled by the author as *Farā'id al-Uṣūl*. Central to the present discussion is the latter work where he deals exclusively with the methods of application of rational principles to juridical cases.

Anṣārī's point of departure in this work is epistemological, and begins with the question of how legal knowledge should be attained. He proposes that the position, which a *mukallaf* (capacitated person) usually takes in the understanding of the legal norms is: 1) one of certainty (*qaṭ*^{c}), 2) a valid conjecture (*ẓann*) or 3) of doubt (*shakk*).[17] The first category applies essentially to certain knowledge of things which are subjects of the legal norms. It is possible that certainty could be acquired within the context of things (i.e. rational premises). As such, knowledge then can be just mediums (*awsāṭ*) between man and the legal norm (*ḥukm*).[18] The validity of this category, therefore, derives from itself rather than the law. Then, Anṣārī raises the question of whether certainty acquired from the rational premises is valid or not? He concludes in the affirmative and adds that the tradition reports should not be taken as opposing "rational certainty." Here, he challenges the *Akhbārī's* position of refuting logical premises and defends the use of syllogism in legal methodology, which he applies in this part of his work.[19] He includes "general knowledge" (*al-ʿilm al-ijmālī*) in the category of relative certainty although its validity appears to be speculative.

The second category, the valid conjecture, according to him, is an avenue to reach the reality of things, and it includes contextual signs (*al-amārāt al-maʿmūlah*) which attach validity to the outward meanings of the revealed texts. These signs either have rational bases or entail a rational argument. Even in cases when they are not considered valid, he tries to obtain another perspective from them.[20] The third category of understanding the proper legal norms is based on doubt. The practical way to find out the appropriate legal passage in case of doubt rests on taking one of the following two positions:

1) Without taking the past situation (*sābiqah*) into consideration, one of the three rational principles should be employed as practical avenues for solving problems: a) *Iḥtiyāṭ* (to be prudent in case of doubt resulting from ignorance of the law or its subject matter): The principle of prudence requires that the one in doubt either attempts to discover the true application of the law or repeats his legal action. Anṣārī tends to restricts its application to relevant cases only.[21] b) *Barā'ah* (lit. the state of being discharged from liability): If doubt in the subject matter constitutes a valid case for the principle of *barā'ah*'s application, three situations should be taken into consideration: First, there is a punishment for not searching to find the law even though the action may be considered legally correct. Second, the action can be considered legally correct (*aṣl al-ṣiḥḥah*) in contracts only as a declaratory law (*al-ḥukm al-waḍʿī*). Third, the principle of *barā'ah* cannot be applied in rituals where the intention of pious act (*qurbā*) is a constituent element.[22] c) *Takhyīr* (juristic choice): He includes this among the practical principles but does not elaborate on it in this part. In the epilogue of his work, he sets the condition that the choice should be made after exhausting all avenues of juridical investigation, since the intellect alone is *ḥākim* (the ruler) in the case.[23]

2) Taking the past situation into consideration, and that is *istiṣḥāb* – the principle of presumption of continuity or status quo when there is no proof to indicate any change from the past situation. Anṣārī introduces *istiṣḥāb* as a rational practical principle whose authority resembles that of induction and deduction in logic. The *sharʿī* legitimacy of *istiṣḥāb* is analogous to several principles understood from the Qur'an and the Sunnah, such as "doubt never invalidates certainty" (*lā tanquḍ al-yaqīn bi al-shakk*).[24] Here, he deals in detail with varieties of *istiṣḥāb*: positive or negative and subject or normative ones. He considers it to be the key principle which takes priority over other practical principles. Through *istiṣḥāb*, one either proposes a new solution or supports the existing norms. In the epilogue, he deals with the issue of conflict of laws under the heading of "equivalence and preponderence" (*al-taʿādul wa al-tarājīḥ*). Among other things, he tries to shed more light on problems of intervention (*wurūd*), governance (*ḥukūmah*) and particularization (*takhṣīṣ*).[25]

Anṣārī's frequent use of rational principles gives the impression that he did not consider the existing sources of the law adequate to respond to newly arising questions. The negative presumption of continuity (*istiṣḥāb al-ʿadam*), *per se*, implies the lack of any applicable rule and a return to existing practices which are mainly based on customs. The frequent application of this kind of *istiṣḥāb* seems to aim at equipping the Shariʿah with customary laws rather than at sticking to remotely applicable *aḥkām* (legal norms). However, his theoretical elaboration on the rational avenues for arriving at a plausible solution impressed the Shiʿi milieu of his time, and the practical principles found a distinct place in the articulation of subsequent Shiʿi law and legal methodology. Most of the succeeding Shiʿi authors added several chapters to their works in order to include the aforesaid rational principles into their legal methodology.[26] It seems, nevertheless, that they had problems with how and to what extent they should incorporate these principles into their legal methodology since Anṣārī had not determined their place in the overall composition of *uṣūl al-fiqh*.

Khurasani

One of the most celebrated works in the field of legal methodology is *Kifāyat al-Uṣūl* by a student of Anṣārī named Mullā Muhammad Kazim Khurasani (d. 1329/1911) whose unyielding fatwas in support of Constitutionalism were crucial for the triumph of the Iranian Constitutional Movement of 1906–1911. His work is heavily imbued with semantics of the legal texts to the extent that the authority of sources of the law and rational reasoning appear only in the context of discussion on literal interpretations. In his introduction he explicitly states that the objective of *uṣūl* is to draw generalization out of various subject matters, not merely to elaborate on the four sources of the law. He explains that if one focuses on the sources, the argument would ultimately turn into how to establish the textual authority and applicability of the four legal indicants (*al-adillah al-arbaʿah*). However, the scope of literal interpretation is much wider than remaining confined to the *adillah* or the fixed texts.[27]

Khurasani opens his discourse with a new heading: *"waḍʿ al-alfāẓ"* (lit. to lay down words) under which he states that words are laid down by either designation or convention (*al-taʿyīnī aw al-taʿayyunī*). With this point of departure, he presents a linguistic discussion on varieties, meanings and differences between the statement and composition.[28] He employs his knowledge of theology for the sake of a weighty analysis on linguistics as he refers to Avicenna and Khwājah Naṣīr al-Ṭūsī's conceptions of *al-dalālah al-taṣdīqiyyah* (lit. confirmative denotation) to highlight the importance of human will (*irādah*) in understanding the implications of a word which can go beyond its literal meanings.[29] As such, Khurasani presents an amply elaborated account on various ways of reading the real, intended, implied, and sometimes intricate meanings of the legal texts. This part of his work attracted later authors, some of whom considered this kind of approach as the beginning of Shiʿi hermeneutics, if its logical and theological backgrounds were well understood.[30]

Legal Command (*amr*) is the title of the first chapter where Khurasani elaborates on its varieties and methods of understanding and application.[31] *Muqaddimat al-wājib* is the necessary prerequisites of legal commands which are as obligatory to carry out as the commands themselves. The same rule applies to the contrary (*ḍidd*) cases in his categorization,[32] which are part of "prohibition" on which he focuses in the next section. The problem of applicability of conflicting laws to a case is discussed under the heading of *ijtimāʿ al-amr wa al-nahy*. For instance, the place of prayer by law should not be usurped (*maghṣūb*). As such, there is tension between the application of the command to perform the prayer on time and the prohibition of appropriating other's property without the owner's consent.[33] The next question is how and when the prohibition entails the nullification of an act. In this chapter, he discusses a number of legal principles which fit in the category of legal maxims' (*qawāʿid al-fiqh*) rather than *uṣūl al-fiqh*.[34]

In pursuit of his literal approach, Khurasani then puts forward the topic of "implied meanings" (*mafāhīm*) in the third chapter. This topic, which was propounded into legal methodology by the early Ḥanafī authors, deals with the scope of meanings of the legal norms (*aḥkām*). The expressed (*manṭūq*) meaning, of course, enjoys the authority of proof (*dalīl*). The implied meaning, too, generally bears the same authority. Only divergent meanings (*al-mafhūm al-mukhālif*) are matters of argumentation, and he elaborates on the meaning of some of them.[35] "General and particularization," "abstract and qualified" and "symbolic and lucid" are topics of the next two chapters which do not vary from the previous forms of presentations, save for his meticulous elaboration. With the five above-mentioned chapters, he completes his account on the textual evidences and their legal authority. Thereafter, he turns to contextual evidences.

"The Valid Contextual Evidences" (*al-amārāt al-muʿtabarah*) can be derived from either the revealed or rational sources. In both cases, they usually enjoy the authority of legal proof pending the way they are characterized. In this context, he distinguishes the legality of "certain knowledge" (*qaṭʿ*), "explicit meanings of words" (*ẓawāhir al-alfāẓ*), "contextual sign" (*qarīnah*), consensus (*ijmāʿ*), fame (*shuhrah*), solitary tradition-reports (*āḥād*), varieties of valid conjecture (*ẓann*) and preference (*tarjīḥ*).[36] As shown above, some of the evidences are reduced to the category of *ẓann* rather than *ʿilm*, yet they bear the same legal validity because of contextual factors. The validity of contextual evidences have their root in the Qur'an and the Sunnah and in the early presentations of *uṣūl al-fiqh*. However, with his linguistic approach, he re-conceptualizes ways of evaluating the contextual evidences.

After dealing with *dalīl* and *amārah*, Khurasani turns to *aṣl* (the principle) which should be considered legally valid in the absence of any other evidence. The authority of the *aṣl*, which was later re-titled as the practical principle (*al-aṣl al-ʿamalī*), derives from discursive reasoning, which is in line with the spirit of the Shariʿah rules. Following the pattern set by Anṣārī, Khurasani discusses the four general and practical principles (*al-uṣūl al-ʿamaliyyah*) in the seventh chapter. His treatment of the issues is similar to his master except when he elaborates on *takhyīr* (juristic choice) and a number of juristic maxims such as 'lā ḍarar wa lā ḍirār' (no harm shall be inflicted or reciprocated).[37]

The last chapter explores cases of conflict of laws under the title of *taʿāruḍ al-adillah wa al-amārāt*. Khurasani acknowledges the hierarchy of the evidences for he generally sees no possibility that a contextual evidence (*amārah*) may conflict with a text-based evidence, or for a juridical maxim (*aṣl*) to be applicable while a valid proof or contextual evidence is presentable. Indeed, the *aṣl* inevitably prevails where two equally valid evidences negate each other. Discussing these issues, he also points to the "secondary designation" (*al-ʿunwān al-thānawiyyah*) of an action that may exceptionally overrule or postpone the first and direct application of the law in cases of difficulty, constrain, exigency, or compulsion.[38] This argument provided an *uṣūlī* pretext for some Shiʿi governments to excuse themselves from carrying out the law whenever it was expedient to do so. As an epilogue, he brings to the fore the question of ijtihad and *taqlīd*. These two topics became so pronounced in the nineteenth and twentieth centuries that no Shiʿi jurisprudential work could ignore them. In this part, he endorses the necessity of following the opinion of the most learned *mujtahid*.[39]

In his two last chapters, Khurasani appears to be much engaged in the contents of the texts and the sound judgment of the jurisprudent in charge, in spite of the fact that his overall format rests on the literal form of textual expressions. He actually deals with common sense and the human rational faculty for recognizing and interpreting the proper legal norm. Rubrics such as contextual evidences, signs, or priorities refer to juridical pretexts which allow both customary law and human preference to decide the applicability of the proper legal norm. Nevertheless, the methodological authority of his work is essentially centered on the "literal demonstration of the texts."

Al-Muzaffar
Shaykh Muhammad Rida al-Muzaffar (d. 1383/1964), aware of the twentieth century educational changes, attempted to simplify both the language and contents of Islamic legal methodology so as to make it available to a wider range of readers and students. We will focus on his achievements after a survey on the structure of his presentation of *uṣūl al-fiqh*.

Al-Muzaffar's Presentation of Legal Methodology
Al-Muzaffar divides his legal methodology into four sections preceded by a prelude and an introduction, and followed by an epilogue.

Prelude: Definition, subject matters and setting the topics of *uṣūl*.
Introduction: Linguistic bases of legal texts. How words are laid down to convey meanings; real or metaphor; intention and expression.

A. Semantics (*mabāḥith al-alfāẓ*)
   1. The derived words (*al-mushtaqqāt*).
   2. The commands. He presents varieties of obligatory (*wājib*) norms.

3. The prohibitions and their varieties.
4. Implied meanings (*al-mafāhīm*) which are divided into six kinds.
5. The general and the particular (*al-ʿāmm wa al-khāṣṣ*).
6. The absolute and qualified meanings (*al-muṭlaq wa al-muqayyad*).
7. The ambiguous and lucid terms (*al-mujmal wa al-mubayyan*).

B. Rational Entailments (*al-mulāzimāt al-ʿaqliyyah*)
This is a new title under which al-Muzaffar juxtaposes two sets of never previously related topics:
1. Independent analytic reasoning (*al-mustaqillāt al-ʿaqliyyah*): human intellectual perception of good and evil.
2. Dependent analytic reasoning (*ghayr al-mustaqillāt al-ʿaqliyyah*): They include rules of necessity (*idṭirārī*), expediency (*maṣlaḥah*), and the principle that entails an obligation from obligatory premises.

C. The Proofs (*ḥujaj*)
The authority to validate legal norms is derived from:
1. The Holy Book: The problem of abrogation is discussed here.
2. The Traditions of the Prophet and infallible Imams.
3. Consensus: The opinion of the majority indicative of the *ḥujjah*.
4. The Rational Proof (*al-dalīl al-ʿaqlī*).
5. The Validity of the Manifest Meanings (*ḥujjiyyat al-zawāhir*).
6. Fame (*shuhrah*): The Widespread Circulation of Legal Maxims.
7. The Practice of People (*al-sīrah*) which resembles *ʿurf* (custom).
8. *Qiyās*: He defines it as expansion of *ratio legis* to new cases.
9. Equivalence and Preponderance (*al-taʿādul wa al-tarājīḥ*).

D. The Practical Principles
   1. The principle of presumption of continuity of the past (*aṣl al-istiṣḥāb*).
   2. *Barā'ah*: the state of being discharged from liability.
   3. *Iḥtiyāṭ*: to be prudent in case of ignorance of the law or other matters.
   4. *Takhyīr* or juristic choice, after exhausting all legal proofs and signs.[40]

As shown above, al-Muzaffar constructed a new format for *uṣūl al-fiqh* in which various topics of the discipline are carefully characterized and arranged according to the category of their functions.[41] The first quarter belongs to semantics as much as an understanding of the legal language requires. He follows the traditional pattern, particularly in this part of his work. Nevertheless, he does not extend semantics to be inclusive of the major part of his methodology. The second quarter bears the novel title of "rational entailments" where he puts together two sets of never previously related topics. That is "intellectual reasoning" divided into "dependent" and "independent" juxtaposing the validity of the human intellectual faculty with a number of semi-revealed but rationally understood rules. The latter category includes topics such as necessity (*ḍarūrah*), consideration of public interest (*maṣlaḥah*) and *muqaddimat al-wājib* (the principle that entails an obligation from obligatory premises). The former category (*al-mustaqillāt al-ʿaqliyyah* – lit. independent reasoning) appears with a detailed definition including its role in deduction of appropriate laws from the revealed sources. Al-Muzaffar was the scholar who deeply investigated the scope of "independent reasoning" in Shiʿi jurisprudence, and eventually reduced the Shiʿi conception of independent ʿaql to the human intellectual perception of good and evil.[42]

Ḥujjah or legal authority is the next topic to which al-Muzaffar turns after dealing with ʿaql. He considers this quarter of *uṣūl* as the core and kernel of legal methodology that comprises the major premises of all literal minors discussed in the previous quarters. He even draws a syllogism to demonstrate the importance of the legal authority.[43] Central to his discussion is, of course, the authority of *adillah* particularly the revealed indicants i.e. the Qur'an and the Sunnah. First, however, he focuses on meanings of the legal authority, contextual evidence (*amārah*) and valid conjecture (*zann*). Then he discusses the authority of the Qur'an, the Sunnah and *ijmā'* in a conventional manner. The rational indicant (*al-dalīl al-'aqlī*) as the fourth source of Shi'i law is another focus of this quarter. He attempts to find out what is really meant by this category of legal source and presents a brief historical survey on how some Shi'i authors have confused *'aql* as a source of law with contextual evidences such as *mafāhīm* (literal implications) or rational principles such as *istiṣḥāb* (presumption of continuity). He eventually redefines *'aql* and reduces it to the human intellectual perception of good and evil.[44] In his effort to provide meaningful context for many controversial notions, he does not hesitate to show how some expressions and titles did deceive (*khidā' al-'anāwīn*) both their authors and readers.[45]

As a supplement to the above four sources of authority, al-Muzaffar explores five rational practices which amount to legal authority (*ḥujjah*), though they are not by themselves legal indicants (*adillah*). The manifestation of meanings (*zuhūr*) is a semantic device that he places among supplementary elements of the *ḥujjiyyah* by basing it on juridical syllogism. Some Shi'i authors, as indicated above, confused the function of *zuhūr* with the role of *'aql* as the fourth source of law. Next is the widespread circulation (*shuhrah*) of either tradition-reports or fatwas which amounts to legal authority in respective cases. In a similar manner, he invests authority in the practices of rational people (*sīrat al-'uqalā'*) and some kinds of *qiyās*. He finally includes topics of conflict of laws – under the heading of the equivalence and preponderance (*al-ta'ādul wa al-tarājīḥ*) – among intellectual inferences which serve legal authority for a *ḥukm*.[46] As such, he attempts to expand the scope of *ḥujjiyyah* to cover most components of legal authority.

By exhausting all avenues of revealed and rational reasoning which lead to legal authority, there still remain some juridical problems to be solved by practical principles, which cannot be accepted as *ḥujjah* or *dalīl* but only as contextual evidence (*amārah*). The practical principles constitute the fourth quarter of al-Muzaffar's legal methodology. He propounds the four aforesaid practical principles of Anṣārī, and cautions readers that they are not limited to the four. There may arise new principles pending the context of their application. However, the attention should be focused on the applicability (*majrā*) and suitability of all practical principles.[47]

Overall al-Muzaffar seems to be attempting to reduce the semantics and literal parts of legal methodology in favor of a profound focus on the legal authority (*ḥujjiyyah*) as the central topic of *uṣūl al-fiqh*. Before turning to the legal authority however, he proposes a series of rational entailments (*mulāzimāt*) which also bear on legal authority, but they do not depend on a revealed indicant as directly as the items of the *ḥujjiyyah* do. Thereafter, he deals with another set of rational principles, which in essence are practical solutions ultimately invested with legal authority. If we consider his introductory quarter on semantics as a literal discourse on ways of discerning the legal authority of the texts, we can then see how he defines the whole of *uṣūl al-fiqh* in terms of a search for the legal authority through juristic ijtihad.

Concurrent with al-Muzaffar and after him, a number of Shiʿi authors presented legal methodology in its traditional form with numerous elaborations or modifications. None of them seem to have surpassed the brevity and thoroughness of al-Muzaffar's work. It should, however, be mentioned that the *uṣūl* writings of the twentieth century thinker and jurist Sayyid Muhammad Baqir al-Sadr (d. 1980) offers another delicate arrangement within the juristic tradition. His work, nevertheless, is divided into three rounds of repetitive presentations in order to suit the format of his class and students and, as such, can hardly qualify as a distinctive format.[48]

In the present era, a number of modern authors reproduced *uṣūl al-fiqh* with new proposals, and some of them suggested a new approach to the Shariʿah in reference to legal methodology to which we will focus in the next chapter.

Al-Sayyid Muhammad Baqir al-Sadr

As an original thinker of Islamic law, al-Sayyid Muhammad Baqir al-Sadr (d. 1400/1980) re-oriented Shiʿi legal methodology with lucidity of language and new logical arguments. He also laid the groundwork for modern Islamic banking and the idea of juridical supervision of governmental institutions. Born in al-Kazimayn (Iraq) in 1935, he studied in Najaf under two well-known ayatollahs of the time: al-Khu'i and al-Hakim. Aware of the current socio-economic ideas and trends, al-Sadr proposed such alternatives as Islamic insurance and banking systems as well as infusing juristic checks and balances into Muslim governance, which have become partly grounded in Iran and Iraq. Unfortunately, al-Sadr got deeply involved in politics by synthesizing the ideology of the Daʿwah Party (Ḥizb al-Daʿwah al-Islāmiyyah) and refuting Iraq's ruling Baʿth party, which eventually cost him his life in April 1980.

He wrote three books on the discipline of *uṣūl al-fiqh*, the last of which, namely, *Durūs fī ʿIlm al-Uṣūl* (or *al-Ḥalaqāt*), has become the focal point of current Shiʿi scholarship. It consists of three course teachings (*al-ḥalaqāt al-thalāthah*) in which he progressively enhances his elaboration on *uṣūl al-fiqh*. Below, we will present the gist of his account on Islamic legal methodology.

In the introduction, he offers a new definition of *uṣūl al-fiqh*: "knowledge of the shared elements in the procedure of derivation from the divine law"[49] (*al-ʿilm bi al-ʿanāṣir al-mushtarakah fī ʿamaliyyah istinbāṭ al-ḥukm al-sharʿī*).[50] By "shared elements," he means the general principles that one holds in order to make rulings in different areas of the law, as opposed to special principles (*al-ʿanāṣir al-khāṣṣah*) that are restricted to their specific domain. For example, "It is forbidden for a fasting individual to immerse his head in water" represents a reported tradition-report of the Lawgiver. This ruling addresses the specific elements of "forbid, fasting, and water immersing," all of which are subjects of *fiqhī* discussion; however, its validity and the scope of its applicability are *uṣūlī* problems that can be solved by applying the general principle of *ḥujiyyat al-ẓuhūr al-ʿurfī* (the authority of demonstrating tradition-words in their common usage). This principle is frequently used in all areas of jurisprudence because it determines the applicability of the revealed law throughout the entire legal practice, whereas the forbidden action belongs to a specific category of the law.[51] For this reason, al-Sadr preferred to describe *uṣūl al-fiqh* as "knowledge [of application] of the shared elements." He also compared it with formal logic, characterizing the former as a "juridical way of analytical thinking" and the latter as analytical thinking, and concluded that the *uṣūl* are the logic of fiqh.[52]

After illustrating their interaction, he focuses on the legitimacy of ijtihad or of using the *uṣūlī* methodology in the Shariʿah to regulate the variety of *sharʿī* rulings. He points out that Shiʿi jurists refuted ijtihad up to the seventh/thirteenth century, when al-Muḥaqqiq al-Ḥillī (d. 676/1277) separated it from *qiyās* (analogy) and legitimized the former and parts of the latter. This change altered the term's meaning, he argues, because before al-Ḥilli's time the Shiʿi *ʿulamāʾ* understood it as an application of personal opinion (*raʾy*). The new view of ijtihad as an effort to derive a legal norm (*ḥukm*) from the sources (the Qurʾan and Sunnah) paved the way for them to see it as a "procedure" to determine the law and not a source of the law itself.[53] The possibility of considering ijtihad as such a source points to the Sunni authors who regarded *qiyās* as an additional source of Islamic law. In the latter part of his introduction, al-Sadr tries to briefly clarify the definition of *ḥukm* as the divine-law ruling concerning the Muslims, as opposed to the legal agents' actions (*afʿāl*), unlike the traditional *ʿulamāʾ* who applied *ḥukm* to actions.

Outline of al-Sadr's Presentation of *Uṣūl al-Fiqh*

After al-Sadr's innovative definition of Islamic legal methodology, he divides all *uṣūl al-fiqh* topics into two major parts: legal indicants (*adillah*) and procedural principles (*al-uṣūl al-ʿamaliyyah*), followed by a sum of points on the conflict of legal indicants (*taʿāruḍ al-adillah*).

1. Legal Indicants: Regardless of their being definitive (*qaṭʿī*) or not, all legal indicants can, according to him, be categorized in two parts of *sharʿī* (ordained by the Lawgiver) or *ʿaqlī* (rationally understood).

    a. *Sharʿī* indicants are essentially based on the Qur'an and Sunnah, which include the tradition-reports from the infallible Imams, and divided into verbal and non-verbal categories:

        i. Under the rubric of verbal indicants, al-Sadr covers most problems dealing with the semantics of Arabic language with a somewhat logical approach.[54]

        ii. Non-verbal indicants include the implications of action, silence, and life conduct (*sīrah*) of the Prophet and the infallible Imams.[55]

    b. Rational indicants cover a number of logical and legal principles, which he discusses in a rather new context, such as interrelations among different rulings and the contradiction between obligation and prohibition.[56] In his second course teaching (*al-ḥalaqah al-thāniyah*) he identifies the following principles, among others, as rational indicants:

        i. The impossibility of imposing an obligation beyond a human being's capacity (*taklīf ma lā yuṭāq*).

        ii. The possibility of conditional obligation (*imkān taklīf al-mashrūṭ*).

        iii. The implication of rational necessities (*iḍṭirār*).

        iv. The impossibility of agreement between two opposites (*ijtimāʿ al-'amr wa al-nahy*).

        v. The concomitance between the *sharʿ* and reason.

    Concerning the application of the above indicants, he adds that all cases subject to the rational indicants must be definitive, not speculative (*ẓannī*).[57] It is noteworthy that *ijmāʿ* and *ʿaql* are, so far, missing from his account of *sharʿī* indicants (*adillah*).

2. Procedural Principles (*al-uṣūl al-ʿamalī*) are applied in the absence of a specific ruling. Al-Sadr presents the following four principles

with a different rubric and novel explanations:
a. The primacy of caution (*aṣālat al-iḥtiyāṭ*).
b. The primacy of exemption (*aṣalat al-barā'ah*).
c. The principle of the adequacy of summarized knowledge (*al-ʿilm al-ijmālī*).
d. The presumption of continuity (*istiṣḥāb*).

3. Conflict of Legal Indicants (*taʿāruḍ al-adillah*) includes:
   a. Contradiction between textual indicants. This contradiction, which is verbal (not in content), should not be confused with cases of general (*ʿāmm*) and specific (*khāṣṣ*) ones.
   b. Contradiction between procedural principles (*bayn al-uṣūl*), such as between the above-mentioned principles of *istiṣḥāb* and *barā'ah*, wherein *istiṣḥāb* governs.
   c. Contradiction between textual indicant and procedural principle, wherein the former prevails unless it is downgraded as *amārah* (contextual evidence) due to doubt about its authenticity.[58]

In his second course teaching (*al-ḥalqah al-thāniyah*), al-Sadr puts forth four legal maxims to solve the problems of conflicting laws:
a. Covential clash (*al-jamʿ ʿal-ʿurfī*) of two conflictingrulings.
b. Collapse of both contradictory rulings (*tasāquṭ al-mutaʿāriḍīn*).
c. Preference (*tarjīḥ*) of specific (Shiʿi) traditions.
d. Choice (*al-takhyīr*) of the specific traditions.[59]

The above outline shows that al-Sadr essentially adopted the late Shiʿi method of categorizing the main topics of *uṣūl al-fiqh* into the semantics of legal indicants (*adillah*) and the procedural principles (*al-uṣūl al-ʿamaliyyah*), followed by issues of conflicting laws. He does not give a special title to independent intellectual reasoning (*al-mustaqillāt al-ʿaqliyyah*), which al-Muzaffar reduced to the human perception of good and evil (see above). However, in the course of elaborating the principle of adequacy of summary knowledge (*al-ʿilm al-ijmālī*), al-Sadr comes close to this concept, thereby suggesting that Shiʿi jurisprudence of the nineteenth and twentieth centuries was leaning toward the semantics of Arabic language more than theology. This shift can well be seen by looking at how he reorients the theory of *ḥujiyyat al-ẓuhūr al-ʿurfī* (the authority of demonstration of tradition-words) in their common usage. In his third course presentation, he claims that the apparent meaning of tradition-words is the legal proof for understanding. He then buttresses this with the authority of the Qur'an and the Sunnah, as well as the normative conduct of rational people (*sīrat al-ʿuqalā'*) to qualify his claim as regards the authority of *ẓuhūr*.[60]

Al-Sadr does not give a separate title to *ijmāʿ* (consensus) among *sharʿī* indicants, as most Shiʿi authors did. Rather, he places it in the "case verification" section, in which *tawātur* (successive transmission of hadith) stands first and *shuhrah* (fame) in the third place. It is apparent that he, unlike Mirzā-ye Qummī and Khurasani, does not recognize *ijmāʿ* as a source of law that was attested to in Sunni law and conditionally adopted in Shiʿi law. By making *shuhrah* equivalent to *ijmāʿ*, al-Ṣadr shows his reliance on the procedural function of *ijmāʿ* in the community, regardless of its theoretical value in Islamic jurisprudence as an independent source of law. The way he positions *ijmāʿ* in the "case verification" chapter implies that he was unconvinced by the Shiʿi theory of equating juristic *ijmāʿ* with the very presence of the Twelfth Imam. We know that the *Uṣūlī ʿulamā'* of the nineteenth and twentieth centuries tried hard to preserve the position of *ijmāʿ*; even al-Qummī proposed considering the *ijmāʿ* of the Shiʿi *ʿulamā'* as discovering (*kashif*) the words of the infallible Imams.[61]

Thus we see that al-Sadr, more than either Khurasani or al-Muzaffar, leans toward the practical and procedural aspects of *uṣūl al-fiqh*. In his approach, logic plays a more important role than theology. Compared to the Sunni legal methodologies of that time, we find the Shiʿi ones inclined to incorporate such logical principles as "the procedural principles" (*al-uṣūl al-ʿamaliyyah*), whereas Sunni *uṣūl al-fiqh* was more inclined to adopt the role of such socio-theological concepts as *maṣlaḥah* (consideration of the public interest) and *maqāṣid* (purposes of the law), as we saw in the works of Abu Zahrah and Wahbah al-Zuhayli.[62]

CHAPTER 9

Modern Alternative Approaches to the Theory of Law

AT THE dawn of the twenty-first century, alternative approaches to the sources of Islamic law have become the salient features of the Islamic intellectual discourse. Although overshadowed by political "Islamism," the theoretical changes in contemporary Islamic legal thought appear to be the current intellectual revival's most compelling facet. Islamic law's rise to prominence in recent decades has ignited new approaches to the primary sources together with novel methods of interpretation. At present, several quarters are voicing a desire for an ideal application of Islamic legal norms as their central theme. Some of them even defy the status quo and consider the system to be outdated because it does not address the people's aspiration for social justice. In response, some Muslim scholars and intellectuals have sought to rationalize this pressing aspiration's compatibility with modern proposals and a rehabilitated legal theory that they find suitable for the requirements of modernity.

Islamic approaches to legal theory entered a new phase upon their exposure to modern scholarship, which recognizes a critical role for human rationality in legal corroboration unparalleled in Muslim traditional legal thought. Prior to this, the latter had experienced innovations in its legal methodology via the proposals of the Muʿtazilī "rationalists" such as Abū Ḥamid al-Ghazālī, Abū Isḥāq al-Shāṭibī, and Shāh Walīyullāh. But none of them had ever assigned a central place to human rationality in both perception and analysis, as the modern approaches have.

The modern discourse on legal methodology can be identified with two distinct strains of scholars: 1) those who sought to reform Islamic law and ethics from within the existing system so that it could respond to these new challenges and 2) those who tried to introduce an external approach, namely, to apply the modern disciplines of epistemology or hermeneutics. At the same time, the traditional discourse on law and its methodology still continues, largely oblivious to any new developments. This chapter focuses on new intellectual (non-traditional) approaches only, beginning with those that belong to the first strain.

Muhammad Iqbal

The poet-philosopher Dr. Muhammad Iqbal (d. 1357/1938) approached the legal methodology and some *uṣūlī* concepts with a deep insight into both Western and Islamic legal philosophy. As a Hegelian graduate of Cambridge and Munich universities, and therefore fully aware of the role of "human development" in modern thought, he proposed his theory of "human progress" not only to inspire a new spirit of religiosity among Muslims, but also to warn them of Western modernism's deficiency when it came to meeting one's spiritual needs. He put forward the idea of the ego's (*khudī*) development as a "constant becoming" and "self-realization" based on eternal love (*ʿishq*) and quest (*shawq*).[1] For the ego to develop, it requires its freedom as well as its possible faults, both of which Iqbal found in the Qur'an. He wrote:

Three things are perfectly clear in the Qur'an:
1. Man is the chosen one by God.
2. That man with all his faults, is meant to be the representative of God on Earth.
3. That man voluntary accepted trusteeship at his peril.[2]

Iqbal attached great importance to reconstructing and codifying Islamic law on the grounds that an Islamic renaissance can be realized only after reexamining modern jurisprudence from the Qur'anic viewpoint.[3] In his article "The Principle of Movement in the Structure of Islam," he critically interrogates the place and role of Islamic law's four sources. He maintained that the Qur'an's main purpose was to awaken in each person the higher consciousness of his/her relationship with God. The notions of "human faults" and "free personality" markedly distinguish Iqbal's thought from that of the traditional idealists, who entertained the idea of the perfect man (*al-insān al-kāmil*).

Iqbal's idea of "free personality" stems from his theory of perpetual change and movement in both nature and history. He identifies the principle of movement within the workings of ijtihad[4] and proclaims that the closing of this particular "door" is "a pure fiction suggested partly by [the] crystallization of legal thought in Islam, and partly by intellectual laziness."[5] He suggests that *fiqh* should be opened up for criticism and reevaluation.

Concerning the traditions of the Prophet, Iqbal first upheld Shāh Walīyullāh's view that the Prophet, who sought to convey all-embracing principles, could not possibly reveal different principles for different peoples or leave them to their own devices to work out the rules of conduct. Instead, God's method was to train one particular group and then use it as a nucleus to construct a universal Shariʿah.[6] Iqbal later changed his position and expressed his admiration for Abū Ḥanīfah, whose keen insight into Islam's universal character had caused him to use these traditions only sparingly and to introduce *istiḥsān* (juristic preference) and develop *qiyās*, both of which "necessitate a careful study of actual conditions in legal thinking."[7] Iqbal concluded his argument by stating: "A complete grasp of value [of the traditions] alone can equip us in our endeavor to reinterpret the foundational principles."[8]

Iqbal considers *ijmāʿ*, the third source of Islamic law, to be the most important legal concept and thus is astonished that it had never been institutionalized and thus had remained a mere idea. He regards the political interests of the Umayyad and Abbasid dynasties' absolute rulers as responsible for restricting ijtihad's power to individual *mujtahid*s. For our own time, he proclaims that a legislative assembly is the only possible forum in which *ijmā*ᶜ could be exercised and should inspire Muslims to form a legislative body. To Iqbal, *ijmā*ᶜ means the embodiment of collective ijtihad, whose authority cannot be bound by the community's previous consensus, including that of the Companions, except in matters where they were the sole authority. However, he refutes the idea that *ijmā*ᶜ may repeal the Qur'an.[9]

Iqbal presents a fresh analysis of *qiyās* as the fourth source of Islamic law by relating its development to the possible incursion of Aristotelian logic into the scholarship of second/eighth century Iraq where Abū Ḥanīfah, with his Aryan background, had grown up and was primed to prefer "abstract analogy" over concrete tradition-reports.[10] Iqbal at first refutes this incursion, but finally embraces it due to his belief that the spark of living lay in "the creative freedom and arbitrariness of life," whose presence in man is endorsed in the Qur'an and Sunnah. The pure reason to which the legists of Hijaz rightly reacted can turn Islam into a kind of lifeless mechanism. Because of their criticism, *qiyās* was later adjusted and eventually became a source of life and movement in Islamic law.[11] Iqbal, however, criticized both schools of legal thought: the Ḥijāzīs did not see the full significance of their own position because they had "narrowed their vision to the ᶜprecedents' that had actually happened in the days of the Prophet and his companions" and the modern Ḥanafī legists have "eternalized the interpretation of the founder or his immediate followers much in the same way as the early critics of Abū Ḥanīfah eternalized the decisions given on concrete cases."[12] As seen above, Iqbal has a socio-philosophical insight into the legal schools' various positions on *qiyās*, which may not fully correspond to the juridical understanding of the cases.

One may ask how Iqbal kept "creative freedom" consistent with the "arbitrariness of life" of Arabia? Did he reduce humanity's creative freedom to the arbitrariness or simplicity of life in Arabia?

All of his writings, however, exhibit his full awareness of the various implications of "freedom" and "progress" in both the modern and traditional senses. The above-mentioned example typifies the complexity of his thought in juxtaposing elements of both continuity and change in Islamic tradition. Reacting to those observers who found some contradicting arguments in Iqbal's writings, Fazlur Rahman (d. 1988) writes: "It would not, indeed, be a misuse of Iqbal's own terminology if we say that a creative thinker operates by *ʿishq* rather than by *ʿaql*. It is the task of the serious *interpreter* to enunciate and neatly formulate."[13] The idea of *ishq*, indeed, allows Iqbal to see the whole world as a "holy ground" that cannot be divided into the secular and religious. Rahman, however, concludes that "it may even be said that Iqbal *suggests* rather than *enunciates*."[14]

It is noteworthy that Iqbal deliberately chose the language of poetry (mainly Persian along with Urdu) to communicate his ideas. His choice of Persian was due to its suitability for the complexity of his thought.[15] The latitude of Persian poetry apparently allowed Iqbal to deal with those "secrets of the universe" expressible only in the language of metaphor. A contemporary essayist observes that Iqbal, like some Western thinkers "finds Reality in some respect absurd, of a character that can neither be explained nor explained away."[16] Iqbal, however, seems to believe that the language of poems would reach a wider range of readers with a deeper impression than would prose writing.

As far as Islamic law is concerned, Iqbal's suggestions on implementing *ijmāʿ* and appraisal of *qiyās* seem innovative in both substance and outlook. His proposal of embodying *ijmāʿ* in the form of a state assembly signifies his pragmatism for putting into effect an Islamic theoretical issue. Yet his redefinition of ijtihad as an instrument of Islamic revival appears as his most persuasive contribution to modern Islamic doctrinal movements.

Taha Jabir Alalwani
Among the graduates of Cairo's traditional school of al-Azhar, Taha

Jabir Alalwani (d. 2016) is renowned for his time-honored ideas and command of the Shariʿah and legal methodology (*uṣūl al-fiqh*). His editing and publishing of *al-Maḥṣūl*, the great *uṣūl* work of Imām Fakhr al-Dīn al-Rāzī (d. 1209), catalyzed Alalwani's legal outlook as depicted in several of his later treatises and articles on legal methodology and the history and principles of Islamic jurisprudence. Alalwani taught Islamic jurisprudence in Saudi Arabia for ten years before becoming a founding member, and subsequently the president of, the International Institute of Islamic Thought (IIIT) in 1985. He also wrote at length on the ethics of disagreement in Islam, the appraisal of ijtihad as the practice and knowledge of source methodology, and the Islamization of knowledge. Within the context of legal methodology and particularly ijtihad, as we will see below, he offers new proposals for dealing with the social problems facing today's Muslim societies.

Alalwani asserts the decline of ijtihad as the main cause of the present crisis of Islamic law. In several treatises, he surveys the history of ijtihad and the rise of *taqlīd* (unquestioned following of the opinion and practice of others) and concludes that the present crisis of Islamic jurisprudence started with "closing the door of ijtihad" in the tenth century.[17] He even states the year when this occurred – 310/922, the year of death of al-Ṭabarī, the historian, jurisprudent, and supposedly the last *mujtahid*. This phrase practically came to mean the official banning of public recognition for the existence or appearance of any new *mujtahid*. As a result, Alalwani argues, Islamic law was confined to following the opinions of one of the four early Sunni imams, namely, Abū Ḥanīfah, Mālik, al-Shāfiʿī, and Ibn Ḥanbal.

> It was for this reason that Imām al-Ḥaramayn (d. 478/1086) claimed that there was *ijmāʿ* [consensus] among the scholars of his day and that *taqlīd* of one of the Ṣaḥābah [the Companions of the Prophet] was not acceptable. Rather, people were to adhere to the *fiqh* of the four imams who had probed and examined the Shariʿah, who had classified and given form to questions of *fiqh*, and who had digested the teaching and opinions of the Companions and the Successors.[18]

The circulation of such a supposed consensus among the seventh/
thirteenth-century jurists led Ibn al-Ṣalāḥ al-Shahrazūrī (d. 643/1246)
to claim that "following one of the four imams was obligatory (*wājib*),
as only their teaching had been systematized, clarified and preserved."[19] However, ijtihad as an intellectual exercise could not come
to a complete halt. As a result of the above tacit consensus, it acquired
an oblique path in which several exigent and miscellaneous formulas
were invoked. For example, traditional scholars proposed *al-ḥiyal wa
al-makhārij* (i.e., legal stratagems and loopholes) to provide a way to
resolve day-to-day problems. Alalwani refutes such marginal and
superfluous solutions, which often skirt the issue without setting a
norm to deal with the core problem,[20] and presents his own proposals
in two categories:

1. In his earlier works, he focuses on a critical presentation of the
   history of Islamic jurisprudence and the methodology of ijtihad,
   most of which may be regarded as a traditional examination of
   the concepts. In 1990, he published a treatise on the nature and
   history of Islamic legal methodology's (*uṣūl al-fiqh*) development,
   which he characterized as "the most important method of research
   ever devised by Islamic thought."[21] His evaluation of its nature
   and place centered on the history of *uṣūl al-fiqh*'s development
   and the role it had played in reconciling revelation and reason. He
   emphasized the period of the Companions, who were the second
   source of the prophetic instructions after the Qur'an. His main
   topic, however, is the issues related to ijtihad. To restore this
   practice in the proper sense, he proposes that:

   a. Special attention should be paid to the methods of exercising
      ijtihad by those traditional scholars who developed theories
      for *qiyās* (legal analogy), *istiḥsān* (juristic preference), and
      maṣlaḥah (consideration of public interests).
   b. Given that an absolutely all-inclusive *mujtahid* cannot exist, a
      scholarly collegial council should be established and include
      experts who specialize in all aspects of modern life.

  c. Scholars must take an interest in knowing the Shari'ah's purpose and end-goals and set guidelines to organize the study of problems.[22]

2. More of his "up-to-date" ideas appear in his works on ijtihad and the *maqāṣid.* In an article published in 1991, he proposes that ijtihad's dynamism should be used to structure an Islamic methodology (*al-minhāj*) suitable for the Islamization of contemporary knowledge. To erect such a methodology, he warns, one must do his/her best to become free of the influence of Western scholarship, namely, its categorization and concepts. For this reason, he does not sketch the structure for such a methodology, but only points out the need for definition, perspective, and a proper point of departure.[23] In a panoramic assessment of ijtihad's progression, Alalwani divides methodological (*uṣūl*) studies into specialized and unspecialized studies.

The specialized studies more or less match up with his above-mentioned traditional approach, whereas the unspecialized studies may be subdivided into secular and non-secular. The former, according to Alalwani, comprise those who stretched ijtihad's meaning "to the breaking point to justify their dream of modernization and Westernization."[24] For the latter groups, he offers the following remarks that should be attended to before devising a methodology:

1. One must know the historical background of ijtihad and *taqlīd* to understand the issues related to the division between intellectual [mainly juridical] and political authority in Islam and other matters.
2. The connection between ijtihad and the Shari'ah's higher objectives (*maqāṣid*) is important to illustrating the affinity between ijtihad and *maqāṣid,* or the antipathy between *taqlīd* and the *maqāṣid.*
3. Minute attention is required to realize the multiplicity of opinions under ijtihad and to clarify the truth behind them (*ikhtilāf*).

4. Continuous self-renewal should be preserved through meetings and adjusting to changing circumstances. Ijtihad should not be considered a purely legalistic and legislative function.[25]

The above outline points only to the positive side of Alalwani's appraisal of the Muslims' works. But he also makes sure to equip his arguments with numerous instances of mistakes and shortcomings made by Muslims when calling for ijtihad, especially during recent history. In seeking to make Islamic legal methodology relevant to today's problems, he finds no other avenue better than that of ijtihad in the absolute sense to take the Shariʿah's higher objectives into account to conform to timely requirements. Needless to say, he wanted to see all changes occur within the limits of the Shariʿah parameters and Islamic spirit.

Alalwani's continuous search for how to deal with modern questions from an appropriately Islamic perspective led him to another juridical formula, namely, the "knowledge of priorities" (ʿilm al-awlawiyyāt). In a work published under the rubric of *Maqāṣid al-Sharīʿah*, he both signifies the important role that "knowledge of rational priorities" can play in balancing and stabilizing Islamic jurisprudence and justifies this fact with examples taken from topics of "conflict of laws" (taʿāruḍ) and preferences (tarajīḥ) which originally stem from reason rather than revelation. His interpretation of *awlawiyyāt* in this context is much broader than the literal definition. A comprehensive knowledge of the Shariʿah, namely, Islamic theology as well as jurisprudence, is needed to acquire the wisdom of priorities.[26]

The negative effects that result from disregarding "the priorities" constitute a topic on which Alalwani elaborated and posited twenty-four unwanted outcomes. We will content ourselves with mentioning the five important ones. First, Muslims being plunged so deeply into details (of the Shariʿah) that they cannot neither systematize them nor address the subtle relation between cases and principles. Second, Muslims preferred to adhere to blind imitation (*taqlīd*) rather than carrying out the initiatives (ijtihad). Third, they place too much significance upon supererogatory or optional undertakings, before obligatory actions. Fourth, Muslim jurists often rely upon their presumption and refuse to investigate the causality of things. Fifth, the over-reliance upon the names of iconic (and often deceased) scholars from whom Muslims expect to hear the truth instead of verifying the authenticity of what these people said – a kind of idolatry (*ṣanamiyyah*) that deters them from thorough contemplation. The rest of his elaboration analyzes how trivial trends of thought and superfluous spiritual displays occupied their minds without making a real contribution to religion and society.[27]

Alalwani provides remarkable points and explanations on the principles of *awlawiyyāt*, although their origins go back to al-Ghazālī's formula of *munāsabah* (lit. relevancy) and al-Shāṭibī's theory of *maqāṣid*. In the later part of his book, he acknowledges al-Ghazālī and especially al-Shāṭibī as precursors of the idea. Alalwani argues that priorities were not followed up because trivial notions kept them away from devising a proper course of dealing with substantial problems.[28] He clearly points out the fact that his concept of priorities should be understood along the Shariᶜah's higher purpose (*maqāṣid*) and commands, as the title of his book suggests.

Alalwani is one of few Muslim authors who present scholarly opinions of Islamic thinkers regardless of their sectarian or devotional attachments. He refers to and sometimes incorporates Shiᶜi-oriented works of thinkers such as Sayyid Jamāl al-Dīn al-Afghānī (d. 1315/1897) and Muhammad Hussain Na'ini (d. 1355/1936) and to their Sunni counterparts such as Shaykh Muhammad Abduh (d. 1324/1906) and Abd al-Rahman al-Kawakibi (d. 1320/1902).[29] Due to his pioneering work on *The Ethics of Disagreement in Islam*, he is well aware that he should not expect all Muslims, regardless of their circumstances and backgrounds, to agree on what constitutes an ideal vision of Islam.[30] In this book, one finds examples of more tolerant and open-minded attitudes toward disagreements from Islamic history, particularly from the precedents set by the Companions.

AbdulHamid AbuSulayman

AbdulHamid AbuSulayman (d. 2021) was among the authors who sought to reform Islamic methodology from within the traditional legal methodology and align its application so that it could deal with contemporary requirements. His approach to the Shariʿah is imbued with an assumed crisis in the mind of Muslims, a crisis that prevented them from appreciating Islamic values in light of the time-space factors. In his broad criticism of the traditional methodology, he reevaluated the sources of the law and the method of juridical interpretation with reference to the international relations policies of Muslim governments. Here, we content ourselves with new proposals that he proffered in Islamic jurisprudence.

AbuSulayman called his approach to the Shariʿah *aṣālah*, that is innovative, in contrast to some of the traditional approaches, which he labeled "imitative."[31] This approach unveils itself in his treatment of the authority of the sources of Islamic law; however, he adds many qualifications to bring his approach into line with the orthodox perception of the Shariʿah. He divides the sources into two types: primary (e.g., the Qur'an, the Sunnah, consensus, and *qiyās*) and secondary (e.g., juridical preference, consideration of the public interest, and the obstruction of ostensibly legitimate means [*sadd al-dharā'iʿ*].[32] Concerning the primary source's authority and application, he makes the following novel observations: The Qur'an is the first revealed source of Islamic law and, as such, should neither be considered a subject for abrogation nor divided into Makkan or Madinan verses. Rather, it should be regarded as part of the same whole, whose application must be aligned with the space-time considerations, which are said to be applied "…in the light of changing circumstances in the overall flow of human life and experience."[33] In this way, he implies that this broader context can affect the basic principles of religion. Aware of possible problems, he tries to filtrate his idea through the channel of *uṣūl al-fiqh* by ultimately reducing these considerations into applying the two principles of *ḍarūrah* (lit. necessity) and *talfīq* (lit. piecing together).

In this connection, he acts like some muftis, such as Rashid Rida (d. 1935), who legitimized the charging of interest in today's banking system.[34] AbuSulayman speaks about the necessity of methodological reforms, but elaborates only on the possible changes concerning the rules of abrogation.

The problem of conflicting laws, as we saw in Chapter 1, was the *raison d'être* for forming *uṣūl al-fiqh*. Muslim scholars attempted to solve the problem first by delineating a hierarchical consideration for the law's sources, and then by setting rules for cases of abrogation (*naskh*) and particularization (*takhṣīṣ*) followed by semantical interpretations. According to AbuSulayman, Muslim scholars did not elaborate the philosophy of abrogation well enough to justify the flexibility of the law embedded within the Islamic legal system. He writes:

> The concept of *naskh*, as traditionally elaborated, reflects a static understanding in the methodology of Islamic thought, for it acts without taking notice of the difference between the general and universalistic nature of the Qur'ānic teachings as opposed to the specific and particularized treatment of subjects found in the *sunnah*. The traditional concept of *naskh* also reflects a total lack of appreciation for the elements of time and place in the process of interpreting and applying texts, as well as in comparing and analyzing them.[35]

By emphasizing the late Madinan verses and traditions as a standard for Islam, AbuSulayman describes the prevalent juristic legal methodology as static because it leaves aside many Makkan and the early Madinan verses and experiences. For instance, the universal verse of the early Madinan period, "Let there be no compulsion in religion, truth stands out clear from error" (2:256) was subverted by the late Madinan verse: "When the forbidden months are past, fight and slay the pagans wherever you find them" (9:5). According to Ibn Salāmah (d. 410/1019), this verse alone abrogated 124 earlier verses.[36] AbuSulayman observes that this genre of methodology suited the

Umayyad and early Abbasid's powerful governments during which the jurisconsults standardized their methodologies. "Contemporary Muslim jurists, though they have attempted to reinterpret many cases of *naskh*, seem to accept the same concept of permanent *naskh*." He suggests that one way to solve this problem is "to reconcile verses that seemed to contradict one another in the light of space-time factors."[37] In reality, however, this suggestion has been practiced by past and present-day Muslim societies via *ḍarūrah* and *maṣlaḥah*. By considering both time and space, he nevertheless outlines a formula that is adaptable to the ever-changing situations within contemporary societies.

Second, AbuSulayman's argues that the traditions of the Prophet, more than the Qur'an, reflect this space-time element. In other words, they should be read within their own context. While appreciating al-Shāfiʿī's effort to establish the Sunnah's authority, AbuSulayman nevertheless rejects its validity for today, for instance, the Prophet's view on attacking the *mushrikūn* (pagan Arabs) at least once a year.[38] He finds the patterns set by the prophetic traditions on war expeditions to be not analogous to today's realities.[39] He criticizes the traditions' historical arrangement and finds it amazing that despite the highly technical terminology used in their categorization, the traditions nevertheless appear to be neither well-arranged nor authentic. This often engenders automatic criticism whenever an author cites a hadith that serves little more than to distract readers from the point the author was trying to make.[40]

Finally, AbuSulayman regards the principle of *ijmāʿ* as useless, unless new intellectual approaches to the traditional methodology are developed. Basing *ijmāʿ* on the agreement of *mujtahid*s, who merely cite the authoritative *ʿulamā'* in turn, only adds to the confusion. Today, subjects require the consensus of experts drawn from different segments of society covering various disciplines. By approaching the problems in this way, he employs formulas from other disciplines such as empiricism and systematization in jurisprudence.[41]

AbuSulayman considers *qiyās* to be a product of historical developments during the second/eighth century that sought to support and maintain the basic models espoused by the Caliphs. As a supplement to *qiyās*, later jurisconsults worked out the principles of *maṣlaḥah* and *siyāsah sharʿiyyah* (government legal policy) in response to the political conditions of the time.[42] He does not assign much religious or rational value to *qiyās* and the above-mentioned principles, but does engage in its historical analysis within his space-time theory.

In a chapter entitled "Reform of Methodology" in his *Towards an Islamic Theory of International Relations*, he advocates a new reading of the Qur'an and Sunnah. In his critical reading of Islamic history, he makes a number of interesting observations that may help us understand the present stagnation of Muslim thought. He finds a series of undue rifts not only between religious and political leadership, but also between religious and empirical sciences.[43] He considers the replacement of Caliphate with hereditary kingship as the main cause of the rift between governments and Muslim legal interpretation and their resulting scholarship. In his view, this rift led to the Islamic world's isolation and is "the underlying cause of all the maladies that would later beset the *ummah*."[44] The lack of empiricism within the religious sciences resulted in the latter's disorientation from the time-space dimension necessary for updating legal norms.

Mohammad Hashim Kamali

Mohammad Hashim Kamali (b. 1944) combines aspects of the traditional legal methodology with proposals for adaptation to recent changes within Muslim societies. His consistent engagement with the law has allowed him to not only produce detailed presentations of the field's various disciplines, but also to formulate new proposals that may reconcile the legitimacy of Islamic law with the ruling Muslim governments. He has written several works on various branches of Islamic law, legal methodology, hadith studies, and religious freedom in Islam. His two important works, *Principles of Islamic Jurisprudence* (1989) and *Shariʿah Law: An Introduction* (2008), allow us to observe his contributions to the field. In the 2003 edition of *Principles*,

Kamali first recapitulates most of the topics of legal methodology and then attempts to present a new scheme to reorient some of the sub-disciplines of *uṣūl al-fiqh* to address various contemporary issues.

In his introductory remarks, Kamali defines *uṣūl al-fiqh* as both a "methodology" and "principles." "Methodology," in his view, concerns mainly methods of reasoning such as analogy (*qiyās*) and the presumption of continuity (*istiṣḥāb*), whereas "principles" include general directives that comprise the larger part of the primary sources and can be utilized as raw material in the development of law. The components of both of them are, however, the same and include primarily knowledge of the sources of the law and their order of priority; then legal rules, which may be deduced from the sources; and, finally, the exercise of ijtihad. He separates ijtihad from "the deduction of rules" in order to give the former an independent identity aimed at further adapting and refining responses to the changing needs of Muslim societies.[45] In the introduction's second part, Kamali distinguishes two main approaches to the study of *uṣūl al-fiqh*: theoretical and deductive. He states: "[W]hereas the former is primarily concerned with the exposition of theoretical doctrines, the latter is pragmatic in the sense that deduction is formulated in light of its application to relevant issues."[46] His arrangement of *uṣūl al-fiqh* topics indicates that he has more in common with the latter approach, as will be demonstrated below.

Kamali commences his account with the sources of the law, namely, the Qur'an and Sunnah. This marks his consideration for the theory of Islamic law that derives its legality from these two fundamental sources. He later turns to the much elaborated yet complicated topic of "legal language" (*mabāḥith al-alfāẓ*), which is very important because it is viewed not only as a conduit for "legal norm" (*ḥukm*), but often as the very ingredient of the legal norms themselves. However, by separating "literal indications" and "textual implications" (*al-dalalāt*) Kamali draws a clear picture of what he rightly contends are "rules of interpretation." The former deals mainly with the proposition of words such as allegory (*mu'awwal*), metaphor (*majāz*), clear (*wāḍiḥ*), and unclear (*ghayr wāḍiḥ*), whereas the latter centers on textual implications such as alluded meaning, inferred meaning, or required meaning. Kamali allocates two chapters to the above topics under the rubric of "Rules of Interpretation I" and "Rules of Interpretation II," to distinguish these two sets of implications.[47]

The next chapter on legal language is entitled "Commands and Prohibitions" of the revealed texts. He perceives this issue as a matter of the Qur'anic (and prophetic) language that follows up the discussion on the sources.[48] Nevertheless, from a different perspective these commands and prohibitions could be seen as constituent parts of Islamic legal norms (*aḥkām*) and could transfer the issue of *alfāz* (literal interpretation) to *aḥkām*. But Kamali characterizes the Islamic conception of them as "often coupled with an appeal to the conscience of the individual," thereby distinguishing it from the "imperative rules" of modern laws that are often devoid of such an appeal and confined to tangible results.[49]

In line with his elaboration on the revealed texts is the problem of abrogation (*naskh*). Not content with depicting the opinions of the traditional authors like Ibn Salāmah, he reflects on the views of al-Zuhayli (b. 1932) and AbuSulayman and eventually concludes that "*naskh* is basically factual and has little juridical substance of its own, nor does it seem to have a direct bearing on the substance of legal theory."[50] For the same reason, one can transfer this topic from the *adillah* (indicants) to the "conflict of evidences" – a secondary issue discussed at the end of Kamali's work.

Kamali then turns to two other sources of Islamic law – *ijmāʿ* and *qiyās* – on which he elaborates at length from both the traditional and contemporary viewpoints. Afterwards, he brings to the fore two rather methodologically trivial topics, namely, "Revealed Laws preceding the Shariʿah of Islam" and "The Fatwa of a Companion." Concerning the former, Kamali, on the authority of Abu Zahrah, concludes that "…disagreement among jurists on the authority or otherwise of the previous revelations is of little practical consequence, as the Shari'ah of Islam is generally self-contained and its laws are clearly identified."[51] As for the latter, it either fits into the category of ijtihad or is provided "to be a persuasive source of guidance" and has "priority over the *ijtihad* of other *mujtahids*," which may squeeze into the context of legal norms.

After covering revealed indicants, a number of supplementary indicants remain that can simply be arranged under the rubric of "rational indicants" (*al-adillah al-ʿaqliyyah*), as some Muslim *uṣūlī* authors did (see Chapter 8). These include *istiḥsān* (equity in Islamic law), *maṣāliḥ mursalah* (textually unattested rulings that take into account universal public benefit and welfare), *istiṣḥāb* (the presumption of continuity), and *sadd al-dharāʾiʿ* (blocking the means). Kamali, however, follows the general pattern set by the early Muslim authors and treats each topic as an independent subject matter. He propounds that the main object of analyzing the textual sources and legal indicants is to arrive at a legal norm (*ḥukm sharʿī*). He submits, in order, the five Shariʿah values (i.e., *ḥalāl, mandūb, mubāḥ, makrūh,* and *ḥarām*), the three legal sanctions (i.e., *ṣaḥīḥ, fāsid,* and *bāṭil*) and the three pillars of legal norms – the subject matter referred to (*maḥkūm fihi*) – and the authority of the lawgiver (*ḥākim*), who must be capable of understanding the legal norm (*maḥkūm ʿalayhi*). This pattern of *ḥukm* analysis, which was proposed by al-Ghazālī and elaborated by al-Shawkānī and Abu Zahrah (see Chapter 7), reiterates the status of the legal norm from an individual perspective.

Kamali completes his arrangement of *uṣūl* contents with the three essential topics of *ʿurf* (custom), conflict of evidence, and ijtihad, each of which he characterizes as deserving an independent category. *ʿUrf* is an important social concept and practice that can supplement the legal sources both theoretically and practically. Its theoretical role can be seen in the principle of the presumption of continuity that originates from the people's normal practice. Conflict of evidence encompasses several juridical issues to which the *uṣūl* methodology partly owes its origin. In the early stages, the argument of the legal sources' conflicting authority, especially problems of abrogation and particularization (*takhṣīṣ*), gave birth to *uṣūl al-fiqh* (see Chapter 1).

For his last topic in this section, Kamali not only elaborates on the procedure, variety, and qualification of ijtihad, but also presents an interesting account on how statutory legislation dampens the practice of ijtihad today. He concludes his remarks by referring to Iqbal's proposal for revitalizing it by instituting an assembly of scholars that practices *ijmāʿ* as the fabric of modern government. He also quotes al-Tamawi, who proposed that such governments should provide the necessary education to train "up-to-date" *mujtahids*.[52]

Kamali's conception of collective ijtihad is far broader than the prevailing conventional understanding. Following imam al-Shāfiʿī's concept of the infallibility of the general consensus of the Muslim community at large,[53] he assigns legal authority to collective ijtihad either in the form of *shūrā* (consultation) or *ijmāʿ*. He criticizes the traditional authors who increasingly subjected the issue to such onerous technical conditions that *ijmāʿ* eventually lost its popularity and practicality. To him, the verses on *shūrā* are inspiring enough to be translated into their own workable formula.

In the last chapter of *Principles* Kamali presents a new scheme for *uṣūl al-fiqh*, one that explores novel avenues for this discipline's utility and relevance to today's statutory legislation. Like Alalwani and AbuSulayman, his point of departure here is historical, as he sees a gap created between Muslim governments and the *ʿulamāʾ* due to the historical isolation of Islamic legal scholarship (particularly legal methodology) from the state authority of respective governments. This approach signals the beginning of the struggle to reduce the existing tension between theory and practice in Islamic thought. We shall see below how he entertains ideas to bridge the gap between government and legal scholarship.

The other viewpoint is that the time-space considerations are of no relevance, a position adopted by many traditional scholars. We have already seen how AbuSulayman suggested empiricism to equip Muslim jurisprudence with these considerations. In his "A New Scheme for *Uṣūl al-Fiqh*," Kamali blames *taqlīd*, literalist approaches, and rigid interpretation for ignoring the role of time-space in the understanding the Qur'an and Sunnah. In his paper "Toward a *Maqāṣid*-Oriented Legal Theory," he reintroduces al-Shāṭibī's idea of considering the Shariʿah's end goals (*maqāṣid*) in relation to public and civic interest as a possible method of connecting the elements of time-space to contemporary jurisprudence.[54]

Finally, Kamali evaluates the proposal made by the Egyptian author Jamal al-Din Atiyyah (b. 1928) to strike a balance between the need for the continuity and preservation of Islamic values, and a purposeful move to change the existing impasse regarding *uṣūl al-fiqh*. Kamali sees two Islamic core values, the Qur'anic concepts of consultation and obedience to those in charge of community affairs (*ʿūlū al-amr*), as having been neglected and therefore not fully integrated into *uṣūl al-fiqh*. He expects that governing authorities would extend their reach to theoretical consensus and even place their decisions on the same level as transmitted proofs.[55] Relying on the above premises, Kamali supports the first three of Atiyyah's five suggestions for a new division of the Shariʿah's sources:

1. The transmitted proofs, which include the Qur'an, Sunnah and revealed laws preceding the Shariʿah of Islam;
2. ordinances of the *ʿūlū al-amr*, which include *ijmāʿ* and ijtihad;
3. the existing conditions or status quo, insofar as it is harmonious with the preceding two categories, and this includes custom (*ʿurf*) and the presumption of continuity (*istiṣḥāb*);
4. rationality (*ʿaql*) in areas where full juridical ijtihad may not be necessary (the day-to-day rulings of government departments, for example, [those] that seek to ensure good management of affairs may be based on rationality alone);
5. original absence of liability (*al-barāʾah al-aṣliyyah*), which presumes permissibility and freedom from liability as the basic norm of Shariʿah in respect of things, acts and transactions that have not been expressly prohibited.[56]

This proposal's significance essentially rests on how they contribute to the existing government's legitimacy, something that Muslim states are in desperate need of today. It is worth noting that attempts to include a Muslim government's ordinances in the Shariʿah's legal structure does have precedence in Islamic scholarship. Some scholars have proposed the context of *siyāsah sharʿiyyah* (government legal policy), which can overrule the Shariʿah's textually derived rules; however, such policies lack the universal value and durability required to preserve the tradition.

In his conclusion, Kamali once more attempts to enable the existing instruments of legal methodology to serve today's social realities, that is, to merge "the government ordinances into *ijtihād*, and 'statutory laws' into *ijmāʿ*."[57] In this respect, the government and the legislative assembly are entrusted with the role of being the main repository of ijtihad and *ijmāʿ*, a move that is *per se* considered to incline toward the *maqāṣid*. The *maqāṣid*'s conventional scope, which confined to five or six headings, is evidently not enough and thus should be revised and supplemented in conformity with the new developments and demands of contemporary life.[58] As such, one can see that most of the proposed pretexts seek to bestow more legality on government ordinances. This seems to be a sound proposal, but only as long as it is coordinated with the principles of checks and balances that are mostly absent from Muslim societies. In contrast, one may also expect to see that "the supremacy of the Shariʿah," one of the first principles of *uṣūl al-fiqh*, develops in a manner that guarantees the restrained nature of governmental authority. Kamali contends that *ijmāʿ* and *shūrā* have historically exhausted their traditional importance due to Muslim scholars' long-standing lack of interest in them. Islam encourages public participation in both performing rituals and ful-filling social realities. The latter, nevertheless, has not received as much attention from the *ʿulamāʾ* as the former. As a result, the rules of congregational prayers are, for example, far more elaborate than the principles of *shūrā* that could help shape the consultative part of an Islamic government. Kamali's suggestion, therefore, offers a new outlook for reviving this forgotten sphere of Islamic public law.

Tariq Ramadan

The Egyptian author Tariq Ramadan (b. 1962) offers a new angle to reading those verses that legitimize the observation of time-honored social realities in legal administration. His approach does not necessarily derive from modern hermeneutics, but incorporates a novel perspective in which "outside realities" play a central role in understanding the proper Islamic legal norms (*aḥkām*). In his *Radical Reform* (2009), Ramadan espouses a theological approach to the Qur'anic concept of *āyāt* (lit. signs) by which he equates knowledge of the outside world with that of the revealed scripture. He states that the "…surrounding Creation is a Universe of signs that must be grasped, understood, and interpreted."[59] He refers to Abū Ḥāmid al-Ghazālī's use of the term "outspread book" (*al-kitāb al-manshūr*) as the Book of the Universe, which is a theological as well as a physical mirror of the "written book" (*al-kitāb al-masṭūr*; viz., the Qur'an).[60]

According to Ramadan the universe is also filled with realities, and therefore texts (*al-nuṣūṣ*) and context (*al-wāqiᶜ*) should be balanced to determine all of the consequences of the thesis in light of contemporary scientific knowledge.[61] Therefore, a council of ᶜulamā' specialized in the study of scripture needs to work with scientists, who are on an equal footing with the ᶜulamā', to formulate a ruling or legal opinion (fatwa) about specific issues.[62]

In his legal reading, Ramadan criticizes the methodology that shaped *uṣūl al-fiqh*, which he defines as the "fundamentals and sources."[63] He distinguishes three essential phases that epitomize Muslim classical approaches to legal methodology:

1. The deductive approach of Imam al-Shāfiᶜī's school,
2. The inductive approach of the Ḥanafī school,
3. The school of *maqāṣid* (the law's "higher objectives").

In his final assessment of these phases, he concludes that "knowledge of the environment" is missing in all three approaches, except in some tangential form such as *istiḥsān* (to deem something good), *istiṣlāḥ* (consideration of public interest), ᶜ*urf* (customary law), [and higher objectives] as they allow room for an extra-legal approach in the form of an adjunct to knowledge of the primary texts.[64]

In one of his prior works, Ramadan sought to expand the application of some basic concepts of Islamic legal methodology and to provide a way to connect those legal principles and social realities that change over time and in culture.[65] These concepts included *maslahah* (the common good), ijtihad (juridical exertion), and fatwa (legal opinion), within which he sought to build a framework to justify some "modern judgment" or "progress."[66] Nevertheless, his new legal and theological approach seems inclined to consider all of them as secondary concepts, especially in comparison to his new theological outlook of "knowledge of [the] outside realities of God's creation."[67]

To legitimize the role of sciences in implementing religious rules, he, like Abdolkarim Soroush, distinguishes between the abstract Shariʿah, which is unchanging and immutable, and its interpretations within particular geographical and historical contexts (i.e., fiqh).[68] He makes some references to the concepts of "necessity" (*ḍarūrah*) and "need" (*ḥājah*), but places substantial emphasis on what he sees as the Shariʿah's higher objectives. His views are shared by scholars such as AbuSulayman and Alalwani (see above), who sought to build a "school of higher objectives of the Shariʿah" (*madrasat al-maqāṣid*)[69] out of ideas stemming from the eighth/ fourteenth century pioneering figure al-Shāṭibī.

The scope of these higher objectives should not be limited to the Shariʿah's five traditional objectives (i.e., the preservation of life, religion, intellect, property, and the family). As Kamali and others have mentioned, the primary texts' orientation should account for the modern human context.[70] Ramadan's conception of the higher objectives does not operate in isolation, for he also takes ethics and education into account.[71]

This realistic approach is evident when he criticizes the current pietistic attitude of some Muslim authors toward modern science, which they label "Islamic economics," "Islamic finance," "Islamic pedagogy," "Islamic psychology," and "Islamic medicine" without defining these discipline's relevant rubrics. Ramadan views them as "misleading if not dishonest." He asks "[W]hat is truly 'Islamic' in this economy? its tools, its methods, its norms, or its goals?"[72] Ramadan adds:

One can understand the intent and meaning of this attempt to re-colonize the Universe of knowledge through an inflated use of the term "Islamic," but it is clear that the process is purely formal, that the real problem has not been tackled. Most important, this is not a good way of solving the problem of dichotomy and discrepancy between the different Universes of knowledge.[73]

Overall, Ramadan's proposals point to the core questions of how Islamic textual scholars can better cooperate with scientists and how their respective jurisdictions are to be defined. His innovation lies in his theological approach, which enables him to add the legitimacy of *āyāt* to the previously held notions of *ʿurf* and *maqāṣid*. In the fourth (and final) part of his *Radical Reform*, which he has entitled "Case Studies," he tries to address this interpretation of *āyāt* and explain how it should affect more traditional approaches. Here, he moves away from his prior somewhat sociological approach and blames most of the problem on a "… far-reaching distortion of Islamic teachings in the name of formalism and obsession with norms."[74] As a result, he emphasizes the law's higher objectives as well as legal ethics.

Salihi Najafabadi and Legal Methodology

Among the contemporary authors of Shiʿi jurisprudence, only Ayatollah Salihi Najafabadi (d. 2006) has offered a new mode of interpretation that often suited contemporary realities and the place of religion in society. During the 1970s he raised a storm in Shiʿi seminaries with his *Shahīd-i Jāvīd* (The Eternal Martyr), in which he denied the predestined character of Imām al-Ḥusayn's martyrdom and cast doubts on the doctrine of the Imāms' infallibility. As a proponent of Islamic unity, he wrote treatises in support of juridical rapprochement with mainstream Sunni Muslims. In his post-Revolution works, he provided a new context for the theory of *wilāyat al-faqīh* (guardianship of the jurisprudent) in which he – unlike Ayatollah Khomeini – laid primary emphasis on the role of people in choosing their leader. Ayatollah Najafabadi regarded the process of instituting (*inshā'*) by the people as the basis of the authority of "a qualified leader" in both confirming and validating that figure's position.

By proposing what he calls a "concrete" (*inshā'ī*) context for applying and implementing this particular theory, he implied that Khomeini's presentation of it was based on "abstract" (*khabarī*) or theoretical premises that ignore the people's vital role in validating the *faqīh's* authority. He tried to incorporate their role and interests into the governing institution of "the qualified leadership" by bringing the modern concepts of "majority rule, bilateral contract and the role of human intellect" into conformity with Islamic principles. In his attempt to do so, he sometimes bypassed the prevailing *uṣūlī* maxim of "the verbal demonstration" and thereby allowed the content's higher goal to determine the meaning of the texts.

Majority Rule

As a social norm, majority rule is a pre-requisite for concluding any communal decision, including the Islamic decision-making process known as *shūrā*. Nevertheless, standard Muslim jurisprudence did not accept this social norm, and many jurisprudents repudiated it on the grounds that several Qur'anic verses did not "recognize" the majority's opinion. Among early Muslim scholars, al-Shāfiʿī appears to have corroborated the validity of the community's majority opinion (*akthar al-ʿāmmah*), especially in reporting the prophetic traditions.[75] Later, the Ḥanafī jurist al-Jaṣṣāṣ al-Rāzī (d. 370/980) allocated a chapter to "the majority views" in his work on *uṣūl al-fiqh*. He eventually did not support this idea, but the fact that he both presented and subsequently repudiated its advocates' arguments shows that Muslim scholars have been aware of its importance as a norm, although they have been unable to establish its expected "religious truth" on the basis of majority opinion.[76]

Ayatollah Najafabadi appears to be the first Shiʿi jurisprudent to adopt and justify this concept by a careful examination of relevant Qur'anic verses, which he divided into two categories: 1) Those that contain the phrase "Most of the people have no knowledge (*aktharuhum lā yaʿlamūn*)." These verses, according to him, refer to trans-material affairs and signify only that people neither generally understand nor are informed about arcane matters, and 2) those that contain the phrase "Most of the people lack wisdom (*aktharuhum lā yaʿqilūn*)." These verses, he claims, refer to people who commit immoral and reprehensive acts. According to him, neither of these categories ever suggested that the majority of people could not understand their own problems and devise appropriate solutions for them.[77]

In addition, he established the concept of majority rule according to the following proofs:

1. The Qur'anic verse 5:1 and others that state *awfū bil ʿuqūd* ("fulfill your contracts"): The general application of this divine ordinance includes the contract of *wilāyah*, which must be respected. One of the parties to this contract is 'the people,' which obviously cannot mean all of them numerically speaking, but rather the majority of people. Thus, this concept acquires its validity because it is part of any valid contract.

2. Endorsing a rational practice: Islam traditionally approves of rational practices, and majority rule is a clear case in point. Ayatollah Najafabadi referred to a tradition of the Prophet, cited by the historian al-Yaʿqūbī (d. 897–98), in which he had recommended to the soldiers fighting under Muʾta's leadership (a commander at the time) that if he should be killed in combat, then they should choose one of their own as the new leader. This prophetic tradition endorses the principle of majority rule and is clearly based on rational practice.[78]

As such, Ayatullah Salihi legitimized majority rule according to the *uṣūlī* method of the general or all-inclusive application of legal texts.

Bilateral Contract
Ayatollah Najafabadi used legal methodology to expand the application of some verses to embrace today's requirements, especially in

terms of political legitimacy. The general ruling of "fulfill your contracts" (5:1) served as his argument's pivotal point. He held that *bay*ʿ*ah* (a procedure for recognizing a person's authority or social status) was the legal channel through which the social contract would be concluded. Indeed, he considered it as effectively investing the ruler with authority in contradistinction to the orthodox view that restricted this to a purely confirmatory function.[79] Moreover, according to him, *bay*ʿ*ah* brings about mutual obligations between both parties.[80] In the Shiʿi orthodox view, *bay*ʿ*ah* refers only to the people's obligation to remain loyal to their oath of allegiance, for the leader's position is considered a divine appointment that people should acknowledge and pledge their allegiance to.

The Role of Human Intellect

Ayatollah Najafabadi assigned an independent role to human intellect in terms of understanding social affairs and sought to establish his thesis according to the Qur'an and tradition-reports. In the introduction of his work he spoke about *aṣālat al-*ʿ*aql* (lit. the principality of intellect) and excluded political matters such as *wilāyat al-faqīh* from the jurisdiction of unquestioning religious allegiance (*ta*ʿ*abbud*). To harmonize this rationalism with Islamic principles, he referred to several verses (e.g., 12:2 and 36:68) that advise people to use their own judgment and quoted a tradition-report from Kulaynī's *al-Kāfī* in the chapter on ʿ*aql*. Nevertheless, he considered it necessary to add that the validity of the same rationalism is based on and derived from reason and can only be confirmed by reported traditions.[81]

The standard Shiʿi approach ranks human intellect (ʿ*aql*) as an additional proof only after it has been established by traditional proofs.[82] In contrast, Ayatollah Najafabadi gave it a central role when it comes to addressing social realities. From a methodological point of view, his emphasis in this regard harkens back to the formula of "independent rational reasoning" (*al-mustaqillāt al-*ʿ*aqliyyah*) that many Shiʿi authors, among them Muhammad Rida al-Muzaffar (d. 1964), have had a hard time redefining.

As such, Ayatollah Najafabadi tried to incorporate the people's role into the interpretation of an originally religious doctrine that has been recently brought to light strictly to serve political purposes. The human intellect and the people's practice play a central role in validating and implementing the Muslim theory of governance. The context of *wilāyat al-faqīh* maintains its religious character, despite the fact that the mode of interpretation ultimately changes its source of legitimacy.

Mohsen Kadivar

Mohsen Kadivar is a prominent Shiʿi jurist and theologian who stands between the traditional and modern approaches to Islamic legal thought. As an electronic engineering student at Shiraz University, Kadivar was drawn into religious studies during the 1979 revolution. He studied Shiʿi jurisprudence under Ayatollah Hossein Ali Montazeri in the 1990s when the latter was dismissed from his position as Ayatollah Khomeini's successor. Following his teacher's ideas, Kadivar first concerned himself with the political side of Islamic jurisprudence but later presented his own understanding of Islamic legal philosophy. Thus far, he has published more than 20 works on Islamic law and philosophy. Only in his 2007 article on Islamic legal methodology, however, did he exhibit his command of the limits of Islamic legal language.

Kadivar claims that "understanding the legal text" is the central problem of all Abrahamic religions. In Islamic legal methodology, texts are divided into *nass* (explicit and therefore definitive meaning) and *ẓāhir* (manifest and therefore speculative meaning). Given that the decisive majority of texts are *ẓāhir*, the topic of "the authority of manifest implications" became this discipline's central theme to such an extent that it occupies half of the content of most such works. His argument that the key to understanding the meaning is ʿ*urf* (the customary usage of language) led him to ask how these usages should be understood: "How much [do] a reader's information and presuppositions interfere in such an understanding?" Islamic traditional scholars have never addressed this question, although most authors rewrote Islamic law according to the presuppositions of their time.[83]

Judging the overall topics of Islamic legal methodology (especially the Shiʿi one), Kadivar points to the following shortcomings:

1. The method of restricting the scope of legal language to "the validity of manifest meanings of texts" (*ḥujiyyat al-ẓawāhir*) ignores alternative ways of identifying textual implications.
2. The scope and even definition of topics such as "rational practices" (*sīrat al-ʿuqalāʾ*) and "independent reasoning" (*al-mustiqillāt al-ʿaqliyyah*) are unclear and need rethinking.
3. The argument on "the validity of absolute speculation" (*ḥujiyyat ẓann al-muṭlaq*) is problematic because it is based on the self-contradicting assumption that the gate of knowledge is closed.

He concludes that deliberating on the above problems is necessary for improving legal methodology and considers Mojtahed Shabestari a precursor in this field.[84]

Kadivar's criticism of traditional methodology raises doubt about the very exclusiveness of *uṣūlī* inferences, which are mainly substantiated on speculation rather than analysis. Although speculation in *uṣūlī* language can lead to certainty in knowledge, this is not the case when it is associated with the closure of the gate of knowledge. In fact, due to the absence of a systematic arrangement of topics, *uṣūlī* methodology can foster many contradictory elements in its verbal argumentations.

Kadivar's second criticism involves the Shiʿi topic of "independent reasoning." This criticism shows that the early Shiʿi jurists proposed a useful title – *al-mustaqillāt al-ʿaqliyyah* – but failed to provide enough adequate material to validate it. We saw in Chapter 8 Shaykh Muhammad Rida Muzaffar's strenuous efforts to delineate its application.

Kadivar emphasizes the inadequacy of relying solely on the manifest meaning of legal language, a view that points to the necessity of employing modern ways of expanding and systemizing legal methodology. He notes the necessity of employing modern linguistic skills, hermeneutics, and analytic philosophy, but does not elaborate on them. Nevertheless, Kadivar endorses the modern epistemological steps taken by authors such as Soroush and Shabestari (see next chapter) and compares the difficulty of adopting modern ways to the difficulty of past Muslim scholars who tried to adopt some principles of Greek logic into their own eras' Islamic legal methodology.[85]

CHAPTER 10

Modern Hermeneutics and Legal Language

EVER SINCE 1980, the legal language of Islam has been subjected to not only fresh legal deliberation, but also to a new series of epistemological analyses, i.e., modern hermeneutics – a discipline concerned with the nature and presuppositions of the interpretation of religious texts.[1] Prior to the 1980s, most changes to Islamic law were offered through the channels of interpretive disciplines such as *tafsīr* (exegesis), *ta'wīl* (allegorical interpretation) and ijtihad (independent judgment), all entrenched in the rules of Islamic legal methodology (*uṣūl al-fiqh*). None of these devices were used to extend the meaning of a text beyond the literal demonstration of the text or beyond the religious context in which the texts emerged; whereas the modern epistemological approach seems to essentially rest on "presuppositions" surrounding the understanding of the text. The process of understanding a text, in this approach, does not begin with reading the text, but rather it starts prior to that with the dialogue between the culture shaping the reader's perception (see below). Innovative approaches to the Shariʿah are best reflected in the works of the five figures discussed in this chapter.

Modern hermeneutics has come under heavy criticism by its detractors among post-modernist writers. Schleiermacher and Dilthey believed that correctly interpreting a text meant recovering the original intention of the author. This theory, which postulates a determined meaning in existence became a subject of criticism by two postmodernist thinkers, Heidegger (d. 1976) and Gadamer (d. 2002) who elaborated on "the problem of temporal distance that separates us from meaning of texts."[2] Gadamer, writing on the nature of human understanding, argues that people have a "historically affected consciousness" which influences their understanding. The contemporary Iranian author Ali Mirsepassi comments on the latter radically alternative conception as follows:

> In this way, we see "the meaning of a text" moved from its initial stage of "literal demonstration" to "reconstruction of the original intention of the author," and finally to "historical consciousness of the reader." From among Muslim thinkers the writings of Soroush and Abu Zayd more than others seem to have the flavor of the third stage of understanding the meaning of a text.[3]

Nasr Hamid Abu Zayd

The prominent Egyptian author Nasr Hamid Abu Zayd (d. 2010) was among the first Islamicists who approached the Shariʿah by applying hermeneutics as a method of inquiry into the interpretation of legal texts. His early works centered on evaluating Muslims' methods of semantics, implications in the interpretation of the texts according to the European founders of hermeneutics such as Friedrich Schleiermacher (d. 1834) and Wilhelm Dilthey (d. 1911). To them hermeneutics is a process of reconstruction by the reader of the original intention of the author. Abu Zayd examined the writings of Muslim scholars and grammarian such as al-Jāḥiẓ (d. 255/869), Abū Bakr al-Bāqillānī (d. 403/1013) and ʿAbd al-Qāhir al-Jurjānī (d. 471/1078) in light of their theories of hermeneutics.[4] He attempted to present a fresh and often critical reading of their writings.

The controversial work of Abu Zayd, *Mafhūm al-Naṣṣ*, is one of his discourses on the Qur'anic sciences. In this book, he launched a new way of reading religious texts in light of modern hermeneutics. To signify the importance of the text, he referred to the Islamic Arabian civilization as "Civilization of the Text" (*ḥaḍārat al-naṣṣ*) in contrast to the Greek which he dubs "Civilization of Reason" (*ḥaḍārat al-ʿaql*). His emphasis, therefore, is on the understanding of texts that require interpretative skills to discern the cultural context surrounding the presentation of a text. The Qur'an being the prime source-text of Islam, he categorizes its verses to two: those revealed before the *Hijrah* as "faith building" in contrast to those after the *Hijrah* (622–632) which are more of society building in character.[5] Nevertheless, the textual output of the Qur'an was, in Abu Zayd's view, overshadowed by the immense sanctity later attached to it as the Holy Book.[6]

In one of his later works, *Naqd al-Khiṭāb al-Dīnī*, Abu Zayd notes the abuse of the Holy Book by Muʿāwiyah (d. 60/680), founder of the Umayyad Dynasty, who used a shrewd tactic of raising Qur'anic fragments on lances in an attempt to rescue himself from an imminent defeat by diverting Muslim soldiers' attention from their own ijtihad to an expected direct judgment of the Qur'an: "The Qur'an is just pieces of writings," Abu Zayd quotes the fourth Caliph ʿAlī ibn Abī Ṭālib (d. 40/661) responding to calls for truce in the battle of Ṣiffīn, "it does not speak; only men speak for it." Abu Zayd concludes that texts require a certain scope of rational interpretation that only the human mind can afford.[7]

He claimed that the understanding of a text revolves around the data and perceptions at the time of the reader, and he quotes from *Literary Identity* by Peter W. Nesselroth that the process of understanding a text does not begin with reading the text, but rather it starts prior to that with the dialogue between the culture shaping the reader's perception and the text. In the case of the Qur'an, knowledge of "occasions of revelation" is necessary for eliciting a legal norm (*ḥukm*) or for inferring a meaning from it. But Muslim interpreters often separated the text from the legal norm, and some of them even claimed that the *ḥukm* or the command of God existed before the coming of the text.[8] Abu Zayd drew out three factors that may cause this misunderstanding:

1. The literal implication (*al-dalālah al-lughawiyyah*) was confused by some of the interpreters with the legal implication (*al-dalālah al-sharʿiyyah*), as in the Qur'anic verse 14 in chapter 87: "He will prosper he who purifies himself." "Purification" in this Makkan verse does not imply zakah (legal alms) which, according to the famous Qur'anologue al-Suyūṭī (d. 911/1505) was historically established after the *Hijrah*.

2. Some interpretations were attributed to the Prophet's Companions whose explanations are associated with the Madinan period, whereas the content of the verse belonged to the Makkan era. To solve the problem, the later ʿulamāʾ had to assume that the *ḥukm* existed before the text. Qur'anic verse 33 of Makkan chapter 41 reads: "Who is better in speech than he who calls [people] to God, performs righteous deed and says 'I am of those who bow in Islam.'" It was quoted from ʿĀ'ishah (d. 58/678) that the verse was revealed for the muezzin (announcer of the hour of prayer); where-as history tells us the *adhān* (the call for prayer) was established in the early Madinan period.[9]

3. Confusing the sequence of verses with the occasion of revelation resulted in different readings of a verse, and in gainsay assumptions: firstly that the text was revealed before the occasion arose, and secondly the text preceded its suitability and necessity to be a legal norm. An example is verse 45 in chapter 54: "Soon will their multitude be put to flight, and they will show their backs." Al-Suyūṭī quoted the second Caliph ʿUmar that he had heard the Prophet reciting this verse during the Battle of Badr when the army of Quraysh was defeated. Yet the sequence of verses suggests a similarity between the ancient Egyptian Pharaohs and Makkan pagans, and the verse can be understood as referring to the Pharaoh's army. Another "between the lines" meaning can be understood in conformity with the future tense used in the verse

in that it applies to the Resurrection Day. Abu Zayd concludes that different readings of a text resulted from the reader's standpoint, and that the evolution of one's knowledge opens the way for a new understanding of the text.[10]

In the quest for finding a new meaning or function for legal principles, Abu Zayd drew on a number of methodological topics from *uṣūl al-fiqh* such as "general and its particularization," "occasions of revelation," "abrogation," "implication and divergent meaning" and "absolute and qualified." For instance, he evaluated abrogation as the main proof for a dialectical relationship existing between the revelation and external realities, and said that its function is to adapt to changes and to advance law giving.[11] He considered both the generalization and particularization of the Qur'anic verses as a means to maintain the unity of the law and to fully understand them, both the literal expressions and the occasions in which the law was given should be taken into consideration.[12] The relationship of "real to metaphor" also is a relationship of change and transformation with which Abu Zayd finally concluded his arguments in *Mafhūm al-Naṣṣ* with a Sufi type explanation.[13]

To pave the way for exploring alternative concepts for the religious texts, Abu Zayd tried to refute some Islamic legal maxims such as "there is no room for ijtihad wherever a text is available." He claimed that the statement (*manṭūq*) of the Qur'an was fixed and permanent, but its conception (*mafhūm*) was changeable and open to variable approaches. To establish this claim, Abu Zayd refers to the history of Muslim rational approaches (especially the Muʿtazilī approach) in addition to practical principles of legal methodology such as: the priority of consideration of public interest (*maṣlaḥah*) over the text, preservation of objectives (*maqāṣid*) of the law and suitability (*munāsabah*) of *ratio legis* in analogous applications. These principles were mainly proposed by the eighth/fourteenth-century jurist al-Shāṭibī and endorsed partly by Ibn Taymiyyah and others (see Chapter 5). Pursuing different objectives or grounding themselves on variable information, Muslim jurists historically presented varying conceptions emanating from certain texts.[14]

A legal case in point is a daughter's share of inheritance which principally should curtail (*ḥajaba*) the right of all second degree relatives in the absence of other first degree heirs such as brothers. According to most Sunni schools of law, a daughter is not entitled to inherit more than her determined share (*farḍ*), which is *half*, from her parents' bequest. The rest should be returned to either *ʿaṣabah* (paternal male residuary) or to the public treasury (*bayt al-māl*) in the absence of other first degree heirs. Only the Shiʿi school of law (especially the Jaʿfarī school) clearly gives the right to the daughter to appropriate the second half of the bequest by returning (*radd*) it to her, regardless of the presence of the *ʿaṣabah*. The above problem was strongly debated in Egyptian media in the 1980s. Abu Zayd supported those writers who had advised the government to enhance women's rights by adopting the Shiʿi position in the law of inheritance. He argued that the different understanding of the same Qur'anic verses by Shiʿis (and some Ḥanafīs) point to the fact that there was room for ijtihad and new understanding of the Qur'anic verses. He drew two spheres for understanding the verses: 1) to find out the meaning (*maʿnā*) and 2) to delineate the end goal (*maghzā*) of the law. It was the focus of the first/seventh century Muslims, Abu Zayd opines, to adjust the meaning of the verses according to the existing Arab customs. They sometimes sacrificed the spirit and overall objectives of the Qur'an for its literal consistency; but, this was not the case for some authors with Sufi proclivities.[15]

Abu Zayd claimed that today's Muslim juridical understanding of the religious discourse (*al-khiṭāb al-dīnī*) was often more strict than that of their predecessors. He quoted al-Suyūṭī's account on literal categorization of the Qur'anic verses as an example of a historical approach to the text of the Qur'an. In his *al-Itqān*, al-Suyūṭī plainly claimed that all general legal verses of the Qur'an were particularized except verse 23 of chapter 4: "Forbidden to you [for marriage] are your mothers." According to Abu Zayd, al-Suyūṭī divided levels of clarity of the Qur'anic verses as follows: 1) a clear verse is the one which does not bear two meanings, and this is a *naṣṣ* (established text), 2) the verse bears two meanings but one of them is preferable, and that is *ẓāhir* (apparent), 3) should both meanings bear equal weight then the verse is *mujmal* (generalized), 4) if both meanings are not equal, but the stronger (*aqwā*) does not fit into the overall apparent meaning closely, then a remote meaning is preferable; and that is called *mu'awwal* (allegorically interpreted).[16] He concluded that the concept of *naṣṣ* according to al-Suyūṭī and most traditional authors meant nothing but "clear verse," whereas *naṣṣ* appears often as a "fixed and over-sacralized verse" in the writings of the later, and especially present, juridical authors, and this leaves practically no room for a rational reflection of the text.[17]

In 2006, Abu Zayd published an analytic history of reformation of Islamic thought in which various phases of reform after the Muslims' encounter with the West are examined. He concluded his work with reference to the setback of Iranian intellectuals in the 2005 presidential election. He blamed the defeat on the "advanced level of an intellectual debate that currently touches on so many issues previously considered taboo."[18] He then plainly identified this intellectual debate with hermeneutics that was discussed by scholars like Soroush and Shabestari (see below). Abu Zayd describes the discussion as more than rethinking of the Qur'an, rather it was "humanizing the Qur'an by formulating a liberal theology."[19] Here, we see Abu Zayd (exiled for his rethinking of the Qur'an methodology), was concerned about Iranian "advanced rethinking" that can simply go beyond the traditional frame.

Abu Zayd's works on reading and rethinking Islamic texts have produced a plausible criticism of some Muslim traditional methods in approaching the Shariʿah. This criticism proposes a drastic change in both the application and functions of traditional methods so as to be able to keep up with timely considerations of his era. In comparison with rational approaches of the past such as the *maqāṣid* theory of al-Shāṭibī, it does not, however, provide enough religious basis to legitimize or compromise the application of a new approach within the well-founded structure of the Shari'ah. His writings, nevertheless, influenced some Muslim communities in North Africa and Indonesia. One may draw parallels between his writings and some new legal proposals for reform in the civil law of the Maghrib (Morocco, Algeria and Tunisia). This proposal reads: "... the idea of an immutable and sacred 'Muslim law' is the fruit of a doctrinal development, and a dominant version of history that presents it as a compact and definitive whole."[20]

Mohammed Arkoun

As a precursor in the application of critical analyses in the religious sciences, Mohammed Arkoun (d. 2010) influenced the contemporary Muslim mind in rethinking Islamic values. He brought to the fore the idea of historicity and the deconstruction of the Shari'ah. He believed that the development of Islamic law was influenced by Greek philosophy. That is to say that Aristotle's concept of *substance as the primary essence of a thing* introduced to Muslims the notion of *originality* in the sense that concepts have their origins in a reality that is external. This notion not only became a point of departure in Islamic legal methodology but also the very Arabic term *aṣl* derives its methodological meaning from this *origin*.[21] This assertion may be examined in a scholarly manner in the context of correspondence (*ṣidq*), since we know that this idea appeared in Muslims' *uṣūl al-fiqh* in the fifth/eleventh century, and cannot be detected in the works of early Shāfiʿī, Ḥanafī and Muʿtazilī authors. Furthermore, this idea should not be confused with Muslims' commonly believed maxim of *nafs al-amri* (thing in itself) that holds an existing truth behind concepts.

The Indonesian author Amin Abdullah is quoted to claim: "It is Arkoun who is responsible for starting a research in epistemology of Islamic thought."[22] Arkoun applies the principle of "deconstruction" to Islamic orthodoxy. He defines it "as a system of beliefs and methodological representations through which, and with which, a given social group perceives and produces its own history."[23] Or it is also defined as "the system of values which functions primarily to guarantee the protection and security of a certain group."[24] Islamic orthodoxy, in Arkoun's view, suffers from a lack of a system of linguistics and semantics. And that is why it is practically reduced to a religious pluralism. He also discusses Islamic theology as an ongoing process in connection with Arkoun's thought.[25]

In response to the vacuity created by his sharp criticism of orthodoxy, Arkoun proposes Applied Islamology as a phenomenological understanding of Islam. This method seeks out Islam in a society, not the ideology and myth which, in Arkoun's view, are produced by an elite who claim to represent the religion. In Arkoun's writings, Applied Islamology appears conducive to adopting progressive Islam.[26]

Arkoun's thought was translated into the Indonesian language and debated at the academic level by a number of local intellectuals such as Ruslani who translated Arkoun's work, *People of the Book* into Indonesian in 2000. In this book Arkoun tries to redefine *ahl al-kitāb* as people who submit to one God. Suardi Saʿad, another Indonesian scholar wrote about Arkoun's view on Islam and modernism.

Abdolkarim Soroush

Abdolkarim Soroush (b. 1945) is a contemporary Iranian thinker who has thus far offered the most popular proposals for bridging the present gap between modernity and tradition in the Muslim world. Born in Tehran and trained in both the religious (Islamic) and scientific disciplines, Soroush was able to foresee the inevitable conflicts between the two realms, and to come up with widely agreeable proposals to both Western and Islamic modernists. His contributions to Islamic thought include suggestions for humanizing the revealed law, application of modern hermeneutics for setting legal norms, reconstruction of Islamic thought on its innate structure, and emphasizing the mystical beauty of Sufism. Here, we basically focus on his legal approach.

Soroush's first and probably the most controversial proposal was his theory of contraction and expansion of the Shariʿah, which was primarily published in the form of a series of articles in 1987 and later as a book. His point of departure in this book is scientific in the sense that it deals with how knowledge derived from the sciences reshapes our views of the world and affects our understanding of religion. He gives an example of how the discovery of the theory of the Earth's orbit round the sun had shaken some of the existing worldviews not only from the cosmological standpoint but also from philosophical and epistemological ones. Another example is how Emanuel Kant reformed his epistemological philosophy when he learned about Newtonian physics. Muslim jurisprudence, Soroush concludes, was impacted by its surrounding knowledge in the past and subsequently should be more contingent on knowledge of the present time. He quotes an old Sufi expression that "there are as many paths to God as there are people"[27] and, as such, implies a pluralistic approach to religious salvation.

Soroush's epistemological approach to religion seems to have a progressive nature. He periodically introduces new ideas for finding ways of understanding religious norms. His doctrine of "theoretical contraction and expansion of the Shariʿah" by which he questioned the uniformity of Islamic law was introduced in the 1980s and it later appeared in the 2000s as the theory of "evolution and devolution of religious knowledge," questioning the consistency and the very divine nature of the Qur'an. His purpose in addressing both modernity and tradition is to pave the way for cohabitation of reason and revelation, as he finds the fervor of the former to unravel the latter's mystery as an equally beautiful sight.[28] Soroush acknowledges God's dictums via human epistemology: "It is up to God to reveal a religion, but up to us to understand and realize it. It is at this point that religious knowledge is born, entirely human and subject to all dictates of human knowledge."[29]

In this way, Soroush considers any approach to religion subject to the dictates of human knowledge of that time. And as for today's approaches, he makes "modern sciences" in charge of evolving the understanding of both religious rules and spiritual experiences. Soroush bestows a defining role to modern sciences as, in his final analysis, they define the very nature of "modernity" and "new rationality."[30] The revelation too, in his approach, can be extended to a "human prophetic experience."[31] As such, the theory of contraction and expansion of religious knowledge attempts to reconcile the categories of tradition and modernity. To realize this, we can take from both perspectives and not reject modern sciences under the guise of protecting the purity of religion.[32]

In applying his theory of contraction and expansion to the Qur'an, Soroush discriminates between personal and impersonal or spiritual verses of the Qur'an, which has precedents among Muslims. Here, he resembles the Prophet to a teacher who speaks in accordance with the level of his audience. For example, he considers the verses: "To God all affairs are returned" (35:4) and "God is the light of the heavens and the Earth" (24:35) and "Wherever you turn there is God's face" (2:115) as the peak of prophetic voyage. In contrast, verses such as "Perish the hands of Abu Lahab, perish he" (111:1) which are, in his estimation, personal.[33]

It is evident that by expansion of the role of human conception, Soroush aims at juxtaposing reason with revelation within a new scope much broader than the historical Mu'tazilīs. He does not reduce religion to "spiritual experience" neither does he indicate what is left out from "the prophecy" of human conception. The way he admires the beauty of spirituality indicates the mysterious effects of religious rituals and experiences in the mind, and this is combined with allegorical expressions from Persian mystical literature. In no way, however, does he consider that the temporal culture can be a substitute for religion.[34]

Another revolutionary idea in Shī'ism offered by Soroush is the denial of the position of Shi'i Imams as sources of legal norms (*aḥkām*) in jurisprudence. He presents his idea in the context of finality (*khātamiyyah*) of divine assignment with Prophet Muhammad. He refutes the notion of "infallible Imam" as a work of exaggerative (*ghulāt*) Shi'is of the third/ninth century, and claims that the Prophet could not bestow upon the members of his family a position that would contradict the finality of prophethood.[35] Here, Soroush expressively borrows this idea from the Muslim poet and philosopher Mohammad Iqbal (d. 1938) who gave an innovative interpretation to the Islamic principle of the finality of the revelation in the person of Muhammad. That is, Islam should produce enough rationality and mobility among Muslims thus enabling them to substitute "human reason" for prophecy.[36]

In his recent writings, Soroush puts emphasis on the extra-religious values which, in his view, are independent of religion but without being incompatible with it. He blames Muslim epistemological inflexibility on the prevalence of the Ashʿarī theological tradition: "One of the main principle of immoderate Ashʿarī Islam is that there are no objective, external values; all values must come through religion."[37] In contrast, the defeated Muʿtazilī school of thought attempted to show that rationality *per se* was acceptable in Islam, even when not based on religion. Soroush admires reformist thinkers of Sunni Islam such as Nasr Hamid Abu Zayd who strove to revive Muʿtazilī thought. By emphasizing extra-religious values and appropriating them in religious contexts, Soroush signals the non-applicability of dichotomous distinction of all values between secular and religious. In fact he speaks about obviating such a distinction on political governance.[38]

Soroush's emphasis on the epistemological dimensions of knowledge is considered by Farzin Vahdat as a detour around the direct metaphysical discussion of subjectivity: "In doing so, he added a hermeneutic element, likening the external world to a text in need of interpretation."[39] Subjectivity as a pillar of modernity is defined here as "the property characterizing the autonomous, self-willing, self-defining and self-conscious individual agent."[40] In Islamic tradition, "the human subjectivity" is grounded in "God's subjectivity," and is characterized as "mediated subjectivity."[41] Soroush's distinction between "religion in itself" and our "knowledge of religion" seemed to this author as parallel to "Kant's distinction between noumena and phenomena" as Soroush writes, "religion is sacred and heavenly, but knowledge of religion is mundane and human."[42] Another observation on Soroush's theory of utilizing science to comprehend religion is that he has overlooked the main difference between religion as a worldview and science as an approach:

> As a world-view, religion comes to know the world *a priori*. The world it wants to comprehend is an invention of religion itself. Its interest, however, lies not so much in a praxis based on these bigger truths, but rather in accepting and cultivating in them. The scientific outlook on the other hand sees the world *a posterior*. The world it wants to understand is not a creation of itself, since it regards nature as an independent entity.[43]

Due to his epistemological approach, Soroush's ideas on government cannot be based on the prefixed texts. He dismisses the idea that forming a government was a necessary part of revelation. "The Prophet," Soroush claims, "has left no rulings on governance. It is up to the people to decide their government."[44] The relationship between man and God is direct, and no mediating position in spirituality or faith is conceivable. He does not find any support in the tradition-sources for the *ʿulamāʾs* claim to governance. He even refutes the use of the term *wilāyah* (originally: amity, closeness) for political leadership as it conveys several profoundly esoteric meanings, none of them appropriate for political authority.[45]

Soroush's perception of religion, especially that of Islam, is much broader than the traditional legalistic approach affords. The jurisprudential growth of fiqh as it captured the core and kernel of the Shariʿah, according to Soroush, has undermined the spiritual dimension of the religion. He frequently quotes al-Ghazālī who viewed the legalistic approach to the Shariʿah as a worldly (*dunyawī*) look at the religion which should be revised till the ultimate spirit of Islam was revived.[46] He does not hesitate to assert that the Islamic world needs a new approach to foster a dynamic jurisprudence based on a new *uṣūl* (primary principles) rather than on *furūʿ* (secondary principles) or minor issues of fiqh.[47]

As such, Soroush aimed to change the common understanding of a fixed Islam and Shariʿah through an epistemological distinction between religion and religious knowledge. It is a truism that knowledge of religion requires human interpretation based on their rational ability. As he said, God is the One who reveals religion and people are the ones to understand God's work. This seems to be another avenue to allow for the cohabitation of revelation and reason which has had precedents in Islamic thought. Through reason, nevertheless, Soroush allows the intrusion of modern sciences, which can offer various perspectives for an already established belief system. Here, we find he is able to criticize religious knowledge without touching upon the very essence of religion or tradition.

Mojtahed Shabestari

An amazing adoption of modern hermeneutics into religious thought is displayed in the writings of Sayyed Mohammad Mojtahed Shabestari (b. 1937), a retired professor of theology at Tehran University. He was trained in the Shiʿi seminary of Qum, but he also studied German philosophy and Protestant Theology during 1968–77 when he was the director of the Islamic (Shiʿi) Center at Hamburg, Germany. In spite of his jurisprudential background and devotional attachment to Islam, Shabestari's writings increasingly lean towards modern hermeneutical understanding of the religion and its socio-legal norms. He published many works in Persian, among which four of his books in addition to some of his recent interviews demonstrate his approach to the Shariʿah and Muslim society.

Shabestari deliberates on the tendency of the human mind towards conceptualizing things before they turn into beliefs or into established knowledge. He emphasizes presuppositions, which play a vital role in the formation of premises that build one's understanding of a discipline: "Without knowledge of hermeneutics," he argues, "a defensible fiqh and legal methodology cannot theoretically take shape."[48] He considers as "human phenomena" all topics of legal methodology (*uṣūl al-fiqh*) such as "general and its particularization," "statement and conception," and "authority of literal demonstration" (*ḥujiyyat al-ẓuhūr*). These topics and principles, by which the rules of the

Shari'ah are established, belong entirely to the spoken human language even though they communicate "God's words." Nevertheless, the meanings derived from God's words are characterized by Muslim jurists as meta-historical, meta-spatial and self-existing (*wāqi'ī wa nafs al-amrī*). He sees these characteristics to be beyond the capacity of spoken language and contradictory to the humanistic nature of the words used to interpret them. He sees the lack of a clear Islamic theory of "God's words" as the core of the problem.[49]

> More than eight hundred years have passed that Muslim theologians have not produced a new theory on the meaning of "God's words" including His commands and prohibitions (*awāmir wa nawāhī*). The old theories do not fit in our present context.[50]

Shabestari argues that Muslim theologians and philosophers of the early period discussed the nature of God's words with a broader scope than the present day. In his *Nihāyat al-Iqdām fī 'Ilm al-Kalām*, Shahristānī (d. 548/1153) presents a variety of scholarly opinions which have no parallels today. Peripatetic Philosophers (such as Avicenna) eventually attempted to solve the problem by considering "God's words" and the Prophet's speech to be one and the same, and connected them to "the active intellect" (*al-'aql al-fa''āl*). According to this theory, "revelation" emanates from "the active intellect," which is heard by prophets in rhythmic voice, and is only metaphorically called "God's words."[51] This theory contrasts with the view held by Muslim theologians, both the Mu'tazilīs and Ash'arīs. The former maintain that God's words are created by God directly; that is to say they are beyond "the law of causality," thus, constitute an extraordinary phenomena (*khāriq al-'ādah*). Whereas Ash'arīs generally believe that God's words are parts of God's essential attributes and therefore eternal. They are not words or voices, rather they are eternal truth that exists (*kalām nafsī*) within God's essence.[52] Among Muslim gnostic theologians Ibn 'Arabī, according to Shabestari, has a different view on God's words. He claims that the

Qur'an was "God's words for the Prophet; for others it would be ʿGod's words' if it produces a similar prophetic experience for them."[53] That is to say, the impression left by God's words upon individuals is the set criterion to determine whether they constitute divine words. Given this individual experience, Ibn ʿArabī claims that "revelation" is, in general, a continuous phenomenon although "the law-giving revelation" was completed by the Prophet of Islam. Even the very esoteric understanding (*fahm bāṭinī*) of the Qur'an can be a revelation. Shabestari finds surprising similarity between Ibn ʿArabī's view on the impact of "God's word" on the individual and that of Protestant theologians Carl Barth and Paul Tillich.[54]

Concerning the semantics of religious texts, Shabestari does not see the traditional literal interpretation (*mabḥath al-alfāz*) as flexible enough to capture the variety of contextual meanings. He argues that the traditional semantics deems "words" as representing the external realities, and it is enough to know the grammar of the language and verbal rules of legal methodology to understand the meaning and applicability of legal norms. Whereas the modern theory of semantics defines "meaning" as a tool in the structure of each language which *speaks about* external realities, but these are *not the same* realities.[55]

Shabestari frequently demonstrates a great fascination with religiosity, faith and devotion; nevertheless, he confines them to "personal prophetic experience." He bases faith on the divinely associated free will which is part of one's existence but different from his belief (*iʿtiqād*).[56] He sees no application for a religion in people's day-to-day social life except in taking a moral direction (*jahatgīrī*), which is to observe justice.[57] This view originates from his conviction in the free will of the human being and in his continuous motion of "becoming."[58] Shabestari exhibits good familiarity with the Hegelian conception of free will and individual subjectivity. He identifies human existence with freedom of mind, whose subtle nature emanates from the Divine.[59] His commitment to freedom of conscience appears more than just basing individual subjectivity on God's subjectivity in the form of "God's successor on earth" (*khalīfat Allāh fī al-arḍ*) as understood from the writings of some contemporary Muslim authors.

Shabestari's conviction in the freedom of conscience as being the necessary constituent of the faith does not allow him to seek any sanctity for religious knowledge save for the spiritual experiences of devoted individuals. He considers all branches of religious knowledge such as fiqh and its legal methodology as human disciplines which are open to challenges and interpretations. He raises the question of "what is meant by sanctity (*qadāsah*)"? He finds the popular respect for religious figures as the only source for their holiness. "This depends on people's choice" Shabestari concludes "and does not enjoy the divine sanction."[60] At this point, Shabestari's idea draws parallels with that of Abu Zayd who opined that "the textual output of the Qur'an had been overshadowed by the immense sanctity attached to it as the Holy Book."[61]

Shabestari's accounts on religion, modernity and freedom of conscience are not void of inconsistency. Regarding modern values, he does not employ the same critical scrutiny as he does on Islamic values. For instance on examining human rights criteria, he appears too optimistic and willing to ignore its manipulation and political implications in human rights theory,[62] whereas he does not spare any shortcoming in Islamic approaches. As a Muslim religious figure he seems uncertain about the limits to the adoption of modern values by Muslims. He actually refers to the Muslim crisis of combining identity with modernity. "No one yet," Shabestari says, "gave a clear pre-scription to accommodate both modernity and Islamic identity on the one hand, and continuity and change on the other."[63]

In his later interviews and writings, Shabestari claims the Qur'an is *the product* of revelation and not the very revelation itself. The function of the Qur'an is to present a prophetic reading of the world, and its natural and human phenomena, not setting laws for them. The Qur'anic expressions on legal issues, therefore, do not mean that the Qur'an has set law for all people in all ages. Such an understanding of the Book is the work of later jurisprudents who wanted to stabilize society with so called Islamic law.[64]

Jasser Auda

We now turn to the work of a promising contemporary Egyptian author Jasser Auda (b. 1966), who claims to be introducing a new approach to Islamic law particularly to the theory of *maqāṣid*, which he translates as "purposefulness." He dismisses "Islamic modernism" as being unnecessarily apologetic about traditional Islam because it was by and large a reaction to European modernism which endorsed the ideas of centrality and supremacy of modern sciences.[65] Furthermore he criticizes the way Muslim reformists (such as Abduh, Tahtawi and Mohammad Iqbal) incorporated the concept of "causality" in order to re-interpret or re-word the philosophy of religion in Islam. That is to say they "re-interpreted" Islamic articles of faith (the Qur'an and Sunnah) in a way to fit the conclusions of (pre-twentieth century) science, and "causality" which was the logic of modernist *kalām* (philosophy of religion). Abduh's *Risālat al-Tawḥīd* is the clearest example of the above changes in attitude.[66] Auda then explains the contemporary changing status of philosophic thought as follows:

In the west, the second half of the twentieth century witnessed post-modernism's complete rejection of all modernist "meta-narration." ..[A]ll streams of postmodernism agreed on the ʿdeconstruction of centrism'. Thus, according to postmodernists, the center should remain void of anything, whether it is science, man, the west, or even God. 'Rationality' itself, according to postmodernists, became an undesirable form of centrism and marginalization. 'Irrationality' became a desirable and 'moral' alternative. 'Islamic postmodernism,' in turn, utilized deconstructionist concepts in order to criticize central and basic Islamic articles of faith in a radical way. The centrality of the Qur'an and the Prophet in Islam and Islamic law was made subject to a 'free play of the opposites,' to borrow an expression from Derrida.[67]

He then defines "systems theory" before offering his proposal for an

"Islamic systems philosophy" as a rational and non-Eurocentric "postmodern" philosophy:

> Systems theory and philosophy emerged in the second half of the twentieth century as an anti-thesis of both modernist and postmodernist philosophies. Systems theorists and philosophers reject the modernist reductionist view that all human experiences could be analyzed into indivisible causes and effects. On the other hand, systems philosophy also rejects postmodernist irrationality and deconstruction, which are 'meta-narration' in their own right. Thus according to systems philosophy, the universe is neither a huge deterministic machine nor a totally unknown being, complexity can be explained-neither via a series of 'nothing-but' cause and effect operation nor via claims of 'non-logocentric irrationality,' and the problems of the world could be solved neither via more technological advances nor via some sort of nihilism. Hence, thanks to systems philosophy, the concept of 'purposefulness,' with all of its teleological shadows, was back to philosophical and scientific discourses.[68]

By appropriating "the concept of purposefulness," Auda provides a space for the *maqāṣid* theory in his "systems approach." He first refers to the difference between goal and purpose as the latter produces the same outcome in different ways and different outcome in the same or different environment. Thus, purpose-seeking systems could produce different outcomes for the very same environment as long as these different outcomes achieve the desired purpose.[69] Islamic theology (*kalām*) has discussed this problem in the context of "causation" in divine actions (*taʿlīl afʿāl Allāh*). After quoting some Muʿtazilī and Ashʿarī views, Auda finally arrives at Māturīdī's view that "divine actions have causes/purposes out of God's grace."[70] Finally as the core of his methodology of systematic analysis, Auda presents the following outline of the relationship between purposefulness and other features of the system of Islamic law:

1. Purposefulness is related to the cognitive nature of Islamic law

because various proposals for the nature and structure of the purposes of the Islamic law (*maqāṣid al-sharīʿah*) reflect cognitions of the nature and structure of law itself.

2. Universal purposes of Islamic law (*al-maqāṣid al-ʿāmmah*) represent the law's holistic characteristics and universal principles.

3. Purposes of the Islamic law play a pivotal role in the process of ijtihad, in all of its various forms, which is the mechanism by which the system of Islamic law maintains its 'openness.'

4. Purposes of the Islamic law are perceived in a number of hierarchical ways, which correspond to the hierarchies in the system of Islamic law.

5. Purposes provide multiple dimensions that help resolve and understand 'apparent contradictions' and 'opposing tendencies' in the scripts and the fundamental theories of the law.[71]

As seen above, Auda relates his doctrine of purposefulness to "the cognitive nature" of Islamic law, and to a "pivotal role of various forms of ijtihad." By "cognitive nature," he means that Islamic law (fiqh) is a result of human reasoning and reflection of ijtihad upon the scripts.[72] This way of characterization of Islamic law seems to be in line with what a number of Muslim reformist thinkers had already offered, but Auda refuted them as deconstructionists of the modern and post-modern periods. It is not clear to what extent "the human reasoning and reflection" could or should use modern disciplines and methods without ignoring the centrality and superiority of the revealed sources. Number four of Auda's outline refers to a number of hierarchical ways, which correspond to that "in the system of Islamic law," i.e., they should be observed in a purpose-based reading of the law. If these hierarchies refer to those presented in the traditional *uṣūl al-fiqh*, then, a conventional limitation is discernable in the proposed system. He acknowledges that there are "apparent contradictions" and "opposing tendencies" in the script which require multiple dimensions to assist in understanding the fundamental theories of the law and in resolving problems arising from purpose-based reading of the Shariʿah.

Criticizing the application of modern hermeneutics on legal language, Jasser Auda offers his doctrine of purposefulness of the Shariᶜah which in essence is another modern multi-dimensional approach based on "systems theory." The doctrine of purposefulness, according to him, not only looks for the wisdom behind rulings, but provides links between the Islamic law and today's notions of human rights, development and civility. Despite the modern reductionist reading of the law, the multi-dimensional reading will include the literal meanings of either *muḥkamāt* (perspicuous words conveying unequivocal meanings) or "indirect implication" (*ishārah*), "omitted expression" (*iqtiḍā'*) and alluding to the appropriateness factor (*īmā'*). These concepts presently lack juridical authority (*ḥujjiyyah*) because of their uncertainty (*ẓanniyyah*).[73] As such we see Jasser Auda validating the elements which had been kept aside due to lack of textual basis. These elements, in a sense, resembling situations surrounding the meaning of a text called "presuppositions," nevertheless espouse more textual support in a reconstructionist spirit.

Conclusion

MUSLIMS' PERCEPTION of law and the authority of the Shariʿah finds its best expression in *uṣūl al-fiqh*, a discipline developed over time to set up a legal methodology. The objective of the methodology in the beginning was to identify the sources of that law, its hierarchical order, to establish its supremacy, and facilitate the text deducing process by way of literary interpretation and rational explanation. In time it emerged as a broad discipline not only to introduce Islamic approaches to the law but also to train Muslim minds for further critical analysis. In this effort, *uṣūl al-fiqh* adopted a number of principles from Arabic semantics and Greek syllogism, and developed its own literal-rational doctrines (see Chapter 5). However, none of the above developments changed its character, which essentially remained a discipline deeply based on the literal demonstration of the texts. In essence, it always remained the method of conforming the law to its revealed sources. Nevertheless, the contemporary hermeneutical readings of the Shariʿah, and new proposals to incorporate "statutory laws" into the sources suggest an extra dimension for the legal methodology.

The method of conforming the law to its Shariʿah sources functioned as the philosophy of *uṣūl al-fiqh* during its long history. The *raison d'être* of legal methodology was to refine and discipline the flow of individual opinions by filtering them through the channel of text-based deliberations. Historically, the main purpose of al-Shāfiʿī's reaction to the overflow of individual opinions of his time was to advance the Muslim perception of legality which led up to the categorization of the sources (see Chapter 1). This objective was consolidated by the incorporation of parts of formal logic into *uṣūl al-fiqh* in the fifth/eleventh century. This imbued the methodology with an intellectual sophistication that could have led to its further isolation; however, the concurrent Ḥanafī elaboration of legal methodology shifted the emphasis from theoretical discussions to practical solutions for ongoing contingencies (Chapter 3).

A new dimension blossomed in legal methodology since the eighth/ fourteenth century, namely to merge the social notion of public welfare (*maṣlaḥah*) into the process of deducing legal norms from the sources. The important figure in this effort was Abū Isḥāq al-Shāṭibī who combined consideration of the exterior factor of *maṣlaḥah* (public welfare) with an interior factor which was the aims and objectives of the law (*maqāṣid al-sharīʿah*). In Chapter 6, we observed how he legitimized common practices (*al-taṣarrufāt al-ʿādiyyah*) on a wider scope and in light of their main socio-philosophical end-goals for human good. The tendency to merge social notions into legal methodology finds another boost in the eighteenth century with Shāh Walīyullāh of Delhi whose revivalist approach to the Shariʿah proposed the notion of human development (*irtifāq*) that can turn into the advancement of human society (Chapter 7).

Aiming to make the methodology more practical, the Jaʿfarī Shiʿi school has turned to literal-rational presentation of *uṣūl al-fiqh* since the nineteenth century. The interplay of *uṣūlī* principles became the pivot around which most legal problems revolved to arrive at cogent solutions. This method is best manifested in the works of Shaykh Murtaḍā Anṣārī who matured the so-called *Uṣūlī* trend in the seminary situated in the shrine city of Najaf. This trend led to another kind of literary sophistication which only qualified students at the seminaries could exploit to their advantage. It contributed to the rise of a series of Shiʿi intellectuals who rarely addressed contemporary issues; rather they preferred to use this methodological sophistication for self-serving socio-political gains.

In the face of modern developments in legal spheres, *uṣūl al-fiqh* seems to have lost much of its relevance to contemporary legal needs, and instead has been reduced practically to a literary interpretive skill.

A number of modern legal changes occurred without taking into consideration the principles of *uṣūl al-fiqh*: two of them are developing legislation of statutory law and the introduction of procedural law, both of which aim at setting legal rules or reshaping legal truth through human facility. This is in sharp contrast with classical Islamic legal methodology which mainly attempts to find out the already established truth with limited regard to the role of human conceptions. After the Islamic revivalist movements of the 1980s and 1990s, however, the restoration of Shariʿah laws in some Muslim states brought to the fore the significance of a legal methodology for a better understanding of the Shariʿah.

Present approaches to the Shariʿah can be grouped in two sets: conventional and modern. The conventional approach belongs to those who sought to reform the Islamic methodology from within the Shariʿah, that is to say, to align the methods of understanding the Shariʿah with contemporary requirements. Modern approaches on the other hand chose hermeneutical readings of the Shariʿah to incorporate the findings of the human mind beyond "the text" and obviously beyond the conventional legal methodology. Both groups allow the use of modern sciences and methods in religious learning but with different scopes and perspectives. More than the hermeneutical readers, the Shariʿah aligners blame *uṣūl al-fiqh* for losing touch with social realities.

It should be borne in mind that *uṣūl al-fiqh* as part of the Islamic legal system is structured on the premise that it only discovers "the existing truth" (*iḥrāz al-wāqiʿ*) and, as such, does not directly give any scope to human conceptions in reconstructing such truth. To assign an institutive authority to the principle of *ijmāʿ*, for instance, one must first build upon the human faculty of its "constant self-realization," as Muhammad Iqbal proposed.[1] Secondly, one needs to redefine "right" as a "totality of conditions under which the will of one person can be unified with the will of another under a universal law of freedom."[2] Thus, for instituting a meaningful assembly of *ijmāʿ* or the like, a self-assertive attitude and an understanding of our common rights in the public sphere are needed, which Muslims still appear to be lacking. A glance at the history of *ijmāʿ* points to the fact that owing to their faith-based self-realization, the Prophet's Companions and their following generation (*al-tābiʿūn*) developed both the idea and practice of *ijmāʿ* to settle important issues such as the collection of the Qur'an and choice of the Rightly-Guided Caliphs. Because of their strong commitment to Islam, they were able to appreciate the value and authority of their own agreement, whereas appreciation of such a value on any possible agreement was lost in subsequent generations.

Consensus exhausted its applicability in the third/ninth century when al-Bukhārī and Muslim al-Naysābūrī began to systematize and codify hadith. As a result, they entertained the notion of *shuhrah* (lit. widely known) in place of *ijmāʿ*. In fact, what we had thereafter was in practice "prevalent or commonly accepted opinions" which functioned in the same way that *ijmāʿ* was intended to do. Thus, what Muslims lost was their creative claims to *ijmāʿ* and later to ijtihad, rather than their actual consensus and practical ijtihad. The loss of self-assertion in ijtihad and *ijmāʿ* is a major turning point in Islamic legal history which hardly any Muslim author to date has dared to elaborate on its phenomenological causes. In my humble opinion, the prevalence of a self-existing (*nafs al-amrī*) assumption of truth after the waning of the Muʿtazilī school of thought in the fourth/tenth century left little room for Muslims to assert any re-conceptualization of truth in accordance with the knowledge of their time. Were we to compare the attitude of the second Caliph ʿUmar ibn al-Khaṭṭāb in re-formulating several Qur'anic-based legal issues according to his own ijtihad with the seventh/thirteenth century proclamation of the closure of the door of ijtihad, we would see how different attitudes in perceiving religious knowledge yield differing perspectives towards the same knowledge.

For this reason, we believe that any reform in Islamic legal methodology should be modeled on the creative attitude of the Muslim precursors, and must assign a constructive role for human rationality in the elaboration of the legal system of society. This goal cannot be achieved without understanding the history of Islamic legal methodology which explains the philosophy of its structure and changes. In this survey, we have seen how Muslim authors proposed new topics such as *maslahah*, *maqāṣid*, *sadd al-dharā'iᶜ*, *istiḥsān* and *istiṣḥāb* in order to provide more rational forms in adapting to social realities of their time. As we mentioned on several occasions, the type of Islamic legal methodology was a function of the extent of the role played by human intellect. That is to say, it commences with the sources of law and their literary interpretations, it develops the scope of *qiyās* to include topics such as "relevance" and considerations of public interest, then it moves to more distant (from the sources) rational topics like *maqāṣid* and *sadd al-dharā'iᶜ*, and ends up with the independent judgments of ijtihad and juristic preferences in case of conflict of laws.

However, none of these contexts assign a creative authority to the human mind except what was seen in al-Shāṭibī's theory of *maqāṣid*. The success of his doctrine lies in his insight into the philosophy of Islamic law rather than his knowledge of the sources and traditions. His analysis of the philosophy of the *mubāḥ* category (based on the tradition-reports concerning the Prophet's reluctance to be questioned on every aspect of people's social relationships; see Chapter 6) reveals that in his approach the avenue was open for the human mind to exercise its rational authority. It is evident that al-Shāṭibī would not argue for such an understanding of the philosophy of the law if he believed in the self-existing (*nafs al-amrī*) status of socio-religious truth. His method of justifying the law according to its end-goals did not affect the long entrenched juristic pattern of strict attachment to rigid interpretation of the sources. Muslims had to wait until the impact of Western intellectual achievements forced them to open the gate for fresh ijtihad, new statutory laws and even re-orientation to creative minds of scholars such as the same al-Shāṭibī.

Modern approaches to the Shariᶜah propose certain reforms to legal methodology, either from within, or by borrowing methods beyond the conventional scope such as empiricism and hermeneutics. The clearest proposal for reform from within is offered by Hashim

Kamali who, like AbuSulayman, considers the duality between the *'ulamā'* and government since the Umayyad period as the main stumbling block for the advancement of the legal system among Muslims. Kamali suggests that statutory law and government ordinances should either take the place of *ijmā'* and ijtihad or be incorporated within them. We have seen that *ijmā'* has historically exhausted its conventional components, and it is doubtful that it can add to the legitimacy of parliaments or of statutory law. Although it offers a broad context, ijtihad applies to juridical (*shar'ī*) ijtihad, and it is difficult to identify it with government ordinances without raising more problems and even conflicting with the *mujtahids'* traditional exclusive right to apply it. AbuSulayman's criticism on the lack of empiricism in conventional *uṣūl* is sound, but needs more elaboration on how empirical deduction and induction may be applied to *uṣūl al-fiqh* (Chapter 9).

The application of modern hermeneutics as a critical method to legal texts opened a new window for interpretation of the Shari'ah. This discipline is essentially concerned with not only the content of a text, but also with the presuppositions that fostered ideas underlying such a text. It claims that there can be no knowledge without pre-supposition nor pure access to reality.[3] A survey of the accounts of Arkoun, Abu Zayd, Soroush and Shabestari show that they are in agreement that the conventional literal interpretation of the law is not flexible enough to capture the variety of contextual meanings of a given text. On the criticism of the present methodology, they claim that *uṣūl al-fiqh*, as traditionally conceived, ignores the fact that the development of one's knowledge opens the way for a new understanding of the text. Concerning new readings of the Shari'ah, they have yet to offer a concrete proposal other than the general theory of the timely contraction and expansion of the Shari'ah. This theory may serve in opening the ground for the application of other relevant disciplines for fresh readings of texts, but it can hardly propose a formula for such applications. In fact, the manner in which these theorists question the growth of fiqh and authority of the traditional

ʿ*ulamā'* gives the impression that they are aiming at the contraction of conventional jurisprudence through the expansion of the application of other disciplines into the Shariʿah.

Challenging the above modernist approach, we saw Jasser Auda offering his doctrine of the purposefulness of the Shariʿah, which in essence is another modern multi-dimensional approach based on "systems theory." This doctrine, according to him, not only looks for the wisdom behind rulings, but provides links between the Islamic law and today's notion of human rights, development and civility. Despite the modern reductionist reading of the law, the multi-dimensional reading will include the literal meanings of *muḥkamāt* (perspicuous words conveying unequivocal meanings) as well as "indirect implication" (*ishārah*), "omitted expression" (*iqtiḍā*) or alluding to the appropriateness factor (*īmā*). These concepts presently lack juridical authority (*ḥujjiyyah*) because of their uncertainty (*ẓanniyyah*).[4] As such, we see that Jasser Auda validates the elements which had been disregarded due to lack of textual basis. These elements, in a sense, resemble conditions surrounding the meaning of a text called "presuppositions"; nevertheless, they espouse more textual support in the reconstructionist spirit.

All the above observations and criticism may serve to foster the belief that Islamic legal methodology is moving beyond its conventional limits of the *uṣūl al-fiqh*. This methodology now offers several different conduits such as "consideration of higher objectives," "hermeneutics" and "systems" besides the traditional text-based reading of the Shariʿah. The juxtaposition of interdisciplinary skills with legal methodology can shift the focus of *uṣūl al-fiqh* from the authority of literal demonstration of a text to the authority of higher purpose of such a text. The purpose-oriented ijtihad, consideration of public interest and the presupposition of a text, as we saw above, can be seen as the "omitted expression" of the text which should be heard in due time. The ability to read the implied expressions of the Shariʿah needs not only the intervention of human reasoning, but also a strong conviction in human aptitude to re-fashion divine instructions according to the requirements of time. This is what the Muslim societies seem to be in pressing need of today.

The concept of "omitted expression" (of a text) which Jasser Auda has chosen to denote *iqtiḍā*, in a peculiar but possible sense, reminds us of Gadamer's argument that people have a "historically effected consciousness" and that they are embedded in the particular history and culture that shaped them (see Chapter 10). *Iqtiḍā* or its plural participle *muqtaḍiyāt* are untold conditions which arise with the passage of time, and affect the process of understanding and re-understanding of the meaning of a text.

The last point which we had occasion to address in this research is the structural problem in the Muslim methodological approach to the Shariʿah. That is, the theological assumption adopted by most *uṣūlī* authors that "societal realities" have a meta-historical and self-existing (*wāqiʿī wa nafs al-amrī*) character beyond that of any identifiable interaction with the human mind. By this assumption "the social truth" must merely be discovered from the fixed texts, and literally demonstrated. This vantage point in practice leaves no room for the human mind to venture into timely adjustments of the divine law for changing societies. By offering alternative outlooks, as we saw above, a number of contemporary authors attempted new proposals to align legal methodology with the requirements of time. It still depends on the contemporary Muslim thinkers to develop more practical perspectives on how to conform today's social realities to the revealed sources.

Notes

Introduction

1   The distinction between Shariʿah and fiqh is blurred in popular usage.

2   This applies only to matters dealing with relations among people (*muʿāmalāt*) and not to acts of worship (*ʿibādah*). See Ahmed Fekry Ibrahim, *Pragmatism in Islamic Law: A Social and Intellectual History* (Syracuse, NY: Syracuse University Press, 2015), p. 2 and pp. 58–60. The five normative categorizations are obligatory (*wājib*), recommended (*mustaḥab*), permissible (*mubāḥ*), discouraged or abominable (*makrūh*), and prohibited (*ḥarām*).

3   Bernard Weiss: "We thus have two levels of law: Sharīʿa law and *fiqh* law. Sharīʿa law is law considered as residing in the being of God and as embedded within revelation without acquiring a fully articulated form therein. *Fiqh* law is law considered as something articulated by scholars, something residing in their formulations. Sharīʿa law is a sort of Platonic ideal that scholars try to realize, however imperfectly and fallibly, in their *fiqh*. *Fiqh* law accordingly derives its validity from its characer as the closest approximation of Sharīʿa law that scholars are capable of achieving." Bernard G. Weiss, *The Search for God's Law: Islamic Jurisprudence in the Writings of Sayf al-Din al-Amidi* (Salt Lake City: University of Utah Press, 2010), p. 15.

4   David R. Vishanoff, *The Formation of Islamic Hermeneutics: How Sunni Legal Theorists Imagined a Revealed Law* (New Haven, CT: American Oriental Society, 2011), p. 9 (footnote 16) and pp. 41–42.

5   Rumee Ahmed, *Narratives of Islamic Legal Theory* (Oxford: Oxford University Press, 2012), p. 6.

6   *Ḥujjiyyat al-Ẓuhūr lil-Alfāẓ*, see Chapter 8.

7   Robert Gleave, *Islam and Literalism* (Edinburgh: Edinburgh University Press, 2013), p. 99.

8   Mohammad Hashim Kamali, *Principles of Islamic Jurisprudence* (Cambridge: Islamic Texts Society, 2003), p. 518.

CHAPTER I

1   See Abū ʿUbayd al-Qāsim ibn Sallām, *Kitāb al-Nāsikh wa al-Mansūkh*, ed., John Burton, (Cambridge: Gibb Memorial Trust, 1987), p. 3. "*Inna ʿAlī b. Abī Ṭālib (raḍiya Allahu ʿanhu) marra bi qāṣṣ...*" The term *qāṣṣ* has several intricate meanings, among which "Biblical storyteller" is more common. In view of the old Arab storytellers' judicial function, we have translated it as "mediator." Ibn Sallām (d. 224/838) was a theologian, jurist, and philologist who traveled from Khurāsān to Syria and Egypt and died in Makkah.

2   Shaykh Muhammad Abu Zahrah, *Uṣūl al-Fiqh* (Cairo: Dār al-Fikr al-ʿArabī, n.d.), p. 8.

3   Ahmed El Shamsy, *The Canonization of Islamic Law: A Social and Intellectual History* (New York: Cambridge University Press, 2013), p. 11.

4   Muḥammad ibn Isḥāq (known as Ibn al-Nadīm), *al-Fihrist*, ed., Rida Tajaddud (Tehran: Nashr-e Asāṭīr, 1973), pp. 257, 281–84. For example, Makḥūl Shāmī (d. 160/776) and ʿAbdullāh ibn al-Mubārak (d. 181/797) wrote *Kitāb al-Sunan fī al-Fiqh* (pp. 283 and 284), Abū ʿAbd al-Raḥmān Muḥammad ibn ʿAbd al-Raḥmān (d. 159/775) wrote *Kitāb al-Sunan* (p. 281), Abū al-Ṣilt Zāʾidah ibn Qudāmah (d. 161/777) wrote *Kitāb al-Sunan*, and ʿAbd al-Raḥmān ibn Zayd ibn Aslam (d. c. 170/786) wrote *Kitāb al-Nāsikh wa al-Mansūkh* (p. 281).

5   Ibid., p. 258. We know that al-Shaybānī wrote on "the legal commands" of the Qur'an and the Sunnah, upon which al-Sarakhsī (490/1096) based his work. See Muḥammad ibn Aḥmad al-Sarakhsī, *Uṣūl al-Sarakhsī*, 2 vols., (Istanbul: Dār Qahramān, 1372/1952), vol. 1, pp. 10–11.

6   Al-Khaṭīb al-Baghdādī, *Tārīkh Baghdād* (Beirut: Dār al-Kutub al-ʿIlmiyyah, 1986), vol. 14, pp. 245–46. Also see Ibn Khallakān, *Wafiyyāt al-Aʿyān* (Qum: Manshūrāt al-Raḍī, 1985), vol. 6, p. 382.

7   Al-Shāfiʿī, *Kitāb al-Umm* (Beirut: Dār al-Maʿrifah, n.d.), vol. 7, pp. 300 and 302.

Notes

8 El Shamsy, *The Canonization of Islamic Law*, p. 216.

9 Ibid., p. 169.

10 Al-Shāfiʿī employs *bayān* in its structural sense and not, as was later understood by jurists, as a clarification or an attempt to make something completely unambiguous. See Joseph E. Lowry, "Some Preliminary Observations on Shāfiʿī and Later Uṣūl al-Fiqh: The Case of the Term *bayān*," *Arabica* vol. 55, no. 5 (2008): 509. Vishanoff defines *bayān* as "the act of revealing or making something known." Vishanoff, p. 39 and pp. 40–44. See also Rachel A. Friedman, "Clarity, Communication, and Understandability: Theorizing Language in al-Bāqillānī's *Iʿjāz al-Qurʾān* and *Uṣūl al-Fiqh* Texts," PhD dissertation, University of California, Berkeley, 2015.

11 Al-Shāfiʿī, *al-Risālah*, edited by Aḥmad Shākir (Cairo: Dār al-Fikr, 1979), pp. 21–53.

12 Ibid., pp. 53–105.

13 Ibid., pp. 106–46.

14 Ibid., pp. 107–209.

15 Ibid., pp. 210–356.

16 Ibid., pp. 357–370.

17 Ibid., pp. 471–75.

18 Ibid., pp. 476–86.

19 Ibid., pp. 487–502.

20 Ibid., pp. 503–59.

21 Ibid., pp. 560–601.

22 This term should not be confused with "vague," "unclear," "opaque," or "inexact." Rather, it is used in the sense of a word or utterance that lends itself to multiple meanings or is polyvalent.

23 Al-Shāfiʿī, *al-Risālah*, p. 9 and pp. 19–25.

24 Ibid., pp. 22–24 and pp. 476–559; Al-Shāfiʿī, *al-Umm*, vol. 7, p. 277.

25 El Shamsy, *The Canonization of Islamic Law*, p. 9.

26 See Ahmad Pakatchi, "*Ijmāʿ*," in *Dāʾirat al-Maʿārif-e Buzurg-e Islāmī* (Tehran: Markaz-e Dāʾirat al-Maʿārif-e Buzurg-e Islāmī, 1994), v. 6, pp. 615–32.

27 El Shamsy, *The Canonization of Islamic Law*, pp. 169–85.

28 Vishanoff, *The Formation*, p. 64.

29 Sherman Jackson, "Setting the Record Straight," *Journal of Islamic Studies*, vol. 11/2 (2000), p. 122.

30 Murteza Bedir, "An Early Response to Al-Shāfiʿī: Īsā b. Abān in the Prophetic Report (*Khabar*)," *Islamic Law and Society*, vol. 9/3 (2002), pp. 285–311.

31 Wael Hallaq, *A History of Islamic Legal Theories: An Introduction to Sunni Usul al-Fiqh* (Cambridge: Cambridge University Press, 1997), p. 31.

32 Ibid., p. 29. Also see Hallaq, "Was al-Shafiʿi the Master Architect of Islamic Jurisprudence?" in *International Journal of Middle East Studies*, vol. 25 (1993), pp. 591–92.

33 See Majid Khadduri, *Islamic Jurisprudence: Shāfiʿī's Risāla* (Baltimore: The Johns Hopkins University Press, 1961), p. 41.

34 Ibid., p. 35. Also see Norman Calder, *Studies in Early Muslim Jurisprudence* (Oxford: Clarendon Press, 1993), p. 233. "… the concepts of generality and particularity, for example, appear together in the *Muwaṭṭaʾ* attributed to Malik (d. 179/795), but this might represent a third/ninth-century addition, …" (Vishanoff, *The Formation*, p. 27.).

35 Ibn al-Muqaffaʿ, *al-Manṭiq*, ed., M.T. Daneshpezhuh (Tehran: Iranian Academy of Philosophy, 1978), pp. 29–31, 63ff. Ibn al-Muqaffaʿ translated *Peri Hermeneias* from the Persian (Pahlavī) version into Arabic. According to Ibn al-Nadīm, Iranians had translated parts of classical Greece's logical and medical texts into Persian (Pahlavī) just before the advent of Islam, probably during the reign of Anowshirvān (531–79). See ibid., introduction, p. 11 and Ibn al-Nadīm, *al-Fihrist*, p. 303. It should be added that the above-mentioned translation is considered the oldest Arabic version of the *Manṭiq*. In later versions, the terms ʿ*āmm/khāṣṣ* were replaced by *kullī/juzʾī*.

36 Calder, *Studies*, p. 11.

37 Ibid., p. 242. For a counterargument, see David R. Vishanoff, "Early Islamic Hermeneutics: Language, Speech, and Meaning in Preclassical Legal Theory", (PhD dissertation, Emory University, 2004), pp. 136–42. Also see Ahmed El Shamsy, "Al-Shāfiʿī's Writtem Corpus: A Source-Critical Study," *Journal of the American Oriental Society*, vol. 132/2 (April-June 2012), pp. 199–220.

38 Christopher Melchert, *The Formation of the Sunni Schools of Law: 9th-10th Centuries C.E.* (Leiden: Brill, 1997), p. 68.

39 Wael Hallaq, "The Development of Logical Structure in Sunni Legal Theory," *Der Islam*, vol. 64, (1987), p. 45.

40 Al-Shāfiʿī, *al-Risālah*, "Introduction" by Ahmad Muhammad Shakir, p. 12.

41 Ibid., p. 517.

42 Hallaq, "The Development," p. 47; based on Ibn al-Nadīm and Abū al-Ḥasan al-Ashʿarī's writings.

43 Ibn al-Muqaffaʿ, *al-Manṭiq*, pp. 121–23 compared to pp. 1–93.

44 Norman Calder, *Studies in Early Muslim Jurisprudence*, p. 233.

45 Ibid., p. 234.

46 Jonathan E., Brockopp, "Early Islamic Jurisprudence in Egypt: Two Scholars and their *Mukhtaṣars,*" *International Journal of Middle East Studies*, vol. 30 (1998), pp. 167–82.

47 Ibid., p. 173.

48 Al-Khatīb al-Baghdādī, *Taʾrīkh Baghdād*, vol. 10, p. 449.

49 Joseph Lowry, "Does Shāfiʿī Have a Theory of 'Four Sources' of Law?" *Studies in Islamic Law and Society*, ed., by B. Weiss, (Leiden: Brill, 2002), p. 24.

50 Ibid., pp. 23–50.

51 Concerning the various terms used for *ijmāʿ* during the early period, see Ahmad Pakatchi, "*Ijmāʿ*" *Dāʾirat al-Maʿārif*, vol. 6, pp. 615–32. This entry presents an interesting account of this term's history and variants.

52 "...*Idhā nādaytum ila al-ṣalāh*..." ("...When you proclaim your call to prayer..." [Qurʾan 5:58]) and "...*Idhā nūdiya li al-ṣalāh*..." ("...When the call to prayer is proclaimed..." [Qurʾan 62:9]).

53 Al-Shāfiʿī, *al-Umm*, vol. 1, p. 153.

54 Mālik ibn Anas, *al-Muwaṭṭaʾ* (Beirut: Maktabat al-Thaqāfah, 1988), vol. 1, p. 129.

55 Al-Shāfiʿī, *al-Umm*, vol. 2, pp. 28–29.

56 Al-Shāfiʿī, *al-Risālah*, p. 472.

57 See Melchert, *The Formation*, pp. 91 and 109.

58 Ibid., quoting Ibn al-Nadīm, pp. 294–303; Abū Isḥāq Shīrāzī, *Ṭabaqāt al-Fuqahāʾ* (Beirut: Dār al-Turāth al-ʿArabī, 1981), p. 111 and p. 112.

59 We only know that some of Ibn Surayj's work on the subject matters under *uṣūl al-fiqh*, such as *qiyās*, is referred to in later *uṣūlī* books. See Abū Bakr Aḥmad ibn ʿAlī al-Jaṣṣāṣ al-Rāzī, *Uṣūl al-Jaṣṣāṣ al-Musammā al-Fuṣūl fī al-Uṣūl* (Beirut: Dār al-Kutub al-ʿIlmiyyah, 2000), vol. 2, p. 213.

CHAPTER 2

1   Melchert, *The Formation*, p. 69.

2   George Makdisi, "The Juridical Theology of Shāfiʿī: Origins and Significance of *Uṣūl al-Fiqh*," *Studia Islamica*, vol. 59 (1984), p. 43.

3   Devin Stewart, "Muḥammad b. Dāʾūd al-Ẓāhirī's Manual of Jurisprudence," in *Studies in Islamic Legal Theory* (Studies in Islamic Law and Society series), (ed.), Bernard Weiss (Leiden: E. J. Brill, 2002), p. 106.

4   Ibid., p. 109.

5   Ibid., pp. 104–05; quoting from al-Qāḍī al-Nuʿmān's *Ikhtilāf Uṣūl al-Madhāhib*, (ed.), S. T. Lokhandwalla (Simla: Indian Institute of Advanced Study, 1972), p. 212.

6   ʿAmrū ibn Baḥr al-Jāḥiẓ, *Kitāb al-Ḥayawān*, 7 vols., (Cairo: al-Maktabah al-Ḥamīdiyyah al-Miṣriyyah, 1905–07), 1:9, in Stewart, ibid., p. 106.

7   Al-Jāḥiẓ, *Rasāʾil*, 4 vols., (Beirut: Dār al-Jīl, 1991), 1/309–19, in Stewart, ibid., p. 106.

8   Stewart, ibid., p. 109.

9   Ibid. Also see Abū Bakr Aḥmad ibn ʿAlī al-Jaṣṣāṣ al-Rāzī, *al-Fuṣūl fī al-Uṣūl*, 2 vols., (Beirut: Dār al-Kutub al-ʿIlmiyyah, 2000), 2/206. Al-Jaṣṣāṣ claimed that Abū Isḥāq Ibrāhīm al-Naẓẓām was the first one to deny *qiyās*.

10 George Makdisi, "The Juridical Theory of Shāfiʿī," (1984), p. 31.

11 Abū Bakr Muḥammad al-Bāqillānī, *al-Taqrīb wa al-Irshād (al-Ṣaghīr)* (Saudi Arabia: Muʾassasat al-Risālah, n.d.), v.1, p. 172.

12 Ibid., pp. 195–206.

13 Ibid., p. 281.

14 Ibid., p. 310.

15 Ibid., p. 316, ff.

16 Ibid., p. 310 and p. 311.

17 ʿAbd al-Jabbār al-Asad Ābādī, *al-Mughnī fī Abwāb al-Tawḥīd wa al-ʿAdl*, 20 vols., (Cairo: al-Sharikah al-ʿArabiyyah li al-Ṭabʿ wa al-Nashr, 1960),

vol. 17, p. 5. The title of his work on Islamic legal methodology was *al-Nihāyah fī Uṣūl al-Fiqh*. He refers to it frequently in his *al-Mughnī*. He often states that some of the above-mentioned topics were discussed by certain masters of theology such as Abū Hāshim al-Jubbāʿī (d. 321/933) and Abū Bakr Bāqillānī.

18 Ibid., vol. 17, pp. 39–70.

19 Ibid., vol. 17, pp. 107–52. Chapters "*Fī al-awāmir wa mā yattiṣil bi-dhālik*" and "*Fī al-nahy wa kayfiyyah dalālatihi ʿalā al-qubḥ al-munhā.*"

20 Ibid., pp. 30–38.

21 See Chapter 3.

22 See Chapter 6.

23 Vishanoff, *The Formation*, pp. 140–41.

24 Abū Manṣūr ʿAbd al-Qāhir al-Baghdādī, *Uṣūl al-Dīn* (Istanbul: Dār al-Funūn, 1928), pp. 5–12.

25 Ibid. p. 12.

26 Ibid., p. 14.

27 Ibid., pp. 215–29.

28 Ibid., p. 18.

29 Ibid., p. 184.

30 Ibid., pp. 271–78.

31 Ibid., pp. 279–95.

32 Vishanoff, *The Formation*, p. 223.

33 H. Ansari and S. Schmidtke, "The Muʿtazilī and Zaydī Reception of Abū al-Ḥusayn al-Baṣrī's *Kitāb al-Muʿtamad fī Uṣūl al-Fiqh*: A Bibliographical Note," *Islamic Law and Society*, vol. 20/1–2 (2013), p. 98.

34 Abū al-Ḥusayn al-Baṣrī, *Kitāb al-Muʿtamad fī Uṣūl al-Fiqh*, 2 vols., (Damascus: al-Maʿhad al-ʿIlmī al-Faransī, 1964), v.1, pp. 11–14. It is noteworthy that before writing *al-Muʿtamad*, al-Baṣrī had written in a separate treatise a commentary on al-Qāḍī ʿAbd al-Jabbār's non-extant *Kitāb al-ʿUmad*, which both Fakhr al-Dīn al-Rāzī and Sayf al-Dīn al-Āmidī relied upon extensively. He refers to this commentary in his introduction to *al-Muʿtamad*, stating that after completing the commentary he had composed *al-Muʿtamad*, desiring to make it well-structured, organized, and non-repetitive (vol. 1, p.7). Abd al-Azim al-Dib explored this point in his introduction to Imām al-Ḥaramayn al-Juwaynī's *al-*

Burhān (Qatar: Dār al-Wafā' li al-Ṭabāʿah, 1992), vol. 1, p. 45. However, we still see modern scholars repeating the misunderstanding that *al-Muʿtamad* was the name of al-Baṣrī's commentary. For example, see *Encyclopaedia of Islam*, new edition, (Leiden: Brill, 2000), "*uṣūl al-fikh*," vol. 10, p. 932.

35 Al-Baṣrī, *Kitāb al-Muʿtamad fī Uṣūl al-Fiqh*. For a brief description of his classification of chapters, see v. 1, pp. 11–14.

36 George Makdisi, "The Juridical Theology of Shāfiʿī," p. 43.

CHAPTER 3

1 Mohammad Hashim Kamali, *Principles of Islamic Jurisprudence* (Kuala Lumpur: Pelanduk Pub., 1989), p. 9.

2 See Aḥmad ibn Muḥammad Abū ʿAlī al-Ḥanafī al-Shāshī, *Uṣūl al-Shāshī* (Beirut: Dār al-Kitāb al-ʿArabī, 1982). Also see Jawad Shahrastani's introduction to *Jāmiʿ al-Maqāṣid* by Shaykh ʿAlī Karakī (Qum: Mu'assasah Āl al-Bayt, 1987–90), v. 1, p. 5.

3 See Ibn Khaldūn, *al-Muqaddimah* (Iskandariyyah: Dār ibn Khaldūn, n.d.), p. 319. Muhammad Abu Zahrah, *Uṣūl al-Fiqh* (Cairo: Dār al-Fikr, n.d.), p. 14.

4 Ahmet Temel, "The Missing Link in the History of Islamic Legal Theory: The Development of Usul al-Fiqh between al-Shafiʿi and al-Jassas during the 3rd/9th and Early 4th/10th Centuries," PhD dissertation (Santa Barbara, CA: University of Santa Barbara, 2014).

5 Abū Bakr Aḥmad ibn ʿAlī al-Jaṣṣāṣ al-Rāzī, *Uṣūl al-Jaṣṣāṣ al-Musammā al-Fuṣūl fī al-Uṣūl* (Beirut: Dār al-Kutub al-ʿIlmiyyah, 2000), vol. 1, pp. 29–40.

6 Ibid., vol. 2, pp. 206–41.

7 Nabil Shehaby, "The Influence of Stoic Logic on al-Jassas' Legal Theory," in J. E. Murdoch and E. D. Sylla, eds., *The Cultural Context of Medieval Learning* (Dordrecht, Holland: D. Reidel Pub. Co., 1975), pp. 61–85.

8 Ibid., p. 74.

9 Al-Jaṣṣāṣ, *al-Fuṣūl fī al-Uṣūl*, vol. 2, p. 241.

10 Joep Lameer, *Al-Fārābī and Aristotelian Syllogistics* (Leiden: E.J. Brill, 1994), p. 25.

11 Ibid., vol. 2, pp. 99–105.

12 Ibid., vol. 2, pp. 241–42.

13 Murteza Bedir, "Al-Jassas," in Oussama Arabi, David S. Powers, and Susan A. Spectorsky, eds., *Islamic Legal Thought: A Compendium of Muslim Jurists* (Leiden: Brill, 2013), pp. 159–60.

14 Al-Jaṣṣāṣ, *Uṣūl al-Jaṣṣāṣ*, vol. 1, pp. 3–152. It should be noted that al-Jaṣṣāṣ uses terms such as *khiṭāb*, *kalām*, and *bayān* interchangeably.

15 Ibid., vol. 2, pp. 106–97.

16 Ibid., vol. 2, pp. 367–441.

17 Ibid., pp. 145–46.

18 Abū Zayd ʿUbaydullāh al-Dabbūsī, *Taqwīm al-Adillah fī Uṣūl al-Fiqh* (Beirut: Dār al-Kutub al-ʿIlmiyyah, 2001), p. 18.

19 Al-Dabbūsī uses both *ḥujjah* and *dalīl* interchangeably. He does not include *qiyās* in his general classification of *adillah* (the legal sources); however, at the beginning of the chapter on *qiyās* he remarks that *qiyās* is among the *sharʿī* indicants. See p. 260.

20 Ibid., pp. 448–64.

21 Ibid., p. 392 and 465.

22 "*Ka al-mukhaṣṣiṣ li dalīl al-ʿaql wa yakūnu ḥukmuhu ḥukm al-khāṣṣ yaraddu ʿalā al-ʿāmm ḥujjatan fī mā lam yarid al-khāṣṣ fīh.*" Al-Dabbūsī, *Taqwīm al-Adillah*, ibid., p. 460. Murteza Bedir, "Reason and Revelation: Abū Zayd al-Dabbūsī on Rational Proofs," *Islamic Studies*, vol. 43, no 2 (Summer 2004), p. 240. Bedir states that "Dabbūsī's account of the relationship between reason and revelation is extremely sophistica-ted, which is neglected even in the Ḥanafī *uṣūl* tradition where he was otherwise extremely influential," p. 244.

23 Rumee Ahmed, *Narratives*, pp. 145–47.

24 See Aḥmad al-Bukhārī, *Kashf al-Asrār ʿan Uṣūl Fakhr al-Islām al-Bazdawī* (Beirut: Dār al-Kutub al-ʿIlmiyyah, 1997), vol. 1, p. 33.

25 Ibid., vol. 1, pp. 43–46.

26 Ibid., vol. 2, pp. 477–91.

27 Ibid., vol. 3, pp. 337–93.

28 Ibid., vol. 4, pp. 324–49.

29 Osman Tastan argues that "although *Sharḥ al-Siyar al-Kabīr* is based on Shaybānī's *al-Siyar al-Kabīr*, the *Sharḥ* should be considered as Sarakhsī's

own work." Oussama Arabi, David S. Powers, and Susan A. Spectorsky,
eds., "Al-Sarakhsi," in *Islamic Legal Thought: A Compendium of Muslim
Jurists* (Studies in Islamic Law and Society series) (Leiden: Brill, 2013),
p. 250.

30 Abū Bakr Muḥammad ibn Aḥmad ibn Abī Sahl al-Sarakhsī, *Uṣūl al-
Sarakhsī* (Istanbul: Dār Qahramān li al-Nashr wa al-Tawzīʿ, 1952), vol. 1,
pp. 10–11.

31 Ibid., vol. 2, pp. 118–289.

32 Ibid., vol. 2, pp. 118–149.

33 Ibid., vol. 2, pp. 224. The Qur'anic verse reads: "Say: [O Prophet] 'I find
not in the message received by me by inspiration any (meat) forbidden to
be eaten by one who wishes to eat it, unless it be dead meat, or blood
poured forth, or the flesh of swine.'"

34 Ibid., vol. 2, pp. 223–26.

35 Ibid., vol. 2, pp. 289–353.

36 Wael Hallaq, *A History of Islamic Legal Theories*, p. 135. Al-Sarakhsī,
Uṣūl, vol. 2, pp. 208–15.

37 Al-Sarakhsī, *al-Mabsūṭ* (Beirut: Dār al-Maʿrifah, 1993).

38 Al-Sarakhsī, *Uṣūl al-Sarakhsī*, vol. 1, p. 127.

CHAPTER 4

1 Muḥammad ibn Yaʿqūb ibn Isḥāq al-Kulaynī, *al-Uṣūl min al-Kāfī* (Arabic
with Persian commentary and translation), ed. and trans., S. Jawad
Mustafawi (Tehran: Daftar-i nashr-i farhang-i ahlul bayt, n.d.), 4:120–22,
hadith no. 1 (*Kitāb al-īmān wa al-kufr, Bāb al-ḍalāl*).

2 Liyakat Takim, *The Heirs of the Prophet: Charisma and Religious
Authority in Islam* (Albany: SUNY, 2006), p. 81.

3 Muhammad Ebrahim Jannaati, *Taṭawwor-i ejtihād dar howze-ye
estenbāt* (Tehran: Amīr Kabīr, 2007), vol. 1, pp. 151–52.

4 Hossein Modarressi, *Crisis and Consolidation in the Formative Period of
Shiʿi Islam: Abu Jaʿfar ibn Qiba al-Razi and His Contribution to Imamite
Shiʿite Thought* (Princeton: The Darwin Press, 1993), p. 24.

5 Devin Stewart, *Islamic Legal Orthodoxy: Twelver Shiite Responses to the
Sunni Legal System* (Salt Lake City: University of Utah Press, 1988), p. 17.

6   See Mohammad Va'iz-zadeh Khorasani, Mohammad, "Mosahebeh," in *Cheshm va Cherāgh-e Marjaᶜiyyat* (Qum: Enteshārāt-e Daftar Tablīghāt-e Islāmī, 1379/2000), p. 225. Khorasani, a student of Grand Ayatollah Boroujerdi, quotes him as saying that the Imams' tradition-reports can better be understood if we read them in the light of similar Sunni tradition-reports, because the Imams were reacting to the prevalent Sunni fatwas of the time. Thus, Shiᶜi fiqh can be considered a commentary on Sunni fiqh.

7   See Abu al-Qasim Gorji, *Naẓariyyah fī ᶜIlm al-Uṣūl* (Tehran: Bunyād-i Biᶜthat, 1982), p. 28.

8   Wilferd Madelung, "Authority in Twelver Shiᶜism," in *Religious Schools and Sects in Medieval Islam* (Ashgate, USA: Variorum Reprint, 1985), p. 167.

9   Such as Ibn Abī ᶜAqīl al-ᶜUmānī and Ibn al-Junayd al-Iskāfī. See Ahmad Kazemi-Moussavi, *Religious Authority in Shiᶜite Islam* (Kuala Lumpur: ISTAC, 1996), pp. 21–23.

10 This treatise is named *al-Tadhkirah bi Uṣūl al-Fiqh*. See Abū al-Fatḥ Muḥammad ibn ᶜAlī ibn ᶜUthmān al-Karājikī, *Kanz al-Fawā'id* (Beirut: Dār al-Aḍwā', 1985), v. 2, p. 15.

11 Ibid., pp. 15–30.

12 Martin J. McDermott, *The Theology of Al-Shaikh Al-Mufīd* (Beirut: Dār al-Mashriq, 1986), p. 295.

13 Al-Sharīf al-Murtaḍā Abū al-Qāsim, ᶜAlī ibn al-Ḥusayn, *al-Dharīᶜah ilā Uṣūl al-Sharīᶜah*, 2 vols., (Tehran: Dānishgāh, 1967), v. 1, p. 8.

14 Ibid., pp. 19–24.

15 Ibid., v. 2, pp. 477–603.

16 Ibid., Gorji, *Naẓariyyah*, "Introduction," vol. 1, p. 2.

17 Martin J. McDermott, *The Theology of Al-Shaikh Al-Mufīd* (Librairie Orientale, 1978), p. 381.

18 Mohammad Ali Amir-Moezzi, "al-Ṭūsī," *Encyclopaedia of Islam*, 2nd edn.

19 Ibid., vol. 1, p. 133.

20 Shiᶜi tradition sources include Kulaynī's *al-Kāfī*, Ibn Bābuwayh's *Man lā Yaḥḍurhu al-Faqīh*, and Shaykh al-Ṭūsī's *al-Istibṣār* and *Tahdhīb*. For more information on al-Ṭūsī's position between *Akhbārism* and *Uṣūlism*, see Moussavi, *Religious Authority*, pp. 80–84.

21 Modarressi, *An Introduction to Shi'i Law*, Chapter 4, no. iv, under "Shaykh al-Ta'ifa."

22 Andrew Newman, *The Formative Period of Twelver Shi'ism: Hadith as Discourse Between Qum and Baghdad* (Richmond, Surrey: Curzon Press, 2000), p. 60.

23 Norman Calder, "The Emergence of an Imami Shi'i Theology of *Ijtihād*," *Studia Islamica*, vol. ıxx (1989), p. 63.

24 Muḥammad ibn al-Ḥasan, al-Ṭūsī, *al-'Uddah fī Uṣūl al-Fiqh* (Qum: Anṣārī, 1997), vol. 2, pp. 739–58.

25 Ibn Idrīs al-Ḥillī, *al-Sarā'ir* (Qum: Nashr-i Islāmī, 1989), vol. 1, pp. 46–54.

26 Muḥammad ibn al-Ḥasan al-Ṭūsī, *al-'Uddah fī Uṣūl al-Fiqh*, (ed.), Muhammad Rida al-Ansari al-Qummi (Qum: 1998), vol. 1, pp. 7–11. His categorization is on p. 8.

27 Ibid., vol. 1, pp. 7–60.

28 Ibid., pp. 63–559.

29 Ibid., vol. 1, p. 8 and vol. 2, pp. 601–735.

30 Ibid., vol 2, pp. 752–58.

31 Ibid., vol 1, pp. 236 and 350. Al-Ṭūsī also employed the notion of *'amal* or *ijmā' al-faqīh* in his *al-Khilāf* against various Sunni views. See his *al-Khilāf* (Qum: Nashr al-Islāmī, 1987), vol. 1, p. 514.

32 Ebrshim Jannaati, "Ijtihād dar Jāmi'-yi Islāmī," *Kayhān-i Andīsheh*, vol. 10 (1986), p. 17.

33 Najm al-Dīn Ja'far ibn al-Ḥasan al-Muḥaqqiq al-Ḥillī, *Ma'ārij al-Uṣūl* (Qum: Āl al-Bayt, 1983), pp. 45–58.

34 Andrew Newman, "The Development and Political Significance of the Rationalist (Usuli) and Traditionist (Akhbari) Schools in Imami Shi'i History from the Third/Ninth to the Tenth/Sixteenth Century" (PhD dissertation, UCLA, 1986), p. 195. Quoted in Zackery M. Heern, *The Emergence of Modern Shi'ism: Islamic Reform in Iraq and Iran* (London: Oneworld Publications, 2015), p. 16.

35 Newman, pp. 197 and 206.

36 Ibid., p. 216.

37 Ibid., pp. 179–80. "*Li annhu tabtanī 'alā i'tibārāt naẓariyyah laysat mustafīd min ẓawāhir al-nuṣūṣ fī al-akthār.*" Also see W. Madelung,

"Authority in Twelver Shiʿism," in *Religion, Schools and Sects in Medieval Islam* (London: Variorum Reprints, 1985), p. 168.

38 Ibid., al-Muḥaqqiq, p. 181.

39 Ibid., p. 189.

40 Murtada Mutahhari, *Āshnāʾī bā ʿUlūm-i Isāmī* (Tehran: Intishārāt-i Ṣadrā, 1979), p. 57.

41 Madelung, "Authority." Madelung cites the first reason for the difference in how ijtihad developed in Imāmī Shiʿism and Sunnism: "…[A] consensus of the Shiʿite *ʿulamāʾ*, in contrast to the Sunnite situation, is of no legal consequence. No question open to *ijtihād* can thus ever be settled conclusively through a consensus of the Shiʿite *ʿulamāʾ*; nor can it ever be claimed that the door of *ijtihād* itself has been closed by a consensus."

42 Al-ʿAllāmah ibn al-Muṭahhar al-Ḥillī, *Tahdhīb al-Wuṣūl ilā ʿIlm al-Uṣūl* (Tehran: Litho-graph, 1890), chapter on *qiyās*.

43 Murtada Mutahhari, "Ijtihād dar Islām" *Baḥthī darbāra-yi Marjaʿiyyat va Rūḥāniyyat* (Tehran: Shirkat-i Sahāmī-yi Intishār, 1962), p. 41.

44 Al-ʿAllāmah al-Ḥillī, *Mabādiʾ al-Wuṣūl ilā ʿIlm al-Uṣūl* (Beirut: Dār al-Aḍwāʾ, 1986), pp. 58–67.

45 Ibid., pp. 86–87.

46 Ibid., pp. 166–70.

47 Ibid., compare with pp. 193 and 195.

48 Ibid., pp. 214–27.

49 Ibid., p. 243.

50 Ibid., p. 249.

51 Murtada Mutahhari, *Bahhthī darbāra-yi Marjaʿiyyat va Rūḥāniyyat*, pp. 40–42. Al-ʿAllāmah al-Ḥillī wrote a commentary on Ibn Ḥājib's *Muktaṣar Muntahā al-Suʾāl wa al-Amal*. Entitled *Ghāyat al-Wuṣūl wa Īḍāḥ al-Subul fī Sharḥ Mukhtaṣar Muntahā al-Suʾāl wa al-Amal*, it was his first *uṣūl al-fiqh* work. See Sabine Schmidtke, *The Theology of al-ʿAllama al-Hilli (d. 726/1325)* (Berlin: Klaus Scdhwarz Verlag, 1991), p. 66.

52 Robert Gleave, *Scripturalist Islam: The History and Doctrines of the Akhbari Shiʿi School* (Boston and Leiden: Brill, 2007), pp. 4–8. "ʿAllama al-Hilli on the Imamate and Ijtihad," (translated and edited by John Cooper) in S. A. Arjomand (ed.), *Authority and Political Culture in Shiʿism* (Albany: SUNY, 1988), pp. 240–49; and Ahmad Kazemi

Moussavi, *Religious Authority in Shiʿite Islam: From the Office of Mufti to the Institution of Marjaʿ* (Kuala Lumpur: ISTAC, 1996), pp. 61–77.

53 Al-ʿAllāmah al-Ḥillī, *al-Alfayn* (Najaf: Haydariyyah, 1969), pp. 9, 82, 285, and 290.

54 Al-ʿAllāmah al-Ḥillī, *Mabādiʾ*, pp. 244–250.

55 For an elaborate and detailed scholarly treatment of this subject, see Gleave, *Scripturalist Islam.*

56 Mullā Muḥammad Amīn al-Astarābādī, *al-Fawāʾid al-Madaniyyah* (Bahrain: Litho-print, 1903), pp. 48, 184, and 193.

57 Ibid., pp. 114, 125, 132, and 139.

58 Etan Kohlberg, "Aspects of Akhbari Thought in the Seventeenth and Eighteenth Centuries," *Eighteenth Century Renewal and Reform in Islam*, (ed.), Nehemia Levitzion and John Voll (Syracuse: Syracuse University Press, 1987), pp. 133–61.

59 Rula J. Abisaab, *Converting Persia: Religion and Power in the Safavid Empire* (New York: I.B. Tauris, 2004), pp. 107–8.

60 Abu al-Qasim Gorji, *Nigāhī beh Taḥavvol-i ʿIlm-i Uṣūl* (Tehran: Dānishgāh, 1973), p. 42.

61 Shahid II was his grandson.

62 Ḥasan ibn Zayn al-Dīn al-ʿĀmilī, *Maʿālim al-Dīn wa Milādh al-Mujtahidīn*, (ed.), Mahdi Mohaghegh (Tehran: McGill Branch, 1983), p. 30.

63 Ibid., pp. 33–198.

64 Ibid., pp. 199–209.

65 Ibid., pp. 257–67. Al-ʿĀmilī challenges al-ʿAllāmah's view on the *ratio legis* (*ʿillah*) of *qiyās* by saying that he had never consulted al-Murtada's *al-Iḥtijāj*. See p. 260.

66 Ibid., pp. 268–87.

CHAPTER 5

1 Majid Fakhri, *A Short Introduction to Islamic Philosophy, Theology and Mysticism* (Oxford: Oneworld Publication, 1997), p. 135.

2 Joep Lameer, *Al-Fārābī and Aristotelian Syllogistics* (Leiden: E.J. Brill, 1994), p. 245.

3 Ibid.

4 See Wael Hallaq, "Logical Structure in Sunni Legal Theory," p. 48.

5 Ibid., p. 50.

6 John Walbridge, *God and Logic in Islam: The Caliphate of Reason* (Cambridge: Cambridge University Press, 2011), p. 72.

7 Abū Muḥammad ʿAlī ibn Aḥmad ibn Saʿīd ibn Ḥazm, *al-Iḥkām fī Uṣūl al-Aḥkām* (Beirut: Dār al-Kutub al-Islāmiyyah, n.d).

8 Ibid., vol. 1, pp. 15–30. Also see George Hourani, "Reason and Revelation in Ibn Hazm's Ethical Thought" in P. Morewedge, (ed.), *Islamic Philosophical Theology* (Syracuse: SUNY, 1979), pp. 142–164.

9 Ibn Ḥazm, *al-Taqrīb*, p. 99, recorded in Shams Inati, "Logic," *History of Islamic Philosophy*, (eds.), S.H. Nasr and O. Leaman (London and New York: Routledge, 1996), vol. 1, part 11, p. 809.

10 Ibid., pp. 31–51.

11 Imām al-Ḥaramayn ʿAbd al-Malik ibn ʿAbdullāh al-Juwaynī, *al-Burhān fī Uṣūl al-Fiqh* (Qatar: Dār al-Ṭibāʿah wa al Nashr, 1992), vol. 1, pp. 77–123.

12 Ibid., vol. 1, pp. 79–87.

13 Ibid., vol. 1, p. 107.

14 Ibid., vol. 2, pp. 721–39.

15 Ibid., vol. 2, p. 751.

16 Al-Ghazālī, *al-Mankhūl min Taʿlīqāt al-Uṣūl* (Damascus: Dār al-Fikr, 1980).

17 Al-Ghazālī, *Shifāʾ al-Ghalīl fī Bayān al-Shabah wa al-Mukhīl wa Masālik al-Taʿlīl* (Baghdad: Maṭbaʿat al-Irshād, 1971), p. 8.

18 Al-Ghazālī, *al-Mustaṣfā, min ʿIlm al-Uṣūl* (Beirut: Dār al-Kutub al-ʿIlmiyyah, 1983), vol. 1, p. 4.

19 Ibid., vol. 1, pp. 315–316 and vol. 2, p. 228 and 350.

20 Ibid., vol. 1, pp. 9–54.

21 Ibid., vol. 1, pp. 55–99.

22 Ibid., vol. 1, pp. 105–28.

23 Ibid., vol. 1, p. 315 and vol. 2, p. 350.

24 Ibid., vol. 2, pp. 350–407.

25 Ibid., p. 7.

26 Ibid., p. 3.

27 Al-Ghazālī, *Iḥyā' ʿUlūm al-Dīn* (Beirut: Dār al-Kutub al-ʿIlmiyyah, n.d.), vol. 1, p. 28.

28 Ibid., vol. 1, p. 21.

29 Ibid. Also see Gholam Hosayn Ibrahimi Dinani, *Manṭiq va Maʿrifat dar Naẓar-e Ghazālī* (Tehran: Amīr Kabīr, 1991), p. 411.

30 Imran Ahsan Khan Nyazee, *Theories of Islamic Law* (Islamabad: Islamic Research Institute Press, 1994), p. 202.

31 Al-Ghazālī, *al-Mustaṣfā*, vol. 2, p. 318.

32 Ibid., vol. 2, pp. 318–320.

33 Ibid., vol. 1., p. 287.

34 Ibid., vol. 1, p. 286.

35 Ibid., vol. 1, pp. 284–314.

36 Ibid., vol. 2, p. 350 and vol. 2, p. 387. Concerning al-Ghazālī's influence on some Shiʿi authors, see Chapter four.

37 Ibid., vol. 2, pp. 393–94.

38 Fakhr al-Dīn Muḥammad ibn ʿUmar al-Rāzī, *al-Maḥṣūl fī ʿIlm al-Uṣūl*, (ed.), Taha Jabir Alalwani (Beirut: Mu'assasat al-Risālah, 1992), vol. 1, p. 80., (*majmūʿ ṭuruq al-fiqh ʿalā sabīl al-ijmāl wa kayfiyyah ḥāl al-istidlāl bihā, wa kayfiyyah ḥāl al-mustadill bihā*).

39 Ibid., vol. 1, pp. 78–88.

40 Ibid., vol. 1, p. 82.

41 Ibid., vol. 1, pp. 89–122.

42 Ibid., vol. 1, p. 169.

43 Ibid., vol. 5, pp. 157–166.

44 Ibid., vol. 6, p. 95.

45 Ibid., vol. 6, pp. 95–171.

46 Sayf al-Dīn ʿAlī ibn Abī ʿAlī al-Āmidī, *al-Iḥkām fī Uṣūl al-Aḥkām* (Cairo: Mu'assasat al-Ḥalibī, 1967), pp. 11–14. Also see his *Ghāyat al-Marām fī ʿIlm al-Kalām* (Cairo: Lajnah al-Turāth al-Islāmī, 1971).

47 Al-Āmidī, *al-Iḥkām*, vol. 1, pp. 7–89. Also see Bernard G. Weiss, *The Search for God's Law: Islamic Jurisprudence in the Writings of Sayf al-Dīn al-Āmidī* (Salt Lake City: University of Utah Press, 1993), pp. 31–150.

48 Al-Āmidī, *al-Iḥkām*, vol. 1, pp. 145–255.

49 Ibid., vol. 2, p. 3 and vol. 3, p. 166.

50 Ibid., vol. 3, p. 201.

51 Ibid., vol. 4, pp. 104–20.

52 Ibid., vol. 4, pp. 121–35.

53 Ibid., vol. 4, pp. 206–53.

54 Ibid., vol. 4, pp. 136–140.

55 Ibid., vol. 2, especially pp. 3–9 and p. 119 and 174.

56 Ibid., vol. 4, pp. 104–111.

57 Ibid., vol. 4, pp. 111–120.

58 Abū ʿAmrū Jamāl al-Dīn ibn al-Ḥājib, *Mukhtaṣar al-Muntahā al-Uṣūl: maʿa Ḥāshiyat al-Taftāzānī wa al-Jurjānī ʿalā Sharḥ al-Qāḍī ʿAḍudī* (Cairo: al-Maṭbaʿah al-Kubrā al-Amīriyyah bi Būlāq Miṣr al-Ḥamiyyah, 1898).

59 A. Gorji, *Naẓrah fī Taṭawwur ʿIlm al-Uṣūl* (Tehran: al-Maktabah al-Islāmiyyah al-Kubrā, 1982), pp. 48–50.

60 Ibn al-Ḥājib, *Mukhtaṣar*, vol. 1, p. 5.

61 Ibid., vol. 1, p. 6.

62 The fifth/eleventh century authors such as al-Baṣrī rarely used the term ijtihad for independent reasoning other than *qiyās*. Al-Baṣrī used the title of *muftī* and *mustaftī* in place of ijtihad. Ijtihad has been accorded a distinct chapter in Sunni law since the sixth/twelfth century.

63 See Abd al-Rahman al-Banani, *Ḥāshiyat al-ʿAllāmah al-Banānī ʿalā Sharḥ al-Jalāl al-Maḥallī ʿalā Matn Jamʿ al-Jawāmiʿ lī al-Imām Tāj al-Dīn al-Subkī* (Beirut: Dār al-Kutub, 1998), vol. 1, pp. 7–355.

64 Ibid., vol. 2, pp. 528–550.

65 Ibid., vol. 2, pp. 551–675.

66 For more information, see Ṭāhā Jābir Al ʿAlwānī, *Uṣūl al-Fiqh al-Islāmī: Source Methodology in Islamic Jurisprudence* (Herndon, Virginia: International Institute of Islamic Thought, 1990), p. 57.

CHAPTER 6

1 Najm al-Dīn Sulaymān ibn ʿAbd al-Qawī al-Ṭūfī, *Sharḥ Mukhtaṣar al-Rawḍah* (Beirut: Muʾassasat al-Risālah, 1987), vol. 1, pp. 98–100.

2 Ibid., vol. 1, p. 101.

3 Ibid., vol. 1, p. 409; *Tarjīḥ min ghayr murajjaḥ*.

4 Ibid., vol. 2, p. 5.

5 Ibid., vol. 3, p. 169. *Al-uṣūl al-mukhtalif fīhā arbaʿah: al-awwal: sharʿ min qablinā, al-thānī: qawl al-ṣaḥābī, al-thālith: al-istiḥsān, al-rābiʿ: al-istiṣlāḥ*. It seems that the legality of the past religions appears here for the first time among the *adillah*.

6 An excerpt of al-Ṭūfī's *Sharḥ al-Arbaʿīn* is published under the title of *Risālah fī Riʿāyat al-Maṣlaḥah* (Dār al-Maṣriyyah al-Lubanāniyyah, 1993), pp. 13–18.

7 Al-Ṭūfī, *Sharḥ Mukhtaṣar al-Rawḍah*, vol. 2, pp. 147–168.

8 Ibid., vol. 3, p. 217.

9 Ibid., vol. 33, pp. 575–749.

10 Ibid., vol. 3, p. 148.

11 Ibid., vol. 3, p. 148 and pp. 160 and 166.

12 Ibid., vol. 3, p. 159. Reference is to Qur'an 7:172: "When thy Lord drew forth from the Children of Adam – from their loins – their descendants, and made them testify concerning themselves, (saying): 'Am I not your Lord (who cherishes and sustains you)?'–They said: 'Yea! We do testify!' (This), lest ye should say on the Day of Judgment: 'Of this we were never mindful'."

13 Ibid., vol. 3, pp. 204–217.

14 Al-Ṭūfī, *Risālah fī Riʿāyat al-Maṣlaḥah*. The excerpt from *Sharḥ al-Arbaʿīn*, p. 23.

15 Ibid.

16 Ibid., pp. 25–28.

17 Ibid., pp. 37–39.

18 Abū Isḥāq Ibrāhīm al-Shāṭibī, *al-Muwāfaqāt fī Uṣūl al-Aḥkām* (Cairo: Dār al-Fikr, n.d.). Al-Shāṭibī notes that he had initially entitled his work "The Secrets of Religious Obligation" (*al-Taʿrīf bi Asrār al-Taklīf*), but eventually changed it to *al-Muwafaqāt* in response to a dream on what he had proposed to discern of the Lawgiver's intention. See vol. 1, p. 7.

19 Ibid., vol. 1, p. 10. *Inna uṣūl al-fiqh fī al-dīn qaṭʿiyyah lā ẓaniyyah*.

20 Wael Hallaq, *A History of Islamic Legal Theories*, p. 164.

21 Al-Shāṭibī, *al-Muwāfaqāt*, pp. 12–17.

22 Muhammad Khalid Masoud, *Muslim Jurists' Quest for the Normative Basis of Shariʿa* (Leiden: ISIM, 2001), p. 8.

Notes

23 Al-Shāṭibī, *al-Muwāfaqāt*, vol. 1, pp. 68–85.

24 Ibid., vol. 1, pp. 20–27.

25 Ibid., vol. 1, p. 213. Hallaq, *A History of Islamic Legal Theory*, p. 177.

26 *Al-Muwāfaqāt*, vol. 2, pp. 2–5. Muhammad Khalid Masoud, *Shāṭibī's Philosophy of Islamic Law* (Malaysia, Kuala Lumpur: Islamic Research Institute, Malaysian reprint, 2000), p. 152.

27 Mohammad Hashim Kamali, *Issues in the Legal Theory of Uṣūl and Prospects for Reform* (Kuala Lumpur: IIUM., 2000), p. 17.

28 *Al-Muwāfaqāt*, vol. 3, pp. 26–27.

29 Ibid., vol. 2, pp. 158 and 280.

30 Al-Shāṭibī claims that he chose *al-Muwāfaqāt* as the title because of the very high degree of consistency and conformity in the Shariʿah's concepts. See Ibid., vol. 1, p. 7.

31 Ibid., vol. 3, pp. 70–80.

32 Ibid., vol. 3, pp. 71–165.

33 Ibid., vol. 3, pp. 166–223.

34 Ibid., vol. 3, pp. 200–205.

35 Ibid., vol. 3, p. 217.

36 Ibid., vol. 3, p. 227.

37 Ibid., vol. 4, pp. 2–46.

38 Ibid., vol. 4, p. 47.

39 Hallaq, *A History of Islamic Legal Theory*, p. 201; Ibid., vol. 4, pp. 50–55.

40 Ibid.

41 Ibid., vol. 4, p. 56.

42 Ibid., vol. 4, pp. 140–141: "*Inna al-muftī shāriʿ min wajh lianna mā yablaghuhu min al-shariʿah. Immā manqul ʿan ṣāḥibihā wa immā mustanbaṭ min al-manqūl. Fa al-awwal yakūn fīhi muballigh. Wa al-thānī yakūn fīhi qā'im maqāmahu fī inshā' al-aḥkām wa inshā' al-aḥkām innamā huwa li al-shāriʿ.*"

43 Ibid., vol. 4, pp. 140–151.

44 Ibid., vol. 4, pp. 151–202.

CHAPTER 7

1 Zayn al-Dīn ibn Ibrāhīm ibn al-Nujaym, *al-Ashbāh wa al-Naẓā'ir* (Beirut:

Dār al-Fikr al-Muʿāṣir, 1985), p. 101.

2   Ibn ʿĀbidīn, *Majmūʿah Rasāʾil ibn ʿĀbidīn* (Lahore: Suhayl Academy, n.d.), vol. 2, pp. 112–115.

3   Ibid., vol. 2, p. 132.

4   G.N. Jalbani, *Teachings of Shāh Waliyullāh of Delhi* (New Delhi: Kitab Bhavan, 1988), p. 59, quoting Shāh Walīyullāh's Persian work *Muṣaffā*, vol. 1, p. 11.

5   Ibid.

6   Saiyid Athar Abbas Rizvi, *Shāh Walī-Allāh and His Times* (Canberra: Maʿrifat Publication House, 1980), p. 248, quoting *ʿAqd al-Jid*, Delhi, 1892, pp. 7–9.

7   Shāh Walīyullāh, *Ḥujjat Allāh al-Bālighah* (Beirut: Dār Iḥyāʾ al-ʿUlūm, 1990), vol. 1, pp. 119–152. Also see the translation of this book by Marcia K. Hermansen, *The Conclusive Argument from God* (Leiden: E.J. Brill, 1995), pp. 113–144.

8   Mahmood Ahamad Ghazi, *Islamic Renaissance in South Asia 1707–1867* (Islamabad: Islamic Research Center, 2002).

9   Ibn al-Ḥājib divides his legal methodology into: 1) elementals (*al-mabādiʾ*), 2) revelational indicants (*al-adillah al-samʿiyyah*), 3) preference (*al-tarjīḥ*), and 4) ijtihad. See Chapter five.

10 Muḥammad ibn ʿAlī al-Shawkānī, *Irshād al-Fuḥūl ilā Taḥqīq al-Ḥaqq min ʿIlm al-Uṣūl* (Beirut: Dār al-Kutub al-ʿIlmiyyah, 1994), particularly p. 10.

11 Ibid., vol. 2, pp. 295–369.

12 Ibid., vol. 1, pp. 178 and 201.

13 Ibid., vol. 2, p. 355.

14 Ibid., vol. 2, p. 358.

15 Ibid.

16 Ibid., vol. 2, p. 377.

17 Ibid., vol. 2, pp. 420–422.

18 Shaykh Muhammad Abu Zahrah, *Uṣūl al-Fiqh* (Cairo: Dār al-Fikr, n.d), particularly p. 22.

19 Ibid., pp. 24–62.

20 Ibid., pp. 63–293.

21 Ibid., pp. 63–67.

22 Ibid., pp. 341–356.

23 Ibid., pp. 362–365.

24 Wahbah al-Zuhayli, *Uṣūl al-Fiqh al-Islāmī* (Damascus: Dār al-Fikr, 2004), vol. 1, p. 35.

25 Ibid., vol. 1, pp. 37–194.

26 Ibid., vol. 1, pp. 195–414.

27 Ibid., vol. 2, pp. 733–949.

28 Ibid., vol. 2, pp. 1045–1057.

29 Ibid., vol. 2, pp. 1197–1242.

CHAPTER 8

1 Shaykh Yūsuf al-Baḥrānī, *al-Ḥadā'iq al-Nāḍirah* (Najaf: Dār al-Kutub, 1957), vol. 1, pp. 35–40.

2 Ibid., vol. 6, p. 301.

3 W. Madelung, "Akhbāriyya," *Encyclopedia of Islam*, new edition (Leiden: E.J. Brill, 1980), Supplement, fol. 1–2, pp. 56–57.

4 Ebrahim Jannaati, "Qiyām-i Akhbārihā ʿalayhi Ijtihād," *Kayhān-i Andāshah*, vol. 13 (1987), pp. 2–22.

5 See al-Baḥrānī, *al-Ḥadā'iq*, Introduction by Ṭabāṭabā'ī, p. ﺝ.

6 See Muḥammad Bāqir Bihbahānī, *Risālat al-Ijtihād wa al-Akhbār* (Tehran: Lithograph, 1895).

7 See Shaykh Abū al-Qāsim al-Qummī, *Qawānīn al-Muḥkamah fī Uṣūl al-Mutqanah* (known as *Qawānīn al-Uṣūl*) (Tehran: Lithograph, 1302 H/ 1884), vol. 1, p. 2.

8 Ibid., vol. 1, pp. 2–81.

9 Ibid., vol. 1, pp. 81–135.

10 Ibid., vol. 1, pp. 155–192.

11 Ibid., vol. 1, pp. 192–345.

12 Ibid., vol. 1, p. 361.

13 Ibid., vol. 1, pp. 393–409.

14 Ibid., vol. 1, pp. 409–496.

15 Muhammad Sulayman Tunakabuni, *Qiṣaṣ al-ʿUlamā'* (Tehran: ʿIlmiyyah Islāmiyyah, n.d.), p. 162.

16 See Abū al-Ḥasan Muḥammadī, *Mabādī-yi Istinbāṭ* (Tehran: University of Tehran Press, 2001), p. 22.

17 See Murtaḍā Anṣārī, *Farā'id al-Uṣūl*, (ed.), ʿAbdullah Nurani (Qum: Mu'assasat al-Nashr al-Islāmī, 1987), vol. 1, p. 2.

18 Ibid., vol. 1, pp. 4–7.

19 Ibid., vol. 1, pp. 15–18. Anṣārī calls logical rules "deterrent from error" (ʿĀṣimah ʿan al-khaṭa') and makes use of syllogism throughout his work, vol. 1, p. 16.

20 Ibid., vol. 1, pp. 41, 54, and 290.

21 Ibid., vol. 2, pp. 506–509.

22 Ibid., vol. 2, pp. 510–527.

23 Ibid., vol. 1, p. 310 and vol. 2, p. 765.

24 Ibid., vol. 2, p. 544.

25 Ibid., vol. 2, p. 750.

26 Muhammad Jafar Jafari Langrudi maintains that since the 19th century, Shiʿi law was overshadowed by *al-uṣūl al-ʿamaliyyah* which were employed by *mujtahids* in place of legal fictions (*furūḍ-i qānūnī*). See his *Maktabhā-yi Ḥuqūqī dar Islām* (Tehran: Ganj-i Dānish, 1991), pp. 48–49.

27 Muhammad Kazim Khurasani, *Kifāyat al-Uṣūl* (Qum: Mu'assasah Āl al-Bayt, 1988), pp. 7–9.

28 Ibid., pp. 9–13.

29 Ibid., pp. 16 and 17. Khurasani had for two years studied theology and philosophy with the theosopher of Tehran, Mirzā Abū al-Ḥasan Jilwah before his departure to Najaf in 1861.

30 The notion of *al-dalālah al-taṣdīqiyyah* (lit. confirmative implication) became part of literal interpretation in *uṣūl al-fiqh* and practically helped the development of the contemporary Shiʿi hermeneutics. See Mohammad Mujtahid Shabestari, *Hermeneutik-i Kitāb va Sunnah* (Tehran: Intishārāt-e Ṭarh-e Now, 2002), p. 115, footnote 2.

31 Khurasani, *Kifāyat al-Uṣūl*, pp. 61–88.

32 Ibid., pp. 89–145.

33 Ibid., p. 150.

34 Ibid., p. 180.

35 Ibid., pp. 193–212.

36 Ibid., pp. 257–336.

37 Ibid., p. 380.

38 Ibid., pp. 437–460.

39 Ibid., p. 475.

40 Al-Shaykh Muhammad Rida al- Muzaffar, *Uṣūl al-Fiqh*, 2 vols., in 1 book (Qum: Markaz al-Nashr, 1993). It should be noted that the very last part of this work (after *istiṣḥāb*) was not completed by Muzaffar himself. See Muhammad Ali Khurasani, *Sharḥ Uṣūl ʿAmaliyyah* (Qum: Dār al-Fikr, 1998), vol. 4, p. 4.

41 Al-Muzaffar mentioned in a footnote that his setting of legal methodology was new, and his master Ayatollah Muhammd Husayn Isfahani (d. 1361/ 1942, a student of Khurasani) had also notified it. See ibid., vol. 1, p. 17.

42 Ibid., vol. 1, pp. 198–270.

43 Ibid., vol. 2, pp. 13 and 14.

44 Ibid., vol. 2, pp. 115–126.

45 Ibid., vol. 1, p. 289 and vol. 2, p. 120.

46 Ibid., vol. 2, pp. 129–235.

47 Ibid., vol. 2, pp. 239–243.

48 See al-Sayyid Muhammad Baqir al-Sadr, *Durūs fī ʿIlm al-Uṣūl* (Beirut: Dār al-Kitab al-Lubnānī, 1986).

49 Muhammad Baqir al-Sadr, *Lessons in Islamic Jurisprudence*, trans. with an introduction by Roy P. Mottahedeh (Oxford: Oneworld, 2003), p. 37.

50 Al-Sayyid Muhammad Baqir al-Sadr, *Durūs fī ʿIlm al-Uṣūl* (or *al-Ḥalaqāt*), (Qum: Mu'assasat al-Nashr al-Islāmī, 1415/1994), vol. 1, pp. 42–43.

51 Ibid., pp. 46–49. In his second course (*al-ḥalaqat al-thāniyah*), Sadr criticizes the definitions presented by earlier Shiʿi *ʿulamā'* for employing the term *qawāʿid* instead of *ʿanāṣir* to characterize *uṣūl al-fiqh*. Ibid., pp.171–72.

52 Ibid., vol. 1, p. 50.

53 Ibid., vol. 1, pp. 57–62.

54 Ibid., vol. 1, pp. 116–79.

55 Ibid., vol. 2, pp. 267–70.

56 Ibid., vol. 1, pp. 117–36.

57 Ibid., vol. 2, pp. 219–313.

58 Ibid., vol. 1, pp. 157–66.

59 Ibid., vol. 2, pp. 422–58.

60 Ibid., vol. 3, p. 198.

61 See above, Chapter 8, section on Mīrzā Abū al-Qāsim al-Qummī.

62 See above, Chapter 7.

CHAPTER 9

1   Muhammad Iqbal, "Asrār-i Khudī" in *Iqbāl Lāhūrī* (Tehran: ʿIlmī, 1991),
    pp. 85–135; *The Reconstruction? of Religious Thought in Islam* (Lahore:
    Iqbal Academy Pakistan, 1989), pp. 76–98.

2   Muhammad Iqbal, *Reconstruction of Religious Thought in Islam*,
    p. 76.

3   See Khurshid Ahmad, "Iqbal and the Reconstruction of Islamic Law," in
    Mohammad Iqbal, (ed.), by Verinder Grover (New Delhi: Deep & Deep
    Pub., 1995), p. 548.

4   Ibid., p. 117.

5   Ibid., p. 141.

6   Ibid., p. 136.

7   Ibid.

8   Ibid., p. 137.

9   Ibid., pp. 137–140.

10 Ibid., p. 140.

11 Ibid.

12 Ibid., p. 141.

13 Fazlur Rahman, "Iqbal's Idea of Progress" in *Mohammad Iqbal*,
    p. 323. Also see his article "Some Aspects of Iqbal's Political Thought,"
    pp. 102–107.

14 Ibid., p. 323.

15 Iqbal, "Asrār-i Khudī," p. 92.

16 Robert Whittemore, "Iqbal's Panentheism" in *Muhammad Iqbal*, p. 161.

17 Taha Jabir al-Alwani, "The Crisis in Fiqh and the Methodology of
    Ijtihad," the *American Journal of Islamic Social Sciences*, vol. 8, no. 2
    (September 1991), p. 317.

18 Ibid., p. 321; based on ʿAbd al-Malak al-Juwaynī, *al-Burhān* (Qatar:

Maṭbaʿah al- Dohah Al-Ḥadīthah, 1399), vol. 2, p.1146. Alalwani does not take into consideration that the very idea of closure of the door of ijtihad was challenged by some contemporary authors such as Wael Hallaq in his article "Was the Gate of Ijtihad Closed?" *International Journal of Middle East Studies*, vol. 16 (Spring 1984), pp. 3–41.

19 Al-Alwani, "The Crisis," p. 321.

20 Ibid.

21 Taha Jabir al-Alwani, *Source Methodology in Islamic Jurisprudence* (London and Washington: IIIT., 2003), p. xi.

22 Ibid., pp. 68–70.

23 Al-Alwani, "Ijtihād and Taqlīd," the *American Journal of Islamic Social Sciences*, vol. 8, no. 1 (March 1991), pp. 130–132.

24 Ibid., p. 134.

25 Ibid., pp. 138–40.

26 Taha Jabir Alalwani, *Maqāṣid al-Sharīʿah* (Beirut: Dār al-Hādī, 2001), pp. 63–66.

27 Ibid., pp. 78–82.

28 Ibid., pp. 123–29.

29 Ibid., pp. 67–69.

30 Al-Alwani, *The Ethics of Disagreement in Islam* (Herndon, VA: IIIT, 1997), p. 131.

31 AbdulHamid AbuSulayman, *Crisis in the Muslim Mind*, trans. by Yusuf Talal Delorenzo (Herndon, VA: IIIT, 1997), pp. 4 and 18.

32 Ibid., pp. 37–38 and AbuSulayman, *Towards an Islamic Theory of International Relations: New Directions for Methodology and Thought* (Herndon, VA:IIIT, 1994), p. 65. Here, he includes ʿurf (custom) and ʿaql (reason) among the sources as well.

33 AbuSulayman, *Towards an Islamic Theory*, p. 117, *Crisis*, p. 53.

34 AbuSulayman, *Towards an Islamic Theory*, pp. 66–69.

35 AbuSulayman, *Crisis*, p. 49

36 Hibatullāh ibn Salāmah ibn Naṣr al-Muqirrī, *al-Nāsikh wa al-Mansūkh min Kitāb Allāh* (Beirut: al-Maktab al-Islāmī, 1984), p. 98.

37 AbuSulayman, *Towards an Islamic Theory*, pp. 83–84.

38 Ibid., pp. 78–79.

39 Ibid., p. 77.

40 AbuSulayman, *Crisis*, p. 57.

41 AbuSulayman, *Towards an Islamic Theory*, pp. 85–87.

42 Ibid., pp. 74–75.

43 Ibid., p. 25 and AbuSulayman, *Towards an Islamic Theory*, p. 87.

44 AbuSulayman, *Crisis*, p. 26.

45 Mohammad Hashim Kamali, *Principles of Islamic Jurisprudence* (Cambridge: Islamic Texts Society, 2003), pp. 1–2.

46 Ibid., p. 9.

47 Ibid., pp. 117–186.

48 Ibid., p. 187.

49 Ibid.

50 Ibid., p. 225.

51 Ibid., p. 312.

52 Ibid., pp. 494–497.

53 Muḥammad ibn Idrīs al-Shāfiʿī, *al-Risālah*, (ed.), Ahmad Shakir (Cairo: Dār al-Turāth, 1979), p. 472.

54 Hashim Kamali, *Issues in the Legal Theory of Uṣūl and Prospects for Reform* (Kuala Lumpur: International Islamic University Malaysia, 2002), pp. 12–25.

55 Kamali, *Principles of Islamic Jurisprudence*, pp. 500–512.

56 Ibid., p. 509.

57 Ibid., p. 518.

58 Ibid., p. 517.

59 Tariq Ramadan, *Radical Reform: Islamic Ethics and Liberation* (New York: Oxford University Press, 2009), p. 88.

60 Ibid.

61 Ibid., p. 113.

62 Ibid., p. 114.

63 Ibid., p. 3.

64 Ibid., pp. 79–80.

65 Tariq Ramadan, "Ijtihād and Maṣlaḥa: The Foundations of Governance," in *Islamic Democratic Discourse*, (ed.), M. A. Muqtedar Khan (Lanham, MD: Lexington Books, 2006), p. 4.

66 Ibid., pp. 3–20.

67 Ibid.

68 Tariq Ramadan, *Radical Reform*, p. 122.

69 Ibid., p. 127.

70 Ibid., pp. 134–135.

71 Ibid., p. 218.

72 Ibid., p. 117.

73 Ibid., pp. 127–128.

74 Ibid., p. 248

75 Al-Shāfiʿī, *al-Risālah*, pp. 140, 142, 322, 472, and 510.

76 Abū Bakr al-Jaṣṣāṣ al-Rāzī, *al-Fuṣūl fī al-Uṣūl*, (2000), pp. 146–48.

77 Nimatullah Salihi Najafabadi, *Velāyat-i Faqīh: Ḥukūmat-i Ṣāliḥān* (Tehran: Rasā, 1984), pp. 104–112.

78 Ibid., p. 105.

79 Ibid., pp. 123–125.

80 Ibid., pp. 125–129.

81 Ibid., pp. 36–38.

82 For example, Mullā Aḥmad Narāqī refers to self-evidency and human rationality to reconfirm the doctrine only after quoting nineteen tradition-reports to support his doctrine on *wilāyat al-faqīh*. See his *ʿAwāʾid al-Ayyām* (Qum: Lithograph, 1903), p. 188.

83 Mohsen Kadivar, "Mujtahid dar Uṣūl," in *Madreseh* (a quarterly cultural-philosophical journal), no. 6, vol. 2 (2007), p. 62.

84 Ibid., p. 63.

85 Ibid.

CHAPTER 10

1 See Van A. Harver, "Hermeneutics" *The Encyclopedia of Religion*, 16 vols. (New York: Macmillan, 1987), vol. 6, p. 279–287.

2 See Ali Mirsepassi, *Political Islam, and the Enlightenment* (Cambridge: Cambridge University Press, 2011), p. 76.

3 Ibid.

4 See Nasr Hamid Abu Zayd, *Ishkālāt al-Qirāʾah wa al-Āliyyāt al-Taʾwīl* (Cairo: al-Markaz al-Thaqāfī al-ʿArabī, n.d.). This book is a collection of seven articles published in the Egyptian journals between 1981–1988.

5 Ibid., p. 15.

6 Abu Zayd, *Mafhūm al-Naṣṣ* (Cairo: al-Markaz al-Thaqāfī al-ʿArabī, 1987), pp. 9–13.

7 Abu Zayd, *Naqd al-Khiṭāb al-Dīnī* (Cairo: Sīnāʾ li al-Nashr, 1992), p. 74.

8 Abu Zayd, *Mafhūm al-Naṣṣ*, p. 89.

9 Ibid., pp. 93–94.

10 Ibid., pp. 89–95.

11 Ibid., pp. 117, 120.

12 Ibid., p. 195.

13 Ibid., pp. 245–297.

14 Abu Zayd, *Naqd al-Khiṭāb*, pp. 82–86, also see p. 59.

15 Ibid., pp. 85–86, 105 and 219–20.

16 Shams al-Dīn, al-Suyūṭī, *al-Itqān fī ʿUlūm al-Qurʾān* (Cairo: Muṣṭafā al-Bābī al-Ḥalibī, 1951), vol. 2, p. 16, in Abu Zayd, *Naqd al-Khiṭāb*, p. 92.

17 Abu Zayd, *Naqd al-Khiṭāb*, pp. 91–94.

18 Abu Zayd, Nasr Hamid, *Reformation of Islamic Thought* (Amsterdam University Press, 2006), p. 79.

19 Ibid., pp. 78–9.

20 Collectif 95 Maghreb Egalite, *Dalil pour l'egalite dans la famille au Maghreb*, Edition, 2003, p. 14.

21 See Mohammed Arkoun, *Rethinking Islam: Common Questions, Uncommon Answers*, trans. by Robert D. Lee (Colorado: Westview Press, 1994), pp. 18–23.

22 Ibid.

23 Amin Abdullah, *Falasafah Kalam: Di Era Postmidernisme* (The Philosophy of Islamic Theology in Post-modernism Era), (Yogyakarta: Pustaka Pelajar, 1997), pp. 19–20 in Malki Ahmad Nasir, "Indonesians' Scholars' Reception of Arkoun's Thought," *Khazanah: Journal Ilmu Agam Islam*, Bandung (Indonesia) Program Pascasarjana, vol 1, no 6 (July-December 2004), p. 1197.

24 Mohammed Arkoun, "*The Notion of Revelation*" *Die Welt Islami* XXVIII, no. 63 (1988) in Malki Ahmad Nasir., p. 1191.

25 Ibid.

26 Mohammed Arkoun, *Tārīkhiyyat al-Fikr al-ʿArabiyyah al-Islāmiyyah* (Beirut: Markaz al-Qawmiyyah, 1994) in Malki Ahmad Nasir, p. 1193.

27 Abdolkarim Soroush, *Qabḍ va Basṭ-e Theoric-e Sharīʿat* (Tehran: Ṣirāṭ, 1992), pp. 83–88.

28 Abdolkarim Soroush, *Reason, Freedom and Democracy in Islam*, trans. by Mahmoud Sadri and Ahmad Sadri (Oxford: Oxford University Press, 2000), p. 30.

29 Ibid., p. 31.

30 Interview with *Sharq* (Persian newspaper), vol. 3, no. 838 (20 August 2006), p. 17.

31 Abdolkarim Soroush, *Bast-e Tajrabeh-ye Nabavī* (Tehran: Ṣirāṭ, 2004), p. 7. This work has recently been translated into English by Katajun Amirpour. See *The Expansion of the Prophetic Experience: ʿAbdolkarim Sorush's New Approach to Qur'anic Revelation* (Leiden: E.J. Brill, 2011).

32 Interview with *Sharq*, p. 35.

33 "Parrot and Bee," the second letter of Abdolkarim Soroush to Ayatollah Jafar Sobhani, www.drsoroush.com, Persian (May 2008), pp. 4–6.

34 See his *Rāzdānī va Rowshanfekrī va Dīndārī* (Tehran: Ṣirāṭ, 1992), pp. 63–103.

35 "Peyravī az Ahl-e Sonnat ra Mojaz Mīshomāram," Second response of Dr. Soroush to Mr. Bahmanpoor, Sept. 2005, www.drsoroush.com, p. 2.

36 Mohammad Iqbal, *Reconstruction of Religious Thought in Islam* (Lahore: Institute of Islamic Culture, 1986), p. 101.

37 "Reason and Freedom in Islamic Thought," a lecture delivered by Abdolkarim Soroush in CSID Second Annual Conference, *Islam Democrat*, vol 4, no 1 (Jan 2002), pp. 2–3.

38 Ibid.

39 Farzin Vahdat, *God and Juggernaut: Iran's Intellectual Encounter with Modernity* (Syracuse, New York: Syracuse University Press, 2002), p. 200.

40 Ibid., p. 1.

41 Ibid., p. 140.

42 Ibid., p. 201.

43 Mehrzad Boroujerdi, "The Encounter of Post-Revolutionary Thought in Iran with Hegel, Heidegger, and Popper," *Cultural Transition in Middle East*, edited by Sarif Mardin (Leiden: E.J. Brill, 1994), pp. 257–58.

44 Ibid.

Notes

45 Soroush, "Velāyat-e Bāṭinī va Velāyat-e Siyāsī," *Kiyān-e Farhangī*, vol. 44, no. 20 (Nov 1998).

46 Abū Ḥāmid Muḥammad al-Ghazālī, *Iḥyā' ʿUlūm al-Dīn* (Beirut, Dār al-Kutub al-ʿArabiyyah, n.d.), vol. 1, p. 28.

47 Soroush, *Farbihtar az Ideology, Ṣirāṭ*, 1996.

48 Mohammad Mojtahed Shabestari, *Ta'ammolātī dar Qarā'at-e Insānī az Dīn* (Tehran: Ṭarḥ-e Now, 2004), p. 162.

49 Ibid., pp. 160–162.

50 Ibid., p. 60.

51 Mojtahed Shabestari, *Hermeneutik, Kitāb va Sunnat* (Tehran: Ṭarḥ-e Now, 2002), pp. 138–39. Here, Shabestari refers to Mullā Ṣadrā Shīrāzī, *al-Asfār al-Arbaʿah* (Qum, n.d.), vol. 8, p. 25 and ʿAbd al-Razzāq Lāhījī, *Gowhar Morād* (Tehran:1947), pp. 256–58.

52 Shabestari, *Hermeneutik*, pp. 136–37.

53 Ibid., p. 140.

54 Ibid., *Hermeneutik*, pp. 140–144.

55 Shabestari, *Ta'amolātī*, p. 13.

56 Shabestari, *Īmān va Āzādī* (Tehran: Ṭarḥ-e Now, 2000), pp. 37–42.

57 Shabestari, *Ta'mmolātī.*, p. 167, *Hermeneutik.*, p. 236, and *Naqdī bar Qirā'at-e Rasmī az Dīn* (Tehran: Ṭarḥ-e Now, 2002), p. 478.

58 Ibid., *Īmān va Āzādī*, pp. 23–31.

59 Ibid., p. 26. *Insān be maʿnāye andīsha-ye sayyāl-e nowshavanda va khodnavard.*

60 Ibid., p. 84.

61 Abu Zayd, *Mafhūm al-Naṣṣ* (Cairo: al-Markaz al-Thaqāfī al-ʿArabī, 1987), pp. 9–13.

62 Shabestari, *Naqdī bar Qirā'at-e Rasmī*, pp. 199–222.

63 Shabestari, *Īmān va Āzādī*, p. 170.

64 Shabestari, "Qarā'at-e Nabavī az Jahān" *Madraseh*, 6 (July 1997), pp. 92–100.

65 Jasser Auda, *Maqāṣid al-Sharīʿah as Philosophy of Islamic Law: A Systems Approach* (London, Washington: IIIT, 2008), p. 27.

66 Ibid. p. 28.

67 Ibid.

68 Ibid., pp. 28–29.

69 Ibid., p. 51 quoting Jamshid Gharajedaghi's article "Systems
    Methodology: A Holistic Language of Interaction and Design," in *Systems
    Thinking Press* (2004), p. 38.
70 Auda, *Maqāṣid al-Sharī'ah*, p. 53. Auda adds that may Muslim jurists,
    including al-Āmidī, al-Shāṭibī, Ibn Taymiyyah, Ibn Qayyim and Ibn
    Rushd, have been closer to the Māturīdī position than the official Ashʿarī
    position.
71 Ibid., pp. 54–55.
72 Ibid., p. 46.
73 Ibid., p. 228.

CONCLUSION

1 Muhammad Iqbal, *Reconstruction of Religious Thought in Islam*,
   p. 76; Muhammad Iqbal, "Asrar-i Khudī" in *Iqbāl Lāhūrī* (Tehran: ʿIlmī,
   1991), pp. 85–135.
2 See Farzin Vahdat, *God and Juggernaut: Iran's Intellectual Encounter
   with Modernity* (New York: Syracuse University Press, 2002), p. 6
   quoting Kerstin (1992), p. 344.
3 Ali Mirsepassi, *Political Islam, Iran and the Enlightenment: Philosophy of
   Hope and Despair* (Cambridge, UK: Cambridge University Press, 2011),
   p. 75.
4 Jasser Auda, *Maqāṣid*, p. 228.

Bibliography

Abdullah, Amin, *Falasafah Kalam: Di Era Postmodernisme (The Philosophy of Islamic Theology in Post-modernism Era)*, (Yogyakarta: Pustaka Pelajar, 1997).

Abisaab, Rula J., *Converting Persia: Religion and Power in the Safavid Empire* (New York: I.B. Tauris, 2004).

Abu Zahrah, Shaykh Muhammad, *Ta'rīkh al-Madhāhib al-Islāmiyyah fī Ta'rīkh al-Madhāhib al-Fiqhiyyah* (Cairo: Dār al-Fikr al-ʿArabī, 1963).

______, *Uṣūl al-Fiqh* (Cairo: Dār al-Fikr al-ʿArabī, n.d.).

Abū Zayd, Nasr Ḥāmid, *Ishkālāt al-Qirā'ah wa al-Āliyyāt al-Ta'wīl* (Cairo: al-Markaz al-Thaqāfī al-ʿArabī, n.d.).

______, *Mafhūm al-Naṣṣ* (Cairo: al-Markaz al-Thaqāfī al-ʿArabī, 1987).

______, *Naqd al-Khiṭāb al-Dīnī* (Cairo: Sīnā li al-Nashr, 1992).

______, *Reformation of Islamic Thought* (Amsterdam University Press, 2006).

AbuSulayman, AbdulHamid, *Crisis in the Muslim Mind*. Tr. Yusuf Talal Delorenzo, (Herndon, VA: International Institute of Islamic Thought, 1997).

______, *Towards an Islamic Theory of International Relations: New Directions for Methodology and Thought* (Herndon, VA: International Institute of Islamic Thought, 1994).

Ahmad, Khurshid, "Iqbal and the Reconstruction of Islamic Law," in *Mohammad Iqbal*, Verinder Grover (ed.), (New Delhi: Deep & Deep Pub., 1995).

Bibliography

Ahmad Nasir, Malki, "Indonesians' Scholars' Reception of Arkoun's Thought," *Khazanah: Journal Ilmu Agam Islam*, Bandung (Indonesia) Program Pascasarjana, 1 (6) (July-December 2004).

Ahmed, Rumee, *Narratives of Islamic Legal Theory* (Oxford: Oxford University Press, 2012).

Alalwani, Taha Jabir, "The Crisis in Fiqh and the Methodology of Ijtihad," *American Journal of Islamic Social Sciences* 8 (2) (September 1991).

______, *The Ethics of Disagreement in Islam* (Herndon, VA: International Institute of Islamic Thought, 1997).

______, "Ijtihād and Taqlīd," *American Journal of Islamic Social Sciences* 8 (1) (March 1991).

______, *Maqāṣid al-Sharīʿah* (Beirut: Dār al-Hādī, 2001).

______, *Source Methodology in Islamic Jurisprudence* (London and Washington: International Institute of Islamic Thought, 2003).

______, *Uṣūl al-Fiqh al-Islāmī: Source Methodology in Islamic Jurisprudence* (Herndon, Virginia: International Institute of Islamic Thought, 1990).

al-Āmidī, Sayf al-Dīn ʿAlī ibn Abī ʿAlī, *Ghāyat al-Marām fī ʿIlm al-Kalām*. Cairo: Lajnah Turāth al-Islāmī, 1971).

______, *al-Iḥkām fī Uṣūl al-Aḥkām* (Cairo: Mu'assast al-Ḥalibī, 1967).

al-ʿĀmilī, Ḥasan ibn Zayn al-Dīn (Shahīd II), *Maʿālim al-Dīn wa Milādh al-Mujtahidīn*, Mahdi Mohaghegh, (ed.), (Tehran: McGill branch, 1983).

Amir-Moezzi, Mohammad Ali, "al-Ṭūsī," *Encyclopaedia of Islam*, 2nd edn., (Leiden: E.J. Brill, 1980).

Ansari, H. and S. Schmidtke, "The Muʿtazili and Zaydi Reception of Abū al-Ḥusayn al-Baṣrī's *Kitāb al-Muʿtamad fī Uṣūl al-Fiqh*: A Bibliographical Note," *Islamic Law and Society* 20 (1-2) (2013).

Anṣārī, Murtaḍā, *Farā'id al-Uṣūl*, Abdullah Nurani (ed.), (Qum: Mu'assasat al-Nashr al-Islāmī, 1987).

Bibliography

Ansari, Zafar Ishaq, "The Contribution of the Qur'an and the Prophet to the Development of Islamic Fiqh," *Journal of Islamic Studies* 3 (2) (1992).

Arkoun, Mohammed, "The Notion of Revelation: From Ahl al-Kitab to the Societies of the Book," *Die Welt Islami* 28 (63) (1988).

______, *Rethinking Islam: Common Questions, Uncommon Answers*, Robert D. Lee (tr.), (Colorado: Westview Press, 1994).

______, *Tārīkhiyyat al-Fikr al-ʿArabiyyah al-Islāmiyyah* (Beirut: Markaz al-Qawmiyyah, 1994).

al-Asad Ābādī, Qāḍī ʿAbd al-Jabbār, *al-Mughnī fī Abwāb al-Tawḥīd wa al-ʿAdl* (Cairo: al-Shirkah al-ʿArabiyyah li al-Ṭabʿ wa al-Nashr, 1960).

al-Astarābādī, Mulla Muḥammad Amīn, *al-Fawāʾid al-Madaniyyah* (Bahrain: Litho-print, 1903).

Auda, Jasser, *Maqāṣid al-Sharīʿah as Philosophy of Islamic Law: A Systems Approach* (London, Washington: International Institute of Islamic Thought, 2008).

al-Baghdādī, Abū Manṣūr ʿAbd al-Qāhir, *Uṣūl al-Dīn* (Istanbul: Dār al-Funūn, 1928).

al-Baghdādī, al-Khaṭīb, *Tārīkh Baghdād* (Beirut: Dār al-Kutub al-ʿIlmiyyah, 1986).

al-Baḥrānī, Shaykh Yūsuf, *al-Hadāʾiq al-Nāḍirah* (Najaf: Dār al-Kutub, 1957).

al-Banānī, ʿAbd al-Raḥmān, *Ḥāshiyat al-ʿAllāmah al-Banānī ʿalā Sharḥ al-Jalāl al-Maḥalli ʿalā Matn Jamʿ al-Jawāmiʿ lī al-Imām Tāj al-Dīn al-Subkī* (Beirut: Dār al-Kutub, 1998).

al-Bāqillānī, Abū Bakr Muḥammad, *al-Taqrīb wa al-Irshād (al-Ṣaghīr)* (Saudi Arabia: Mu'assasat al-Risālah, n.d.).

al-Baṣrī, Abū al-Ḥusayn, *Kitāb al-Muʿtamad fī Uṣūl al-Fiqh* (Damascus: al-Maʿhad al-ʿIlmī al-Faransī, 1964).

Bedir, Murteza, "An Early Response to Al-Shāfiʿī: ʿĪsā b. Abān in the Prophetic Report (*Khabar*)," *Islamic Law and Society* 9 (3) (2002).

______, "Al-Jassas," in *Islamic Legal Thought: A Compendium of Muslim Jurists*, Oussama Arabi, David S. Powers, and Susan A. Spectorsky (eds.), (Leiden: Brill, 2013).

______, "Reason and Revelation: Abū Zayd al-Dabbūsī on Rational Proofs," *Islamic Studies* 43 (2) (Summer 2004).

Bihbihānī, Muḥammad Bāqir, *al-Fawā'id al-Ḥā'iriyyah* (Qum: Majmaʿ al-Fikr al-Islāmī, 1994).

______, *al-Rasā'il al-Uṣūliyyah* (Qum: Mu'assaseh-ye Nashr-i Āthār-i Waḥīd-i Bibhihānī, 1995).

______, *Risālat al-Ijtihād wa al-Akhbār* (Tehran: Lithograph, 1895).

Boroujerdi, Mehrzad, "The Encounter of Post-Revolutionary Thought in Iran with Hegel, Heidegger, and Popper," in *Cultural Transition in Middle East*, Sarif Mardin, (ed.), (Leiden: E.J. Brill, 1994).

Brockopp, Jonathan E., "Early Islamic Jurisprudence in Egypt: Two Scholars and their *Mukhtaṣars*," *International Journal of Middle East Studies* 30 (1998).

al-Bukhārī, Aḥmad, *Kashf al-Asrār ʿan Uṣūl Fakhr al-Islām al-Bazdawī* (Beirut: Dār al-Kutub al-ʿIlmiyyah, 1997).

Calder, Norman, "The Emergence of an Imami Shiʿi Theology of *Ijtihād*," *Studia Islamica* 19 (1989).

______, *Studies in Early Muslim Jurisprudence* (Oxford: Clarendon Press, 1993).

Cole, Juan, *Sacred Space and Holy War: The Politics, Culture and History of Shiʿite Islam* (London: I.B. Tauris, 2002).

Coulson, N. J., *A History of Islamic Law* (Abingdon: Routledge, 2017).

al-Dabbūsī, Abū Zayd ʿUbaydullāh, *Taqwīm al-Adillah fī Uṣūl al-Fiqh* (Beirut: Dār al-Kutub al-ʿIlmiyyah, 2001).

Dīnānī, Gholām Ḥosayn Ibrāhīmī, *Manṭiq va Maʿrifat dar Naẓar-e Ghazālī* (Tehran: Amīr Kabīr, 1991).

Durrī, Moṣṭafā, *Durūs-i Uṣūl-i Fiqh-i Shīʿeh*. Transcribed lectures of Ayatollah Sayyid Muḥammad Mahdī Mūsavī Khalkhālī, (Mashhad: Bonyād-i Pazhuheshhā-ye Islāmī, 2013).

Fakhri, Majid, *A Short Introduction to Islamic Philosophy, Theology and Mysticism* (Oxford: Oneworld Publication, 1997).

Fayyāḍ, Isḥāq, *Muḥāḍarāt fī Uṣūl al-Fiqh* (Najaf, n.d.).

Gharajedaghi, Jamshid, "Systems Methodology: A Holistic Language of Interaction and Design," *Systems Thinking Press*, 2004.

al-Ghazālī, Abū Ḥāmid Muḥammad, *Iḥyāʾ ʿUlūm al-Dīn* (Beirut: Dār al-Kutub al-ʿIlmiyyah, n.d.).

_____, *al-Mankhūl min Taʿlīqāt al-Uṣūl* (Damascus: Dār al-Fikr, 1980).

_____, *al-Mustaṣfā, min ʿIlm al-Uṣūl* (Beirut: Dār al-Kutub al-ʿIlmiyyah, 1983).

_____, *Shifāʾ al-Ghalīl fī Bayān al-Shabah wa al-Mukhīl wa Masālik al-Taʿlīl* (Baghdad: Maṭbaʿat al-Irshād, 1971).

Ghazi, Mahmood Ahmad, *Islamic Renaissance in South Asia 1707-1867* (Islamabad: Islamic Research Center, 2002).

Gleave, Robert, *Islam and Literalism* (Edinburgh: Edinburgh University Press, 2013).

_____, *Scripturalist Islam: The History and Doctrines of the Akhbari Shiʿi School* (Boston and Leiden: Brill, 2007).

Gorjī, Abū al-Qāsim, *Naẓariyyah fī ʿIlm al-Uṣūl* (Tehran: Bunyād-i Biʿthat, 1982).

______, *Naẓrah fī Taṭawwur ʿIlm al-Uṣūl* (Tehran: al-Maktabah al-Islāmiyyah al-Kubrā, 1982).

______, *Nigāhī beh Taḥavvol-i ʿIlm-i Uṣūl* (Tehran: Dānishgāh-i Tehran, 1973).

______, *Maqālāt-i Ḥuqūqī* (Tehran: Dānishgāh-i Tehran, 1990).

______, *Ta'rīkh-i Fiqh va Fuqahā* (Tehran, 1996).

Hallaq, Wael, "The Development of Logical Structure in Sunni Legal Theory," *Der Islam* 64 (1987).

______, *A History of Islamic Legal Theories: An Introduction to Sunni Usul al-Fiqh* (Cambridge: Cambridge University Press, 1997).

______, "Was the Gate of Ijtihad Closed?" *International Journal of Middle East Studies* 16 (Spring 1984).

______, "Was al-Shāfiʿī the Master Architect of Islamic Jurisprudence?" *International Journal of Middle East Studies* 25 (1993).

Harver, Van A., "Hermeneutics," *The Encyclopedia of Religion* (New York: Macmillan, 1987).

Heern, Zackery M., *The Emergence of Modern Shiʿism: Islamic Reform in Iraq and Iran* (London: Oneworld Publications, 2015).

Hermansen, Marcia K., *The Conclusive Argument from God* (Leiden: E.J. Brill, 1995).

al-Ḥillī, Ibn al-Muṭahhar (ʿAllāmah), *Mabādī al-Wuṣūl ilā ʿIlm al-Uṣūl* (Beirut: Dār al-Aḍwā', 1986).

______, *Tahdhīb al-Wuṣūl ilā ʿIlm al-Uṣūl* (Tehran: Lithograph, 1890).

______, "ʿAllama al-Hilli on the Imamate and Ijtihad," John Cooper (tr.,), in *Authority and Political Culture in Shiʿism*, S. A. Arjomand (ed.), (Albany: SUNY, 1988).

______. *al-Alfayn* (Najaf: Haydariyyah, 1969).

al-Ḥillī, Najm al-Dīn Jaʿfar ibn al-Ḥasan al-Muḥaqqiq, *Maʿārij al-Uṣūl* (Qum: Āl al-Bayt, 1983).

Hourani, George, "Reason and Revelation in Ibn Hazm's Ethical Thought" in *Islamic Philosophical Theology*, P. Morewedge (ed.), (Syracuse: SUNY, 1979).

Ibn ʿĀbidīn, Muḥammad Amīn ibn ʿUmar, *Majmūʿah Rasāʾil Ibn ʿĀbidīn* (Lahore: Suhayl Academy, n.d.).

Ibn al-Ḥājib, Abū ʿAmr Jamāl al-Dīn, *Mukhtaṣar al-Muntaha al-Uṣūl: maʿa Ḥāshiyat al-Taftāzānī wa al-Jurjānī ʿalā Sharḥ al-Qāḍī ʿAḍudī* (Cairo: al-Maṭbaʿah al-Kubrā al-Amīriyyah bi Būlāq Miṣr al-Ḥamiyyah, 1898).

Ibn Ḥazm, Abū Muḥammad ʿAlī ibn Aḥmad ibn Saʿīd, *al-Iḥkām fī Uṣūl al-Aḥkām* (Beirut: Dār al-Kutub al-Islāmiyyah, n.d.).

______, *al-Taqrīb li Ḥadd al-Manṭiq wa al-Madkhūl ilayhi*, Iḥsān ʿAbbās (ed.), (Beirut: Dār Maktabat al-Ḥayāt, 1957).

Ibn Idrīs al-Ḥillī, Muḥammad Mahdī Ibrāhīm, *al-Sarāʾir* (Qum: Nashr-i Islāmī, 1989).

Ibn Khaldūn, Walī al-Dīn ʿAbd al-Raḥmān, *al-Muqaddimah* (Iskandariyyah: Dār Ibn Khaldūn, n.d.).

Ibn Khallikān, Shams al-Dīn, *Wafiyāt al-Aʿyān* (Qum: Manshūrāt al-Raḍī, 1985).

Ibn al-Muqaffaʿ, ʿAbdullāh. *Al-Manṭiq*, M.T. Daneshpezhuh, (ed.), (Tehran: Iranian Academy of Philosophy, 1978).

Ibn al-Nadīm (Muḥammad ibn Isḥāq), *al-Fihrist*, Riḍā Tajaddud, (ed.), (Tehran: Nashr-e Asātīr, 1973).

Ibn al-Nujaym, Zayn al-Dīn ibn Ibrāhīm, *al-Ashbāh wa al-Naẓāʾir* (Beirut: Dār al-Fikr al-Muʿāṣir, 1985).

Ibn Salām, Abū ʿUbayd al-Qāsim, *Kitāb al-Nāsikh wa al-Mansūkh*, John Burton, (ed.), (Cambridge: Gibb Memorial Trust, 1987).

Ibrahim, Ahmed Fekry, *Pragmatism in Islamic Law: A Social and Intellectual History* (Syracuse, NY: Syracuse University Press, 2015).

Inati, Shams, "Logic" in *History of Islamic Philosophy*, S. H. Nasr and O. Leaman, (eds.), (London and New York: Routledge, 1996).

Iqbāl ʿAbbas, *Khāndān-i Nowbakhtī* (Tehran: Tahūrī, 1978).

Iqbāl, Muḥammad, "Asrār-i Khudī" in *Iqbāl Lāhūrī* (Tehran: ʿIlmī, 1991).

______, *The Reconstruction of Religious Thought in Islam* (Lahore: Iqbal Academy Pakistan, 1989).

Jackson, Sherman, "Setting the Record Straight," *Journal of Islamic Studies* 11 (2) (2000).

al-Jāḥiẓ, Amr ibn Baḥr, *Kitāb al-Ḥayawān* (Cairo: al-Maktabah al-Ḥamīdiyyah al-Miṣriyyah, 1905-07).

Jalbani, G.N., *Teachings of Shāh Waliyullāh of Delhi* (New Delhi: Kitab Bhavan, 1988).

Jannātī, Muḥammad Ebrāhīm, "Ijtihād dar Jāmiʿ-yi Islāmī," *Kayhān-i Andīsheh* 10 (1986).

______, "Qiyām-i Akhbārīhā ʿalayhi Ijtihād," *Kayhān-i Andīsheh* 13 (1987).

______, *Taṭawwor-i ijtihād dar howze-ye Istinbāt* (Tehran: Amīr Kabīr, 2007).

al-Juwaynī, Imam al-Haramayn Abd al-Malik ibn Abdullah, *al-Burhān fi Usul al-Fiqh* (Qatar: Maṭbaʿah al-Dohah Al-Ḥadīthah, 1399/1979).

al-Jaṣṣāṣ, Abū Bakr Aḥmad ibn ʿAlī al-Rāzi, *Usul al-Jassas al-Musamma al-Fuṣūl fī al-Uṣūl* (Beirut: Dār al-Kutub al-ʿIlmiyyah, 2000).

Kadivar, Mohsen, *Hukoumat-i Velā'ī* (Tehran: Nashr-i Ney, 1998).

______, "Mujtahid dar Uṣūl," *Madreseh* (a quarterly cultural-philosophical journal) 2 (6) (2007).

Kamali, Mohammad Hashim, *Issues in the Legal Theory of Uṣūl and Prospects for Reform* (Kuala Lumpur: IIUM., 2000).

______, *Principles of Islamic Jurisprudence* (Cambridge: Islamic Texts Society, 2003).

______, *Shariʿah Law: An Introduction* (London, UK: One world, 2008).

______, *The Middle Path of Moderation in Islam* (Oxford, UK: Oxford University Press, 2015).

al-Karājikī, Abū al-Fatḥ Muḥammad ibn ʿAlī ibn ʿUthmān, *Kanz al-Fawāʾid* (Beirut: Dār al-Aḍwāʾ, 1985).

Karakī, Shaykh ʿAlī, *Jāmiʿ al-Maqāṣid*, Introduction by Jawād Shahrastānī (Qum: Muʾassasah Āl al-Bayt, 1987-90).

Kazemi-Moussavi, Ahmad, *Religious Authority in Shiʿite Islam* (Kuala Lumpur: ISTAC, 1996).

Khadduri, Majid, *Islamic Jurisprudence: Shāfiʿī's Risāla* (Baltimore: The Johns Hopkins University Press, 1961).

Khorasānī, Moḥammad Vāʾiz-zādeh, "Mosāḥebeh," in *Cheshm va Cherāgh-i Marjaʿiyyat* (Qum: Enteshārāt-e Daftar Tablīghāt-e Islāmī, 1379/2000).

Khurasani, Muhammad Kazim, *Kifāyat al-Uṣūl* (Qum: Muʾassasah Āl al-Bayt, 1988).

Kohlberg, Etan, "Aspects of Akhbari Thought in the Seventeenth and Eighteenth Centuries," in *Eighteenth Century Renewal and Reform in Islam*, Nehemia Levitzion and John Voll, (eds.), (Syracuse: Syracuse University Press, 1987).

al-Kulaynī, Muḥammad ibn Yaʿqūb ibn Isḥāq, *al-Uṣūl min al-Kāfī* (Arabic with Persian commentary and translation), S. Jawād Muṣtafawī, (ed. and tr.), (Tehran: Daftar-i Nashr-i Farhang-i Ahl al-Bayt, n.d.).

Lameer, Joep, *al-Fārābī and Aristotelian Syllogistics* (Leiden: E.J. Brill, 1994).

Langrūdī, Muḥammad Jaʿfar Jaʿfarī, *Maktabhā-yi Ḥuqūqī dar Islām* (Tehran: Ganj-i Dānesh, 1991).

Bibliography

Lowry, Joseph, "Does Shāfiʿī Have a Theory of ʿFour Sources' of Law?," *Studies in Islamic Law and Society*, B. Weiss, (ed.), (Leiden: Brill, 2002).

Madelung, Wilferd, "Akhbāriyya," *Encyclopaedia of Islam (EI2)*. Second edn. (Leiden: E.J. Brill, 1980).

______, "Authority in Twelver Shiʿism," in *Religious Schools and Sects in Medieval Islam* (Ashgate, USA: Variorum Reprint, 1985).

Makdisi, George, "The Juridical Theology of Shāfiʿī: Origins and Significance of Uṣūl al-Fiqh," *Studia Islamica* 59 (1984).

Mālik Ibn Anas, *al-Muwaṭṭa'* (Beirut: Maktabat al-Thaqāfah, 1988).

Masud, Muhammad Khalid, *Muslim Jurists' Quest for the Normative Basis of Shariʿa* (Leiden: ISIM, 2001).

______, *Shāṭibī's Philosophy of Islamic Law* (Malaysia, Kuala Lumpur, Islamic Research Institute, Malaysian reprint, 2000).

McDermott, Martin J., *The Theology of Al-Shaikh Al-Mufid* (Beirut: Dar al-Mashriq, 1986).

Melchert, Christopher. *The Formation of the Sunni Schools of Law: 9th-10th Centuries C.E.* Leiden: Brill, 1997.

Mirsepassi, Ali, *Political Islam, and the Enlightenment* (Cambridge: Cambridge University Press, 2011).

Modarressi, Hossein. *Crisis and Consolidation in the Formative Period of Shiʿi Islam: Abu Jaʿfar ibn Qiba al-Razi and His Contribution to Imamite Shiʿite Thought*. Princeton: The Darwin Press, 1993.

Mohaghegh Dāmād, Moṣṭafā, "Taḥavvolāt-i Ijtihād-i Shīʿeh: Sayr-i Ta'rīkhī-ye Ḥawzeh-hā va Shīveh-hā," *Majalleh-ye Taḥqīqāt-i Ḥuqūqī-ye Dānesh-kade-ye Ḥuqūq*, 44 (Spring-Summer 2006).

al-Mufīd, Muḥammad ibn Muḥammad ibn Nuʿmān, *Muṣannafāt al-Shaykh al-Mufīd* (Qum: al-Mu'tamar al-ʿĀlamī li Alfīyat al-Shaykh al-Mufīd, 1992).

Muḥammadī, Abū al-Ḥasan, *Mabādī-ye Istinbāṭ* (Tehran: University of Tehran Press, 2001).

al-Muqirrī, Hibatullāh ibn Salāmah ibn Naṣr, *al-Nāsikh wa al-Mansūkh min Kitāb Allāh* (Beirut: al-Maktab al-Islāmī, 1984).

al-Murtaḍā, al-Sharīf ʿAlī ibn al-Ḥusayn, *al-Dharīʿah ilā Uṣūl al-Sharīʿah*, Abū al-Qāsim Gorjī, (ed.), (Tehran: Dānishgāh-i Tehran, 1967).

Mutahhari, Murtada, *Āshnā'ī bā ʿUlūm-i Islāmī* (Tehran: Intishārāt-i Ṣadrā, 1979).

_____, "Ijtihād dar Islām," *Baḥthī darbāra-yi Marjaʿiyyat va Rūḥāniyyat* (Tehran: Shirkat-i Sahāmī-yi Intishār, 1962).

al-Muẓaffar, al-Shaykh Muḥammad Riḍā, *Uṣūl al-Fiqh* (Qum: Markaz al-Nashr, 1993).

Najafābādī, Niʿmatullah Ṣāliḥī, *Shahīd-i Jāvīd* (Tehran: Umīd-i Fardā, 2008).

_____, *Velāyat-i Faqīh: Ḥukūmat-i Ṣāliḥān* (Tehran: Rasā, 1984.

Narāqī, Mullā Aḥmad. *Awā'id al-Ayyām*. Qum: Lithograph, 1903).

Newman, Andrew, "The Development and Political Significance of the Rationalist (Usuli) and Traditionist (Akhbari) Schools in Imami Shiʿi History from the Third/Ninth to the Tenth/Sixteenth Century." PhD dissertation, UCLA, 1986.

_____, *The Formative Period of Twelver Shiʿism: Hadith as Discourse Between Qum and Baghdad* (Richmond, Surrey: Curzon Press, 2000).

Nyazee, Imran Ahsan Khan, *Theories of Islamic Law* (Islamabad: Islamic Research Institute Press, 1994).

Pākatchī, Aḥmad, "*Ijmāʿ*," in *Dā'irat al-Maʿārif-e Buzurg-e Islāmī* (Tehran: Markaz-e Dā'irat al-Maʿārif-e Buzurg-e Islāmī, 1994).

al-Qummī, Shaykh Abū al-Qāsim, *Qawānīn al-Muḥkamah fī Uṣūl al-Mutqanah* (known as *Qawānīn al-Uṣūl*), (Tehran: Lithograph, 1884).

Rahman, Fazlur, "Iqbal's Idea of Progress" in *Mohammad Iqbal*, Verinder Grover, (ed.), (New Delhi: Deep & Deep Pub., 1995).

_______, "Some Aspects of Iqbal's Political Thought," in *Mohammad Iqbal*, Verinder Grover, (ed.), (New Delhi: Deep & Deep Pub., 1995).

Ramadan, Tariq, "Ijtihād and Maṣlaḥa: The Foundations of Governance," in *Islamic Democratic Discourse*, M. A. Muqtedar Khan, (ed.), (Lanham, MD: Lexington Books, 2006).

_______, *Radical Reform: Islamic Ethics and Liberation* (New York: Oxford University Press, 2009).

al-Rāzī, Fakhr al-Dīn Muḥammad ibn ʿUmar, *al-Maḥṣūl fī ʿIlm al-Uṣūl*. (Ed.), Ṭāhā Jābir Al-ʿAlwānī (Beirut: Muʾassasat al-Risālah, 1992).

Rizvī, Saiyid Athar Abbas, *Shāh Walī-Allah and His Times* (Canberra: Maʿrifat Publication House, 1980).

al-Ṣadr, al-Sayyid Muḥammad Bāqir, *Durūs fī ʿIlm al-Uṣūl* (Beirut: Dār al-Kitāb al-Lubnānī, 1986).

_______, *Durūs fi ʿIlm al-Uṣūl* (or *al-Ḥalaqāt*) (Qum: Muʾassasat al-Nashr al-Islāmī, 1994).

_______, *Lessons in Islamic Jurisprudence*. Translated with an introduction by Roy P. Mottahedeh. Oxford: Oneworld, 2003).

al-Sarakhsī, Abū Bakr Muḥammad ibn Aḥmad ibn Abī Sahl, *al-Mabsūṭ* (Beirut: Dār al-Maʿrifah, 1993).

_______, *Uṣūl al-Sarakhsī* (Istanbul: Dār Qahramān li al-Nashr wa al-Tawzīʿ, 1952).

Schacht, Joseph, *An Introduction to Islamic Law* (Oxford: Oxford University Press, 1983).

Schmidtke, Sabine, *The Theology of al-ʿAllama al-Hilli (d. 726/1325)*, (Berlin: Klaus Scdhwarz Verlag, 1991).

Shabestarī, Moḥammad Mujtahid, *Hermeneutik-i Kitāb va Sunnah* (Tehran: Intishārāt-i Ṭarh-i Now, 2002).

_______, *Imān va Āzādī* (Tehran: Ṭarh-e Now, 2000).

______, *Naqdī bar Qarā'at-e Rasmī az Dīn* (Tehran: Ṭarḥ-e Now, 2002).

______, "Qarā'at-e Nabavī az Jahān," *Madraseh* 6 (July 1997).

______, *Ta'ammolātī dar Qarā'at-e Insānī az Dīn* (Tehran: Ṭarḥ-e Now, 2004).

al-Shāfiʿī, Muḥammad ibn Idrīs. *Kitāb al-Umm* (Beirut: Dār al-Maʿrifah, n.d.)

______, *al-Risālah*, Aḥmad Muhammad Shākir, (ed.), (Cairo: Dār al-Fikr, 1979).

Shamsy, Ahmed El., *The Canonization of Islamic Law: A Social and Intellectual History* (New York: Cambridge University Press, 2013).

______, "Al-Shāfiʿī's Written Corpus: A Source-Critical Study," *Journal of the American Oriental Society* 132 (2) (April-June 2012).

al-Shāshī, Aḥmad ibn Muḥammad Abū ʿAlī al-Ḥanafī, *Uṣūl al-Shāshī* (Beirut: Dār al-Kitāb al-ʿArabī, 1982).

al-Shāṭibī, Abū Isḥāq Ibrāhīm, *al-Muwāfaqāt fī Uṣūl al-Aḥkām* (Cairo: Dār al-Fikr, n.d.)

al-Shawkānī, Muḥammad ibn ʿAlī, *Irshād al-Fuḥūl ilā Taḥqīq al-Ḥaqq min ʿIlm al-Uṣūl* (Beirut: Dār al-Kutub al-ʿIlmiyyah, 1994).

Shehaby, Nabil, "The Influence of Stoic Logic on al-Jassas's Legal Theory," in *The Cultural Context of Medieval Learning*, J. E. Murdoch and E. D. Sylla, (eds.), (Dordrecht, Holland: D. Reidel Pub. Co., 1975).

Shīrāzī, Abū Isḥāq, *Ṭabaqāt al-Fuqahā'*, (Beirut: Dar al-Turāth al-ʿArabī, 1981).

Soroush, Abdolkarim, *Bast-e Tajrabeh-ye Nabavī* (Tehran: Ṣirāṭ, 2004). This work has recently been translated into English by Katajun Amirpour. See *The Expansion of the Prophetic Experience: Abdolkarim Sorush's New Approach to Qur'anic Revelation*, Forough Jahanbakhsh, (ed.), (Leiden: E.J. Brill. 2011).

Bibliography

_____, *Farbehtar az Ideology* (Tehran: Ṣirāṭ, 1996).

_____, *Qabḍ va Basṭ-e Theoric-e Sharīʿat* (Tehran: Ṣirāṭ, 1992).

_____, *Rāzdānī va Rowshanfekrī va Dīndārī* (Tehran: Ṣirāṭ, 1992).

_____, *Reason, Freedom and Democracy in Islam*, Mahmoud Sadri and Ahmad Sadri, (tr.), (Oxford: Oxford University Press, 2000).

_____, "Velāyat-e Bāṭinī va Velāyat-e Siyāsī," *Kiyān-i Farhangī*, 44 (20) (Nov 1998).

Stewart, Devin, *Islamic Legal Orthodoxy: Twelver Shiite Responses to the Sunni Legal System* (Salt Lake City: University of Utah Press, 1988).

_____, "Muḥammad b. Dā'ūd al-Ẓāhirī's Manual of Jurisprudence," in *Studies in Islamic Legal Theory*, Bernard Weiss (ed.), (Leiden: E.J. Brill, 2002).

al-Subkī, Tāj al-Dīn, *Jāmiʿ al-Jawāmiʿ* (Beirut: Dār al-Kutub al-ʿIlmiyyah, 2003).

al-Suyūṭī, Jalāl al-Dīn, *al-Itqān fī ʿUlūm al-Qur'ān* (Cairo: Muṣṭafā al-Bābī al-Ḥalibī, 1951).

Taştan, Osman, "Al-Sarakhsi," in *Islamic Legal Thought: A Compendium of Muslim Jurists*, Oussama Arabi, David S. Powers, and Susan A. Spectorsky (eds.), (Leiden: Brill, 2013).

Temel, Ahmet, "The Missing Link in the History of Islamic Legal Theory: The Development of *Uṣūl al-Fiqh* between al-Shāfiʿī and al-Jaṣṣāṣ during the 3rd/9th and Early 4th/10th Centuries." PhD dissertation (Santa Barbara, CA: University of Santa Barbara, 2014).

al-Ṭūfī Najm al-Dīn Sulaymān ibn ʿAbd al-Qawī, *Risālah fī Riʿāyat al-Maṣlaḥah* (Dār al-Maṣriyyah al-Lubanāniyyah, 1993).

_____, *Sharḥ Mukhtaṣar al-Rawḍah* (Beirut: Mu'assasat al-Risālah, 1987).

Tunakābunī, Muḥammad Sulaymān, *Qiṣaṣ al-ʿUlamā* (Tehran: ʿIlmiyyah Islamiyyah, n.d.).

al-Ṭūsī, Muḥammad ibn al-Ḥasan, *al-Khilāf* (Qum: Nashr al-Islāmī, 1987).

______, *al-ʿUddah fī Uṣūl al-Fiqh*. Edited and published by Muḥammad Riḍā al-Anṣārī al-Qummī (Qum: 1998).

Vahdat, Farzin, *God and Juggernaut: Iran's Intellectual Encounter with Modernity* (Syracuse, New York: Syracuse University Press, 2002).

Vishanoff, David R. "Early Islamic Hermeneutics: Language, Speech, and Meaning in Preclassical Legal Theory." PhD dissertation. Emory University, 2004.

______, *The Formation of Islamic Hermeneutics: How Sunni Legal Theorists Imagined a Revealed Law* (New Haven, CT: American Oriental Society, 2011).

Walbridge, John, *God and Logic in Islam: The Caliphate of Reason* (Cambridge: Cambridge University Press, 2011).

Waliyullāh, Shāh, *Ḥujjat Allāh al-Bālighah* (Beirut: Dār Iḥyā' al-ʿUlūm, 1990).

Weiss, Bernard G., *The Search for God's Law: Islamic Jurisprudence in the Writings of Sayf al-Din al-Amidi* (Salt Lake City: University of Utah Press, 2010).

Whittemore, Robert, "Iqbal's Panentheism" in *Muhammad Iqbal*, Verinder Grover, (ed.), (New Delhi: Deep & Deep Pub., 1995).

al-Zuḥaylī, Wahbah, *Uṣūl al-Fiqh al-Islāmī* (Damascus: Dār al-Fikr, 2004).

Index

ʿAbd al-ʿAzīz ibn Yaḥyā al-Kinānī
(d. 240/854), 10
ʿAbd al-Jabbār al-Hamadānī
(d. 415/1024), 18–20, 176n17,
177n34
ʿAbd al-Raḥmān ibn Zayd ibn Aslam
(d. c. 170/786), 172n4
abduction (logic), xiv
ʿAbdullāh ibn al-Mubārak
(d. 181/797), 172n4
abrogation (*naskh*): Abu Zayd, 145;
AbuSulayman, 122–124; conflicting laws, 1; Ibn Salāmah,
123; al-Juwaynī, 57–58; Kamali,
127; al-Shāfiʿī, 4; al-Shāṭibī, 79.
See also Qurʾan
Abū ʿAbd al-Raḥmān Muḥammad
ibn ʿAbd al-Raḥmān (d. 159/
775), 172n4
Abū Bakr al-Ṣayrafī (d. 330/942),
13, 74
Abū Ḥanīfah (d.150/767), 2–3, 83,
114, 115. *See also* Ḥanafī school
and legal methodology
Abū al-Ṣilt Zāʾidah ibn Qudāmah
(d. 161/777), 172n4
Abū Ṭāhir al-Dabbās (d. first quarter
of fourth/tenth century), 28
Abū Yūsuf, 27–28
Abū Yūsuf al-Anṣārī (d. 179/795), 2
Abu Zahrah, Muhammad (d. 1974),
87–89, 127, 128
Abu Zayd, Nasr Hamid (d. 2010),
xviii, 142–148, 152, 157, 168–
169

AbuSulayman, AbdulHamid
(d. 2021), xviii, 122–125, 168,
195n32
ʿādāt (habits): Ḥanafī scholars, 83;
al-Shāṭibī, 77, 78–79; al-Ṭūfī,
75. *See also* ʿurf (customary
practice); social reality and legal
methodology
ʿAḍudī, Qāḍī (d. 756/1355), 69
advent of legal methodology, 1–13;
overview, 1–3; al-Shāfiʿī, 3–7;
al-Shāfiʿī, critique of, 7–13. *See
also* al-Shāfiʿī, Muḥammad ibn
Idrīs
al-Afghānī, Jamāl al-Dīn (d. 1315/
1897), 121
aḥkām (legal rulings). *See* legal
norms (*aḥkām*)
Aḥmad ibn Abī Dāʾūd al-Iyādī
(d. 240–854), 16
Aḥmad ibn Ḥanbal (d. 241/855), 74
Ahmed, Rumee, xiv, 33
ʿĀʾishah bint Abī Bakr (d. 58/678),
144
Akhbārism, 48, 51–53, 91–92. *See
also* sources of law, Shiʿi;
tradition-reports (*akhbār*)
Alalwani, Taha Jabir (d. 2016), xviii,
116–121, 194n18
Alam al-Hudā. *See* al-Murtaḍā, ʿAlī
ibn al-Ḥusayn
Algerian civil law, 148
ʿAlī ibn Abī Ṭālib (d. 40/661), 1, 143
ʿAlī al-Riḍā, 39

hermeneutic tradition, 10; al-Shāfiʿī, 4, 8, 174n34; use by post-Shāfiʿī scholars, 10

al-Ghazālī, Abū Ḥāmid (d. 505/1111), 58–63; arrangement of methodology, xvii; effects of formal logic on, xv, xvi; epistemological approach, 26, 58–63; human rationality, 112–113; ijtihad, 58, 62, 63; ʿillah (efficacious cause), 62; indicants of law (sing. *adillah*), 58, 62; influence of al-Baghdādī on, 20, 23; *istiḥsān* (juristic preference), 63; *istiṣḥāb*, 74; legal norms (*aḥkām*), 128; qiyās, 78

—, influence of: on Alalwani, 121; on Ibn Qudāmah, 73; on Ramadan, 132; on Soroush, 153; on al-Ṭūfī, 74

Gleave, Robert, xvii

"God's words" meaning, 154–156

government, 152, 153

government and legislative bodies, 114–115, 129

government and legitimacy, 130–131, 136–137

government and ʿulamā,' 28, 129–130, 167–168

Greater Occultation, 38–39

Greek philosophers: influence of, 9–10, 29–30, 115, 148; translations to Arabic, 54–55; translations to Persian, 8–9, 174n35. *See also* epistemology and legal theory; formal logic in Islamic methodology; syllogism

Gyekye, K., 55

ḥadd applications, 17

Hadith. *See* tradition-reports (*akhbār*)

Hallaq, Wael, 8, 10, 11, 37, 55, 76–77, 194n18

Ḥanafī school and legal methodology, 27–37; overview, 27–28, 164; al-Bazdawī, 27, 33–35; al-Dabbūsī, 19, 27, 31–33, 179n19, 179n22; Ibn ʿĀbidīn, 83; Ibn Nujaym, 83; Iqbal on, 115; al-Jaṣṣāṣ, 23, 27, 28–31, 176n9, 179n14; al-Sarakhsī, 27, 31, 35–37, 172n5, 179n29; semantics, xiv. *See also* social reality and legal methodology

Ḥanafism and Muʿtazilism, 23

Hanbalism and al-Shāfiʿī's paradigm, 8

Heidegger, Martin (d. 1976), 142

hermeneutics and legal methodology, 141–161; overview, xviii, 141–142, 165–166; Abu Zayd, xviii, 142–148, 152, 157, 168–169; Arkoun, xviii, 148–149, 168–169; Auda, 158–161, 169, 170; and Greek philosophy, 148; Shabestari, xviii, 139, 154–157, 168–169; Soroush, xviii, 142, 149–154, 157, 168–169. *See also* alternative approaches to legal methodology

Ḥijāzī legists, 115

Ḥillah school (Shiʿi), 46–51

Hishām ibn al-Ḥakam (d. c. 190/805), 40

al-ḥiyal wa al-makhārij (legal stratagems and loopholes), 118

ḥujjah (legal authority): al-Dabbūsī, 179n19; al-Muẓaffar, 104–106

human development (*irtifāq*) (Shāh Walīyullāh), 84

human progress theory (Iqbal), 113–114, 115–116

Ḥunayn ibn Isḥāq (d. 260/873), 54

al-Ḥurr al-ʿĀmilī (d. 1104/1693), 52